MOUNT ZION
AND THE
DARKEST VALLEY

DONALD MICHLIN

Sugar Land, Texas

For more information, email Michlin.MZDV@gmail.com

Scripture quotations are taken from the New King James Version.
Copyright © 1979, 1980, 1982 by Thomas Nelson, Inc.
Used by permission. All rights reserved.

Library of Congress Control Number: 2025914903

ISBN: 979-8-9995279-0-5 (hardback)
ISBN: 979-8-9995279-1-2 (paperback)
ISBN: 979-8-9995279-2-9 (ebook)

Cover Design by Donald Michlin

Contents

Preface

One day, my wife and I sat down for a brief devotional at the kitchen table. As she read from her book, she reached the verse that referenced the valley of the shadow of death. On this occasion, I was particularly struck by this reference and thus sought to incorporate this concept into my project, which had become known in our household as *The Project*. I was aware that the reference was to the darkest valley and was convinced that the opposite represented Mount Zion. This inspiration then became the working title of my writings, which has now been adopted as the title of this book.

The project began approximately eight years prior to our devotional. At that time, additional information on the subject of Scripture became accessible via the internet. After eighteen years of learning what was taught from the pulpit at church, I desired to gain a more comprehensive understanding of the books of Moses, Job, and Daniel.

A discernible theme emerged concerning the secret things of God and our responsibility to pursue these insights. In light of this premise, I began investigating the relationship between the celestial bodies and the word of God. This inquiry also facilitated an understanding of ancient civilizations and their geographical placement. While the integration of these subjects presented certain challenges, I was drawn to pursue this line of inquiry.

In the course of my research, I encountered numerous instances where I initially thought the subject could not become any more intricate. However, new areas of inquiry always emerged that required either integration or rejection. My objective was to demonstrate a pattern by presenting illustrative examples drawn as described in the word of God. As I identified more inspirations that aligned with the project, the narrative of the scriptures became increasingly compelling.

The overall design of how creation communicates the word of God is so complex that it is challenging to conceive of an alternative explanation that would account for its existence, except from the divine Creator. It is, therefore, my hope that the reading of this book will demonstrate the concept that the message of God was designed from the very beginning for the reconciliation of humanity and to foster an increase in one's love for God.

Introduction

Creation is patterned after divine purpose, making it both functional and rich in theological application. Examining Scripture, ancient civilizations, cosmology, and biblical festivals reveals its comprehensive design. Within it, there is a pattern that illustrates biblical prophecy, the establishment of the tabernacle and its courtyard, and redemption. These findings provide insight into a pattern that is both observable and repeatable, as well as having a deep spiritual significance. This framework interweaves the heavens and the earth, proclaiming the glory and mysteries of God and calling humanity into fellowship with the Creator.

One might inquire as to the experience of Moses, Aaron with his two sons, along with the seventy elders of Israel on Mount Sinai that led to the construction of the tabernacle and its furnishings. The entire structure was to be erected based on the observations made during that pivotal night, as recorded in the book of Exodus. God presented the pattern for the construction of the tabernacle and its furnishings with the intention that it function as a visual teaching aid. In this manner, the Israelites would interact with God.

In accordance with the instructions they were given, the Israelites proceeded to construct a conceptual framework for understanding the relationship between the earthly and heavenly realms. The pattern presented is relatively simple, yet it exhibits a high degree of sophistication, particularly with regard to its engagement with the geography of the earth and the stars of the heavens. The pattern within the framework can also be demonstrated to correspond to four specific days of the year, which, in turn, correspond to four particular sacred sites around the globe. Thus, the tabernacle and its courtyard involve both the celestial sky and the entire Earth, aligning with other cultures.

The interplay between the stars and the features of the Earth, as it pertains to the pattern, provides illustrative examples that can be repeated for the purposes of understanding the concepts of atonement, prophecy, and the afterlife. This insight is profoundly significant for our perception of the divine. It suggests that the divine Creator is striving to establish communication with humanity so that mankind may gain insight into His nature and engage in a relationship with Him. Furthermore, the presentation of the pattern to the Israelites at Mount Sinai would collectively provide them with the opportunity to serve as a beacon for the rest of the world. Therefore, the fulfillment of this pattern by the nation of Israel would serve to reflect the values of the kingdom of God in heaven.

Furthermore, this comprehensive design can be applied to the book of Revelation to provide a more in-depth study of the descriptions pertaining to much of John's experience, in which he was commanded to write down what he saw. This approach results in a profound understanding of the kingdoms of the beasts, a subject developed in the books of Daniel and Revelation by authors who lived hundreds of years apart. Therefore, these interconnections shed light on the framework for depicting the plan of God, as reflected in the scriptural text.

The application of the pattern makes these concepts clear, which are understood to have been established by God during the act of creation. Moreover, the creation of all things lends support to the notion that humanity is the recipient of divine love. The prevailing expectation is that humanity will return the love that was first given to them. In this regard, the capacity to establish a connection with the Creator has always been a potential aspect of human experience. Therefore, it can be concluded that the complete spiritual journey that an individual is to undertake is revealed by these factors, which have been established from the beginning.

1
Earth and Heaven

The moment, "Let there be light" was spoken, God was already aware of the precise specifications regarding how the Earth and the heavens were to be formed. The same word that spoke the universe into existence would also have His handiwork to communicate the message of the Creator. In this manner, the word of God, the Earth, and the celestial bodies, having been established from a single source, exhibit a unified relationship. This interconnectedness is such that its various elements are mutually connected to each other and depend on each other.

When considered in conjunction with the pattern that will be developed in the next chapters, this interconnectedness illuminates the profound intricacies of the message of the Creator and its underlying purpose. From our vantage point within the universe, this distinct perspective provides insights into the unique relationship between the Creator and humanity. Furthermore, the act of creation is regarded as a manifestation of the divine love of God. Therefore, an investigation into this interdependent relationship will reveal the complex design of the world in which we live.

The concept of redemption is initiated on the first day of creation, when God distinguished light from darkness and subsequently designated them as day and night, respectively. The reference to light and darkness can be understood in spiritual terms, in that humanity has the capacity to choose to walk either in the light or in the darkness. This distinction is evident in the celestial sky, which can be attributed to the rebellion of Satan, who is known as the father of lies, and the foreknowledge that humanity would transgress as well. Thus, this message of light and darkness serves as a reminder of His love and provides the means of salvation, even before the existence of humanity, so that we may walk in the light of His word.

Five Elements of Creation

The philosophies and philosophers of antiquity approached the subject of the elements namely, air, water, earth, fire and spirit in a different way than the application in this study. While these elements are fundamental, ideas will be developed from them, including baptism, which can involve the elements of water and air, as well as narrating the descent of New Jerusalem to earth from heaven, symbolized by the elements of earth and spirit. Moreover, the framework of the elements, as observed throughout the world in its entirety, is set out in a way that will be built upon to reveal the message of the Creator. Therefore, the application of the five elements in this study encompasses not only their observation in the natural world but also the application of the word of God to them.

In order to demonstrate the relationship between Scripture and the natural world, it is first necessary to gain an understanding of the application of the elements to our planet Earth and its effect on the celestial sky. The five elements, each with different characteristics and qualities, are evenly distributed on the earth along the equator based on predominant geographical features of a particular region. Given that both the physical world and the celestial sphere were designed by the Creator, it can be reasonably concluded that the fundamental principles that apply to the five elements on Earth should also be applicable to the celestial sphere.

Delineation of the Elemental Boundaries

The configuration and location of the elements are fixed with respect to predominant geographical features within specific longitudinal boundaries, with the characteristics of these features being identifiable by considering factors such as size, elevation, and depth. Notable examples of such landscapes include the Amazon Jungle, the Sahara Desert, the Himalayas, the Mariana Trench, and the American Great Plains. The ensuing association of elements with distinct geographical features is described as such: the earth element is associated with jungles and tropical forests, the spirit element with hot deserts, the air element with mountain and plateau elevations, the water element with the depths of the ocean, and the fire element with prairies and volcanoes. Therefore, the delineation of elements in relation to the equator unveils a conceptual design.

The area between 92 degrees west longitude and 164 degrees west longitude is designated as the fire element. This region includes the American Great Plains, which is the largest prairie in the world; Yellowstone, which is the largest supervolcano in the world; and the volcanoes of the Big Island of Hawaii. The eastern boundary of the element is delineated by the eastern extent of the American Great Plains in North America. The eight principal islands of Hawaii are situated within the western boundary of this domain. According to the elemental scheme, the predominant association of these geographic features is with the element of fire.

The region is notable for a number of significant volcanic features, including the Yellowstone supervolcano, as well as the volcanoes of

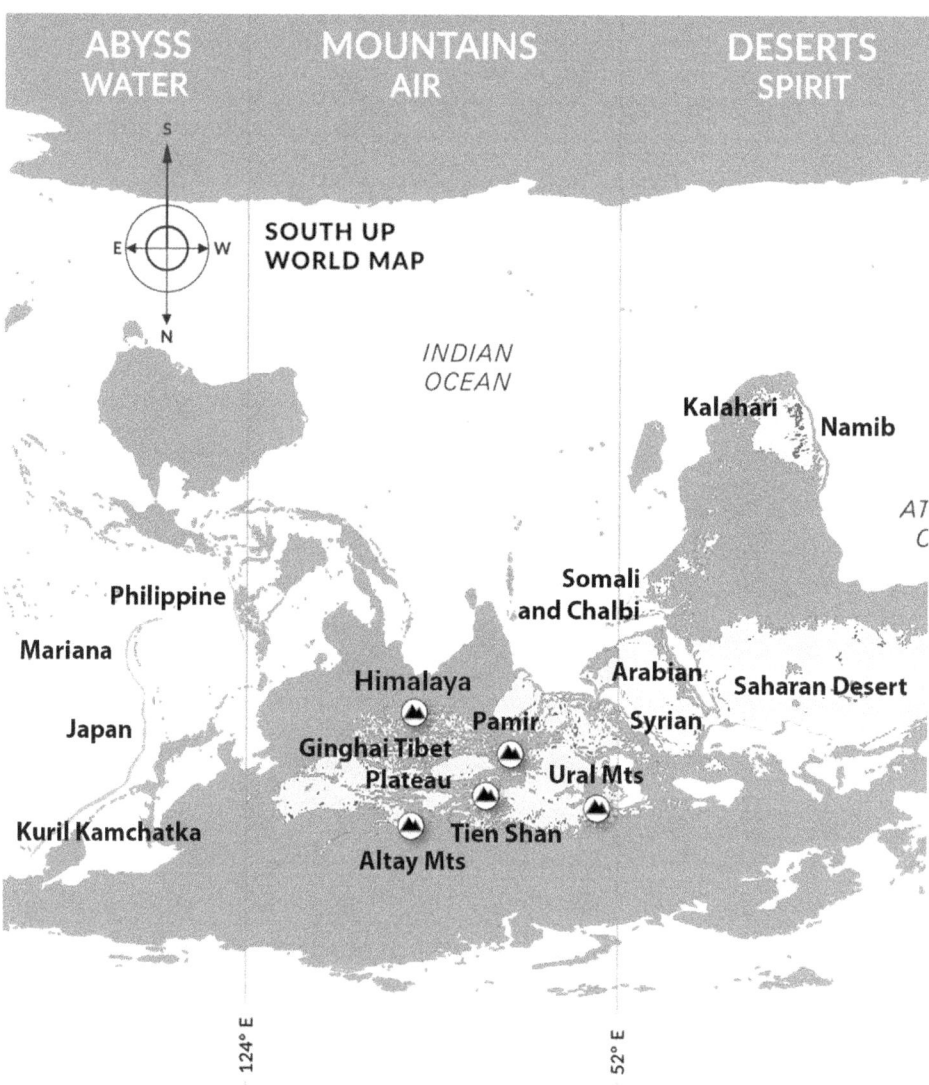

Mauna Loa and Mauna Kea on the Big Island of Hawaii. Yellowstone is situated between 110 degrees west longitude and 111 degrees west longitude, at the convergence of the Great Plains and the Great Basin. The magma chamber beneath Yellowstone is estimated to span approximately fifty-five miles by twenty miles and reach a depth of approximately six miles. Mauna Loa is the largest subaerial volcano in the world in terms of both mass and volume, reaching an elevation of 13,679 feet above sea level. Additionally, Mauna Kea is the tallest volcano in the world, reaching an elevation of 13,803 feet.

The water element extends from 164 degrees west longitude to 124 degrees east longitude and encompasses the seven deepest oceanic formations in the world. The topographic formations include the Mariana Trench, the Japan Trench, the Kuril-Kamchatka Trench, the Tonga Trench, the Kermadec Trench, the Philippine Trench, and the Izu-Ogasawara Trench, which represents a continuation of the Japan Trench. The Challenger Deep in the Mariana Trench represents the deepest known location on Earth, with a depth of 36,037 feet. The next locations with the greatest depths are the Horizon Deep, situated in the Tonga Trench with a depth of 35,433 feet, and the Emden Deep, located in the Philippine Trench. The element of water is thus associated with the concept of depth and the abyss.

The elevation of the mountains and plateaus situated between 52 degrees east longitude and 124 degrees east longitude is associated with the air element. This region encompasses the areas commonly known as High Asia and the Roof of the World. The Himalayan and Pamir regions are home to over one hundred of the highest mountains in the world, with Mount Everest at 29,032 feet, representing the highest point of elevation on Earth. The Qinghai-Tibet Plateau is the largest and highest plateau on Earth, with an average elevation of approximately sixteen thousand feet. Therefore, the air element is indicative of the actual elevation, as opposed to the height of a mountain or plateau.

The geographic features associated with the spirit element are defined by hot deserts situated between 52 degrees east and 20 degrees west longitude. This region encompasses the area between the meridian that bisects the African continent and the Cape Verde Islands, and the meridian off the Horn of Africa. One of the defining characteristics of these sandy deserts is the absence of sound, which is attributable to the exceptional sound-absorbing properties of sand. This characteristic contributes to an experience of quietude, which is unique to these vast, featureless wildernesses and thus associated with the spirit element.

The hot deserts of this region include the Arabian and Syrian deserts in southwest Asia, as well as the Sahara, Kalahari, Namib, Somali, and Chalbi deserts in Africa. The Sahara, which spans approximately thirty-two hundred miles from east to west and eight hundred to fourteen hundred miles from north to south, is the largest hot desert in the world. The Arabian Desert, spanning approximately nine hundred thousand square miles, is the second largest hot desert and the largest in Asia. The Kalahari Desert is a sandy savanna, and its non-wandering dunes form the largest continuous stretch of sand in the world. Therefore, the Sahara, Arabian, and Kalahari deserts are among the most prominent in the world, distinguished by their unique characteristics and vast size.

The primary geographic features of the earth element, situated between 20 degrees west and 92 degrees west longitude, are the rainforests and wetlands. The ecosystems in this region are home to the greatest diversity of plant and animal life, which is unparalleled in other regions of the planet. In consideration of these characteristics, the earth element is associated with the sustainability of physical life.

These biomes include the Amazon Rainforest, the Valdivian Rainforest, the Pantanal, the Corcovado Rainforest, the Everglades, the Okefenokee Swamp, and the Atchafalaya Basin. The Amazon Basin alone spans two million seven hundred thousand square miles and contains half of the world's tropical forests. The Pantanal is the largest tropical wetland in the world, accounting for almost three percent of all wetlands. The Okefenokee Swamp is the second largest freshwater swamp in the world after the Amazon floodplain. Collectively, this region of the Earth is home to a diverse array of wetland ecosystems and accounts for over half of the world's remaining rainforests.

Influence upon the Celestial Sphere

Since antiquity, celestial objects visible in the night sky have served as a source of inspiration for narratives that often convey discernible moral lessons. In many of these accounts, those associated with the heavens are depicted as manifesting a higher form of consciousness in comparison to that experienced by humanity on Earth. It is noteworthy that Enoch states that the angel Uriel imparted knowledge about the constellations to him, as documented in the Book of Enoch. These considerations suggest that the use of the constellations in relation to the Scripture may also serve to reveal the plan of God.

Moreover, the data gathered on the constellations in this study demonstrates a long-standing application of the five elements to the celestial sky. A correlation between the constellations and the elements serves to enhance the visual aspect of the divine plan for humanity, which can be revealed through them. Accordingly, the original intentions behind the constellations, as designed by God, can be revealed in an objective manner.

The distribution of elements along the Earth's equator is discernible in the night sky when projected onto it. In this way, the correlation between the elements used to classify Earth's geographical features can be applied to the attributes of the constellations in the night sky. An intriguing feature that emerges from this projection is the delineation of the path of the Milky Way, which separates the Amazon rainforest from the Valdivian rainforest and traces the shoreline of the Pacific Ocean. The correlation between the elements of the Earth and its effect on the heavens is indicative of a thoughtful design, suggesting an awareness of the characteristics of both the Earth and the heavens in their totality.

It is important to recognize that the illustration portrays several constellations that have been created in recent times. The formation of these constellations is attributed to the grouping of stars and the transfer of stars from older constellations. In light of their recent additions and given the consideration of ancient cultures, these constellations do not contribute to the presentation of the celestial message of salvation.

The constellations Phoenix, Grus, and Crux serve as illustrative examples in this regard. The constellation Phoenix, which derives its name from its brightest star, Ankaa, was formed in the late sixteenth century, circa 1597. The constellation Grus, which is represented by a wading bird, first appeared in 1598 and is composed of stars that were previously part of the constellation Piscis Austrinus, resulting in a smaller southern fish. The constellation Crux, which was formed in the 1600s by stars originally in the constellation Centaurus, is currently the brightest constellation in the southern hemisphere.

Additionally, Argo Navis is no longer officially recognized as a constellation. During the eighteenth century, it was divided into three distinct constellations: Puppis, Carina, and Vela. Each of these constellations is associated with a specific component of the ship: the stern, the keel, and the sail, respectively. However, for the purposes of this study, the three current constellations will be identified collectively under the constellation of Argo Navis.

Delineation of the Celestial Sphere

The western border of the fire element corresponds with the mouth of the Eridanus constellation, marking the end of the river and the transition to the water element. In Greek mythology, the constellation Eridanus represents the path traversed by Phaeton, who is depicted by the constellation Auriga. According to the myth, while in his father's

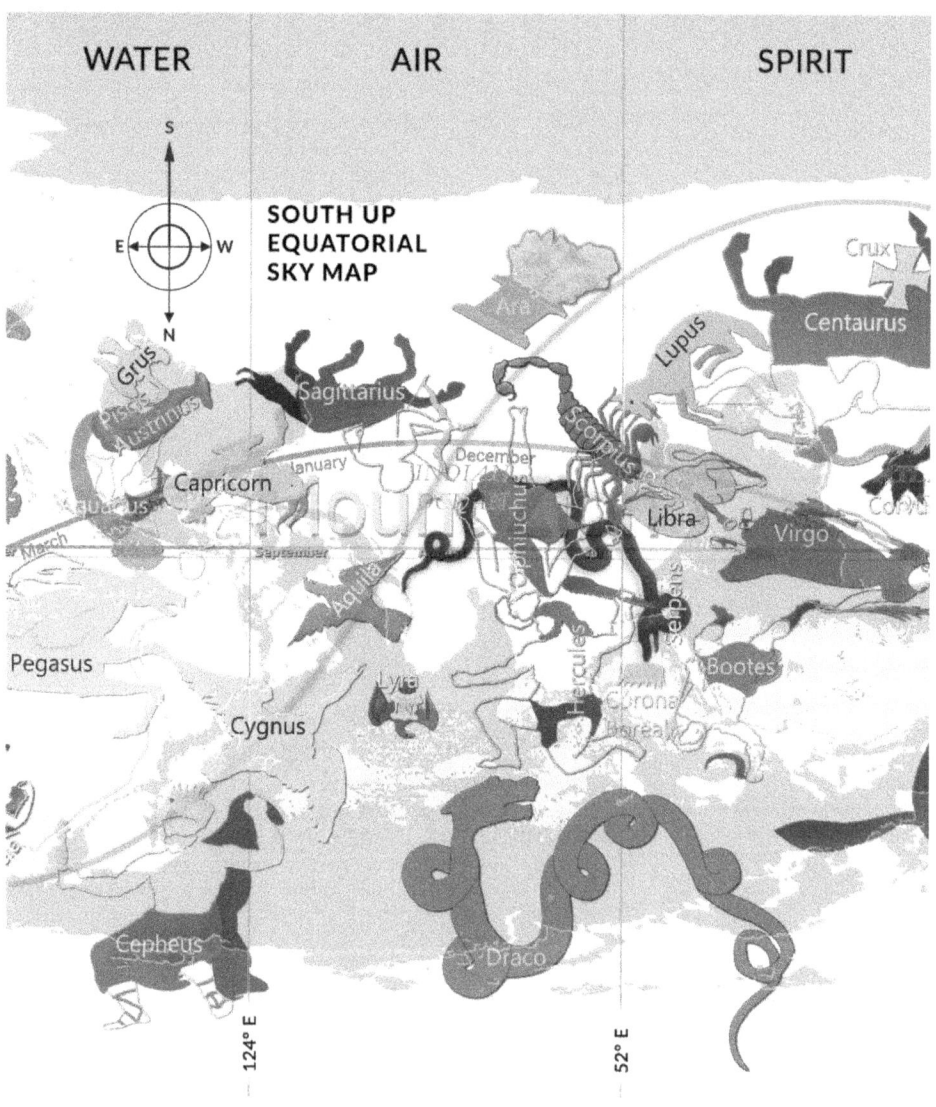

chariot, Phaeton set the world on fire when he drove it too close to the earth. The eastern border of the fire element is associated with the constellation Orion, which, in the context of Maya cosmology, is believed to contain the cosmic fire of creation. Therefore, the celestial region under the influence of the fire element is conceptualized as encompassing the cosmic creation of fire until the flame represented by the path of Phaeton is extinguished.

The constellations of Aries, Taurus, Perseus, and Cetus are associated with the element of fire. The constellation Taurus is associated with the ritual sacrifice of the bull, which is burned as an atonement for sin, while the constellation Aries is linked to the lamb for the Passover meal. This association with the fire element is further reinforced in the Passover ritual, where the lamb is roasted over a fire, as outlined in Exodus 12:8. Additionally, any part of the lamb that is not consumed must be burned before sunrise. Consequently, with regard to the fire element, these constellations are focused on the concepts of judgment and redemption, and the place where atonement is made.

The area influenced by the water element is designated as the Celestial Sea and is represented by the constellations of Cepheus, Cassiopeia, Andromeda, Pisces, Piscis Austrinus, Grus, Aquarius, Cetus, Capricorn, and Pegasus. This region is situated between the piscine tails of Cetus and Capricorn. According to legend, Poseidon is said to have inundated the domain of Cepheus as a consequence of Cassiopeia's assertion that Andromeda was more beautiful than the Nereids. Aquarius is depicted as carrying a jug of water, which he is pouring out, while the winged horse Pegasus emerges from the sea. Thus, this region of the night sky is characterized by an abundance of constellations associated with water.

The constellations of Aquila, Capricorn, Draco, Hercules, Cygnus, Sagittarius, Sagitta, Ara, Lyra, Scorpius, Ophiuchus, and Serpens are associated with the element of air. These constellations represent a range of varying altitudes, from the stinger of Scorpio, which is positioned above its head to the smoke that rises from Ara, which creates the Milky Way. This region of the celestial sky is thus associated with elevation.

Other examples include the depiction of Draco with four legs, a scaly body, and wings in the iconography of the early Sumerians. Additionally, Capricorn is depicted as the front half of a mountain goat, while Serpens is held off the ground by Ophiuchus. Hercules is associated with the concept of the glory of the air from an interpretation attributed to Porphyry. Finally, Sagittarius is depicted holding a bow, while the constellations of Aquila, Cygnus, and Lyra are seen soaring through the celestial sky.

The constellations of Corona Borealis, Libra, Virgo, Centaurus, Crux, Corvus, Bootes, Lupus, and Crater are associated with the spirit element. The constellation Corona Borealis is associated with both freedom and slavery, while Libra represents the celestial scale of truth and justice that serves to measure the worthiness of the conscience. In Greek mythology, Virgo is a goddess of justice who, in disgust at humanity's greed and violence, flees to heaven. The concept of integrity is exemplified in the story of Corvus, who was punished for falsely accusing Hydra as the cause of his tardiness, and in the virtue of Bootes, who was entrusted with the riches of royals and nobles. In light of these considerations, the narratives associated with these constellations underscore the significance of truthfulness and honesty as fundamental tenets of ethical conduct.

The celestial representation of the element of earth can be interpreted to symbolize a garden, which is capable of sustaining a diverse array of living creatures. Gemini is symbolized by biological twins, Cancer is symbolized by the Egyptian scarab beetle, and Canis Major and Canis Minor are referenced as two dogs or wolves. Another noteworthy astronomical association is the sickle asterism, a smaller star grouping that forms the head and shoulders of Leo. The remaining constellations include Argo Navis, Coma Berenices, Leo Minor, Ursa Major, and Hydra.

Putting Two Together

It is important to note that the celestial figures depicted reflect the application of the elements as delineated along the equator of the Earth. The elements of the Earth and their application in the celestial sky, as outlined, provide the correct initial orientation for this study of the word of God. As the Earth rotates on its axis, the constellations transition through the influence of the five elements on a daily basis. However, this pattern is subject to the annual calendar and the Earth's position relative to the Sun during the year. The observable pattern is therefore contingent not only on the effects of the elements on the celestial sky, but also on the consideration of the Earth's orbit during the year and its orientation to the Sun.

The apparent movement of constellations over the course of the year can be evident by its visibility in the sky, which can also correlate to the constellations being influenced by a different element from a fixed vantage point. In this study, the analysis is centered on four specific days that correspond to an established pattern, thereby generating the narrative as found in the word of God. Rather than attributing a wide-ranging set of characteristics to a single instance of a constellation, the position of a constellation influenced by the various elements can engender a more dynamic approach to the constellations and the overall narrative being presented. Thus, the fundamental essence of a constellation is identified in a different manner over the course of the year as its association with the elements changes.

To illustrate this point, consider the constellation Cepheus. Within the context of the narrative, the constellation is interpreted as a symbol of a king, with each instance representing a different figure. These figures, as determined by the pattern, include the following: the

Ancient of Days above the throne, Lord before the tabernacle, Christ's descent to Earth, and Apollyon, who is king over the locust from the bottomless pit. Thus, this dynamic interplay between the Earth and the celestial sky over the course of a year can collectively illustrate the word of God in an informative manner.

2
Heavenly Observances

T he sun, moon, and other luminaries in the heavens were introduced on the fourth day of creation for the purpose of illumination and the measurement of time. The sun emits light and thus governs the day, while the moon reflects light and thus governs the night. The establishment of these astronomical reference points serves to delineate divisions including seasonal cycles, days of the week, and years. The occurrence of sacred times, such as festivals and holy days, can be indicated by these celestial bodies as visual signs. It may therefore be surmised that the luminaries are intended to serve as a reminder of the Creator's message.

There are a number of methods that can be utilized to determine the passage of time. The solar calendar is based on the orbit of the Earth around the Sun, with months assigned a fixed duration. In contrast, the lunar calendar is based on the phases of the Moon as it revolves around Earth, with months of either twenty-nine or thirty days in length. In this regard, the movements of both the Earth around the Sun and the Moon around the Earth are recorded on their respective calendars over the course of the year.

Another calendar system is a celestial coordinate system, known as right ascension, which can be viewed as a yearly calendar. In contrast to measuring time along the ecliptic (the apparent path of the sun), right ascension is directly related to the equator, which is projected on the celestial sphere. As a yearly calendar, it indicates the optimal times for observing a star at a given latitude based on imaginary meridian lines of time. Accordingly, time can be measured in relation to the equator of the Earth, which serves as a reference line for the stars.

The illustration demonstrates the relationship between the two calendar systems. The months in the outer circle correspond to the

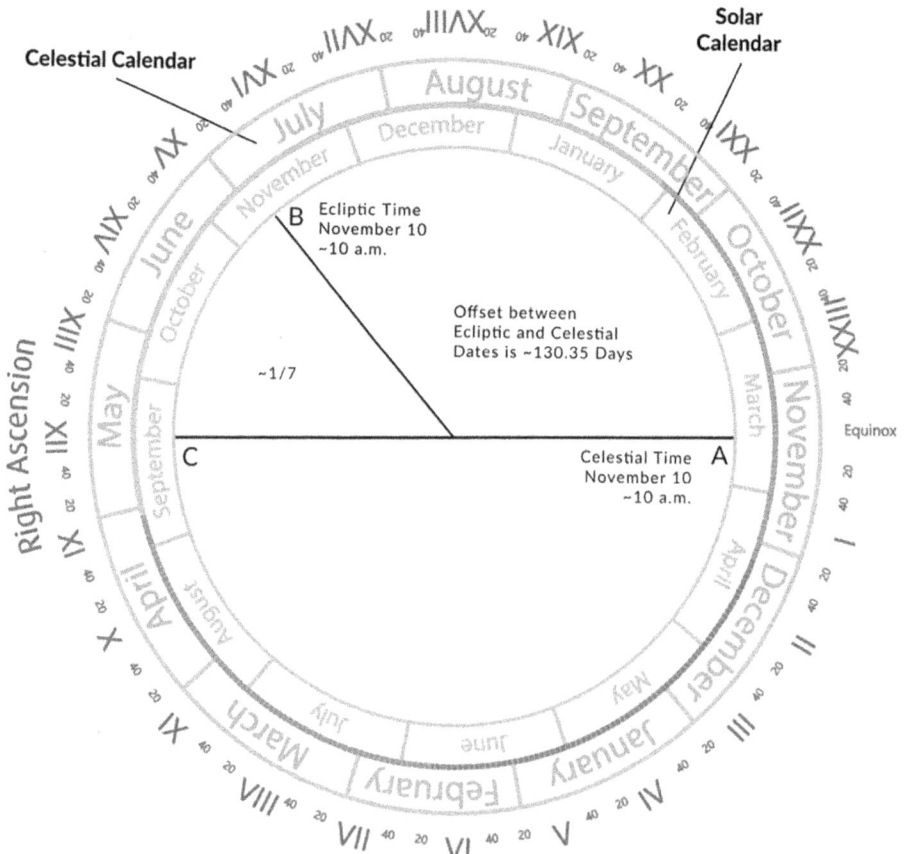

celestial equator, while the months in the inner circle correspond to the solar calendar. It is important to note that a date indicated on the solar calendar may also correspond to the same date on the celestial calendar. Therefore, while each calendar is independent of the other, they can be used in conjunction with one another.

The offset between the solar and celestial calendars is approximately one hundred and thirty and one third days, or one hundred twenty-eight and a half degrees. This offset corresponds to a pattern illustrated at the center of the illustration. To illustrate, the celestial date of November 10, represented by point A, is offset by the specified degree from the corresponding date on the solar calendar, represented by point B. This calendar offset is therefore associated with the overall pattern, which in this case correlates the observances of the sun with the stars.

Roman numerals encircle the calendars that denote the hours of right ascension, expressed in a twenty-four-hour format that corresponds to one revolution of the Earth around its axis. The right ascension is defined as commencing at the zero point, which is the Sun during the March equinox. This point in time also corresponds with the astrological age, which is currently in the constellation Pisces and nearing the constellation Aquarius. The assigned value of right ascension for a specific celestial body is determined by the timing of its passage through the highest point in the meridian as the Earth rotates. Therefore, the measurement of right ascension corresponds with the March equinox, having taken place on that day, and increases towards the east over the course of one day.

Calendar Correlations

The Hebrew lunisolar calendar includes annual holy days that recur on the same dates each year. However, on a solar calendar, these observances will occur on different days each year. It is important to note that the lunar year is typically three hundred and fifty-four days long, while the solar year is approximately three hundred and sixty-five days long. In certain instances, both calendars undergo intercalation to align with the seasons, whereby a lunar month is added to the lunar calendar and a solar day is added to the solar calendar. As a result, the observance of a Hebrew holy day varies within an established thirty-day span on the solar calendar from year to year.

As a consequence of the calendar offset, an intriguing correlation between the solar and celestial calendars is revealed with regard to the Hebrew holy days. In the illustration, the Hebrew spring observances are delineated on the celestial calendar, while the Hebrew fall observances are delineated on the ecliptic calendar. The offset enables

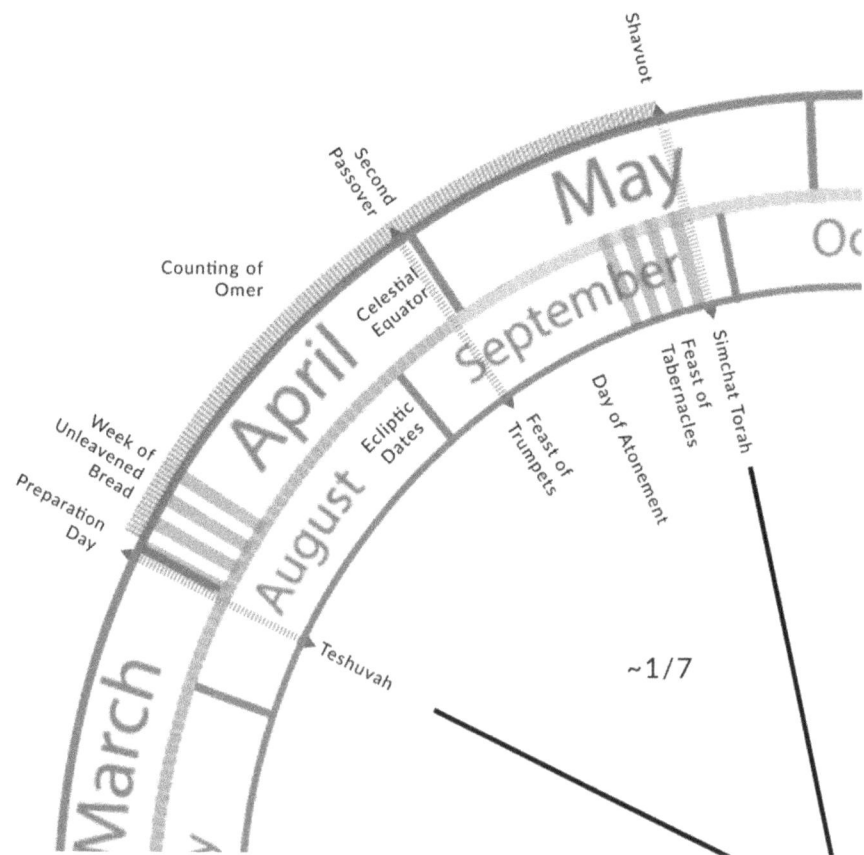

the synchronization of the spring and fall Hebrew observances, which occur forty-one and a half lunar months later. This offset serves to exemplify the interrelationship between the two calendars.

The springtime observances of the day of preparation, the second Passover, and Shavuot are aligned with the fall observances of Teshuvah, the Feast of Trumpets, and Simchat Torah, respectively. The day of preparation is observed on the fourteenth day of the Hebrew month of Abib. The second Passover is observed on the same day in the following month, and Shavuot is the fiftieth day in the counting of the Omer. Teshuvah is observed on the fortieth day prior to the Day of Atonement. The Feast of Trumpets is observed on the thirtieth day following Teshuvah, and Simchat Torah is celebrated on the day which follows the seven-day observance of the Feast of Tabernacles.

Date Methodology

As illustrated, the span of time between the day of preparation and Simchat Torah can be represented as a period of three and a half years. The day of preparation is marked on the celestial calendar as March 31, and Simchat Torah is marked on the ecliptic calendar as September 28. A recent occurrence of these dates is the day of preparation on March 31, 2018, and the Simchat Torah observance in Israel on September 28, 2021, thereby indicating that a three and a half-year offset exists between these two Hebrew observances. Thus, the dating outlined in this study is predicated on this concept.

In the Hebrew calendar, the first month is Abib, later called Nisan. The commencement of this month is contingent upon the observation of a new moon by two witnesses, in addition to the ears of barley being green. There is a possibility that both of these observances may occur before the March equinox, in which case the month of Abib will commence prior to the first day of spring. For the purposes of this study, the first day of Abib is defined as March 18, which occurs prior to the March equinox. Subsequent observances are derived from this reference date.

To facilitate analysis, the table provides the Gregorian dates that will be used in conjunction with the Hebrew calendar. These dates are consistent with the overall complexity of the pattern that will be developed. The dates indicated for the spring and fall observances will be used exclusively on both calendars, which initiate and conclude a period of three and a half years. Thus, the study will recognize a single date for each observance that can be applied to both calendars.

Hebrew Calendar		Observances (3.5 year period)	Calendar	
Abib	1	Rosh Chodesh	March	18
	14	Preparation Day		31
	15	Feast of Unleavened Bread	April	1
	16	First Fruits, Omer 1		2
Ziv	14	Second Passover		30
Sivan	6	Shavuot	May	21
Av	30	Teshuvah	August	8
Tishrei	1	Feast of Trumpets	September	7
	10	Day of Atonement		16
	15	Feast of Tabernacles		21
	22	Simchat Torah		28

This study proposes that the counting of the Omer should commence on the Feast of First Fruits, which occurs on the sixteenth day of the month of Abib. With regard to the Gregorian calendar, it should be noted that the first day of the counting process does not necessarily correspond to the day that follows the weekly Sabbath in the Week of Unleavened Bread. The counting of the Omer, therefore, commences on the Feast of First Fruits, irrespective of the day of the week on which it falls, and concludes on the fiftieth day with the festival of Shavuot.

This approach ensures that the interval between the first day of Abib and Shavuot remains constant on an annual basis, thereby maintaining the correlation between the spring and fall observances on the celestial and ecliptic calendars.

Festival Pairings

As previously illustrated, the day of preparation on the celestial calendar corresponds with Teshuvah on the solar calendar. Despite the discrepancy in the timing of these observations, both share a core principle that strengthens the connections between the two observances. This notion is further reinforced by the observed correlations between the Second Passover and the Feast of Trumpets, as well as between Shavuot and Simchat Torah. Despite the apparent distinction between the spring and fall festivals, their alignment with respect to an aspect of the pattern reveals a shared characteristic, thereby underscoring the significance of this interconnection.

The day of preparation and the day of Teshuvah address the concept of sin and the attitude of the individual toward God. On the day of preparation, all leaven is to be removed from the house. In a similar vein, 1 Corinthians 5:6-8 indicates that the individual must remove sin from their life. The day of Teshuvah is a period of introspection and reflection, during which individuals seek to reconnect with God and examine their lives in the context of Scripture. In light of these considerations, it appears evident that both observances place significant emphasis on the importance of turning to God and confession.

The initial pairing can be understood as an example of the necessity for a relationship with God. It is of the utmost importance to acknowledge sin and return to God in order to engage in worship of the Creator in spirit and in truth. In conclusion, it is evident that both preparation day and Teshuvah underscore the role of freewill in the process of removing sin from one's life.

The second Passover is similarly associated with Teshuvah. The second Passover is observed exclusively by those who were inadvertently ceremonially unclean or who were far away in another land on Passover, but who have since become ceremonially clean on the fourteenth day of the second Hebrew month, Ziv. In accordance with the stipulations set forth in Numbers 9:10-12, the same rules that were outlined in the first Passover are to be observed with the second Passover. This indicates that the lamb is to be consumed with unleavened bread and bitter herbs. Therefore, this Passover offers a second, or perhaps final, occasion for individuals to return and establish a relationship with God.

The second Passover and the Feast of Trumpets are connected by a return theme, with their respective dates corresponding to the transition between the spirit and earth elements. In the case of the second Passover, individuals who have returned from a distant land, having been absent from the Passover in Abib, as well as those who were ceremonially unclean, are now permitted to participate. Furthermore, the Feast of Trumpets may mark the return of the Son of Man, as the specific day or hour of his return is not known except by the Father, as stated in Matthew 24:36. It is noteworthy that this fall observance is referred to as the "day and hour no one knows," marking the beginning of a new year. Therefore, at the junction of the earth and spirit elements, these observances appear to signify a renewal or a return that marks the beginning of a new phase in one's relationship with God.

The festivals of Shavuot and Simchat Torah are observed as occasions to express gratitude for the provision of the Torah, which serves as the foundation for life and sustenance, both physically and spiritually. Originally an agricultural celebration, Shavuot is associated with the establishment of the nation of Israel at Mount Sinai, when Moses returned with the first set of tablets. In contrast, Simchat Torah is a celebration of the joy associated with the possession of the Torah. During this festival, prayers are offered for the rain necessary for the continued existence and vitality of the nation. Therefore, the festival of Shavuot commemorates the giving of the Torah, while Simchat Torah is a celebration of joy in having the Torah.

The Betrothal Alignment

The successive pairings of the Hebrew spring and fall observances present an overarching narrative that parallels the progression from betrothal to the marriage feast. The engagement period is to be concluded on the first day of the seven-day Feast of Tabernacles, which coincides with the consummation of the marriage. After the wedding feast, the festivals of Shavuot and Simchat Torah mark the beginning of their shared life together as husband and wife. Accordingly, the correlation between the Hebrew holy days on the celestial and ecliptic calendars offers insight into the betrothal of those who place their trust in God and adhere to His word.

The observances of the day of preparation and Teshuvah represent the establishment of a relationship between the individual and God. In the context of Jewish tradition, a betrothal is initiated with an agreement on the bride price and consent from the prospective bride. The day of preparation is associated with the ultimate atonement, which is the Lamb of God, who was foreordained before the foundation of the world. The day of Teshuvah, therefore, represents the moment when the bride accepts the marriage proposal by turning to God, thereby establishing a legally binding union between them. This relationship entails the dedication of the individual to God, which is made possible as a result of the ultimate atonement of God, regarded as the equivalent of the bride price.

At some point during the period of engagement, the bridegroom will leave to prepare a wedding chamber in anticipation of the marriage. It is also very important for the bride to have gained a comprehensive understanding of her future husband prior to his return. This same principle can be extended to the relationship between God and His people, in that the people are to gain a deep understanding of His word. It is therefore incumbent upon the bride to endeavor to prepare herself fully, with complete dedication and attention, for her upcoming marriage to her beloved.

In Egypt, the first Passover is associated with the concept of God's ultimate atonement becoming the bride price and the eventual formation of a nation. This observation is supported by the notion that God is distinguishing between those who are His people and those who are not. The acceptance of the Israelites and others to follow the mandates of God resulted in their liberation from slavery. By participating in the

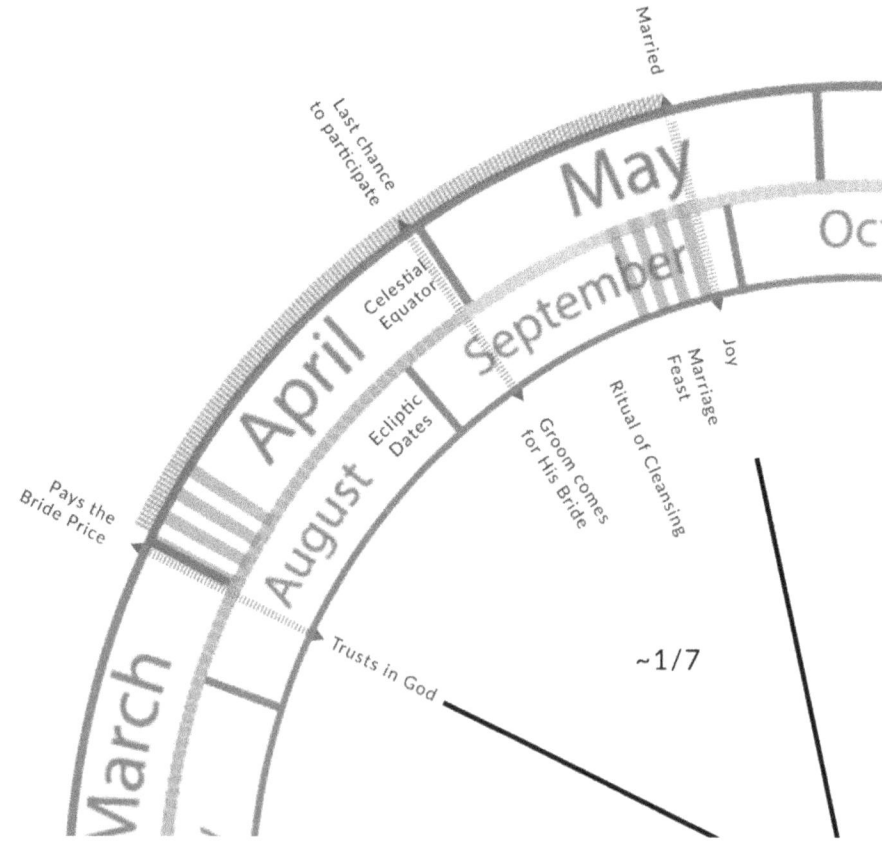

Passover, the Israelites would depart from Egypt in the morning and later become a nation called Israel.

While encamped at Mount Sinai, the Israelites received the Torah and entered into an everlasting covenant with God. This event is said to have occurred on Shavuot and is referred to as the marriage between God and Israel. This event bears resemblance to the future union between the Lamb and his bride as described in Revelation 19:9. Consequently, the covenant between God and the Israelites at Mount Sinai resulted in the establishment of a theocracy with the Creator as their king.

The celebration of Simchat Torah is a later rabbinical addition. The festival is observed in Israel on the same date as Shemini Atzeret, which is a biblically designated occasion known as the eighth day of assembly. This day occurs after the seven-day festival of the Feast of Tabernacles. In this manner, Simchat Torah is integrated with that of Shemini Atzeret.

The Simchat Torah service symbolizes the union between Israel and God, as well as the joy associated with the Torah. On this day, the annual cycle in the weekly reading of the Torah reaches its conclusion and begins anew. This transition is marked by the reading of the final portion of Deuteronomy in the synagogue, which is followed immediately by the first paragraph of Genesis. The festival of Simchat Torah, therefore, signifies a transition to a new phase of life, characterized by the blessing of wisdom derived from active engagement with the study of the Torah.

3

Unveiling the Templet

The significance of adherence to the pattern set forth by God to Moses and the others on Mount Sinai is reinforced in the construction of the courtyard, tabernacle, and its furnishings, which serve to exemplify the nature of His relationship with humanity. This directive is reiterated in several passages, including Exodus 25:9, 25:40, 26:30, and 27:8. In this way, the tabernacle may be regarded as the earthly dwelling place for God, duly functioning as a meeting place between God and humanity. In light of these considerations, it becomes evident that the design of the tabernacle serves the purpose of a visual testament to the authority of God.

This concept of the convergence of heaven and earth is reflected in the design of the courtyard and the tabernacle. In accordance with Exodus 27:18, the dimensions of the courtyard are to be one hundred cubits by fifty cubits. Similarly, a map of the surface of the Earth will have an equator measuring approximately twice the length of the line between the geographic north and south poles. Therefore, it can be proposed that the dimensions of the courtyard are indicative of a correlation with the Earth.

The application of the elemental template of the Earth, which transitions from the earth element, can serve as a model for the courtyard with regard to our relationship with the Creator. The courtyard is surrounded by a wall with a single gate on the eastern side, which is twenty cubits wide. The gate opens to the element of earth and is devoid of any furnishings. When an individual enters the courtyard, their approach can be conceptualized as a metaphor for the process of being born into this world. Therefore, the model of the courtyard can symbolize the spiritual progression of an individual from a state of separation to one of relationship with the Creator.

The tabernacle in the courtyard is designed to serve as a functional model. The structure is subdivided by a veil into two distinct rooms: the Holy Place and the Holy of Holies. Upon entering the tabernacle, the initial room encountered is designated as the Holy Place. This transition from the element of water to the element of air symbolizes the concept of baptism or spiritual awakening to the service of God. In essence, when an individual assumes the role of priest, they enter the Holy Place and begin their service to God.

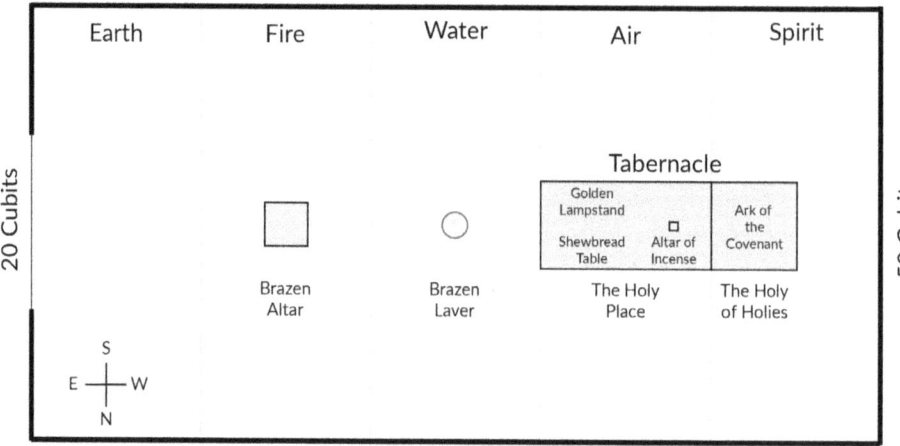

Each room is furnished with items that are distinctive to that particular space. The Holy Place contains the table of showbread, the golden candlestick, and the altar of incense. The Holy of Holies is the location of the Ark of the Covenant, with its mercy seat, which is regarded as an earthly representation of the throne of God and its mercy seat. Therefore, the Holy of Holies is understood to represent a point where heaven and earth converge.

It is noteworthy that the architectural design of the tabernacle and the courtyard, with its surrounding walls, was conceived to be universally applicable, regardless of its specific geographical location. The brazen or bronze altar, measuring five cubits by five cubits, which was used for animal sacrifices, is associated with the fire element. The laver is associated with the water element. The Holy Place, measuring twenty cubits in length, is associated with the air element, while the Holy of Holies, measuring ten cubits in length, is associated with the spirit element. The strategic placement of the tabernacle within the courtyard ensures that its dimensions and orientation effectively model the geographical characteristics of the Earth and the celestial sky.

Cultural Points

The following analysis examines four cultural reference points on Earth that correlate with the pattern. Three of these locations relate to the spiritual journey and provide insight into the function of the courtyard, as well as illustrating all of the judgments by God. The three locations are Teotihuacan in Mexico, Uluru in Australia, and Mount Kailash in Tibet. The fourth reference point is that of Giza in Egypt, which pertains to the afterlife or ultimate fulfillment. By examining these four locations, the construction of a narrative about the plan of God can be further illustrated.

The geographical distribution of ancient cultures across the globe, which exhibit distinctive characteristics in their engagement with the

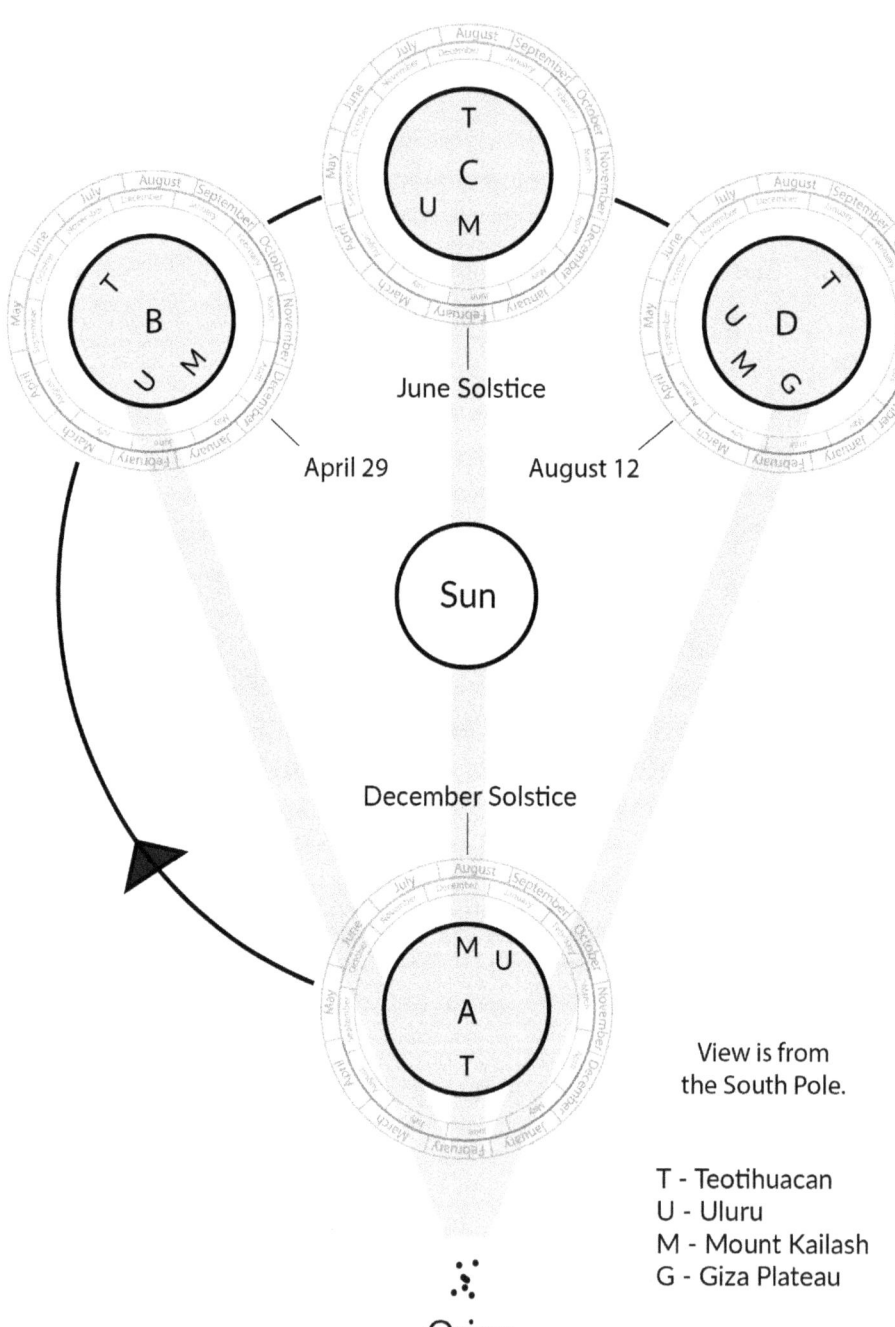

June Solstice

April 29   August 12

Sun

December Solstice

View is from
the South Pole.

T - Teotihuacan
U - Uluru
M - Mount Kailash
G - Giza Plateau

Orion

divine, constitutes an integral aspect of this pattern. In this context, it is a well-documented historical fact that the Maya engaged in the practice of animal and human sacrifice. The Aboriginal people of Australia adhere to a mythological tradition known as the Dreamtime, while both Hinduism and Buddhism espouse the pursuit of enlightenment as a core tenet of their respective belief systems. The ancient Egyptians are regarded as having been particularly devoted to the study of the afterlife. In conclusion, the pattern can be observed in various historical and cultural settings in alignment with Scripture.

The concept is further elaborated in the illustration through the use of an explanatory presentation of the pattern over the course of the year. The four positions of the Earth around the Sun demonstrate that Mount Kailash is oriented in a manner that allows it to face the Sun, whereas Teotihuacan observes the Orion constellation. The line of sight is drawn from Teotihuacan to the Orion constellation, which passes through the longitude of one of the other locations on three occasions. The alignment of these four locations with the pattern is attributed to their longitude, in a manner similar to the assignment of right ascension to a star. Therefore, an interplay emerges between the orbit of the Earth around the Sun and the apparent movement of the constellation Orion in relation to the Sun as observed from Earth.

The accompanying maps, developed for the purpose of this study of the word of God will reference one of the four locations with respect to the placement of the constellations and the stars. The following notations are employed for each location: Teotihuacan (point A), Uluru (point B), Mount Kailash (point C), and Giza (point D). These locations are intended to illustrate the four phases of the spiritual journey of the individual, as exemplified by the constellation Orion. The notations will be applied to the constellation Orion, as well as to the other constellations observed during each corresponding phase. Consequently, a map created from the vantage point of Teotihuacan

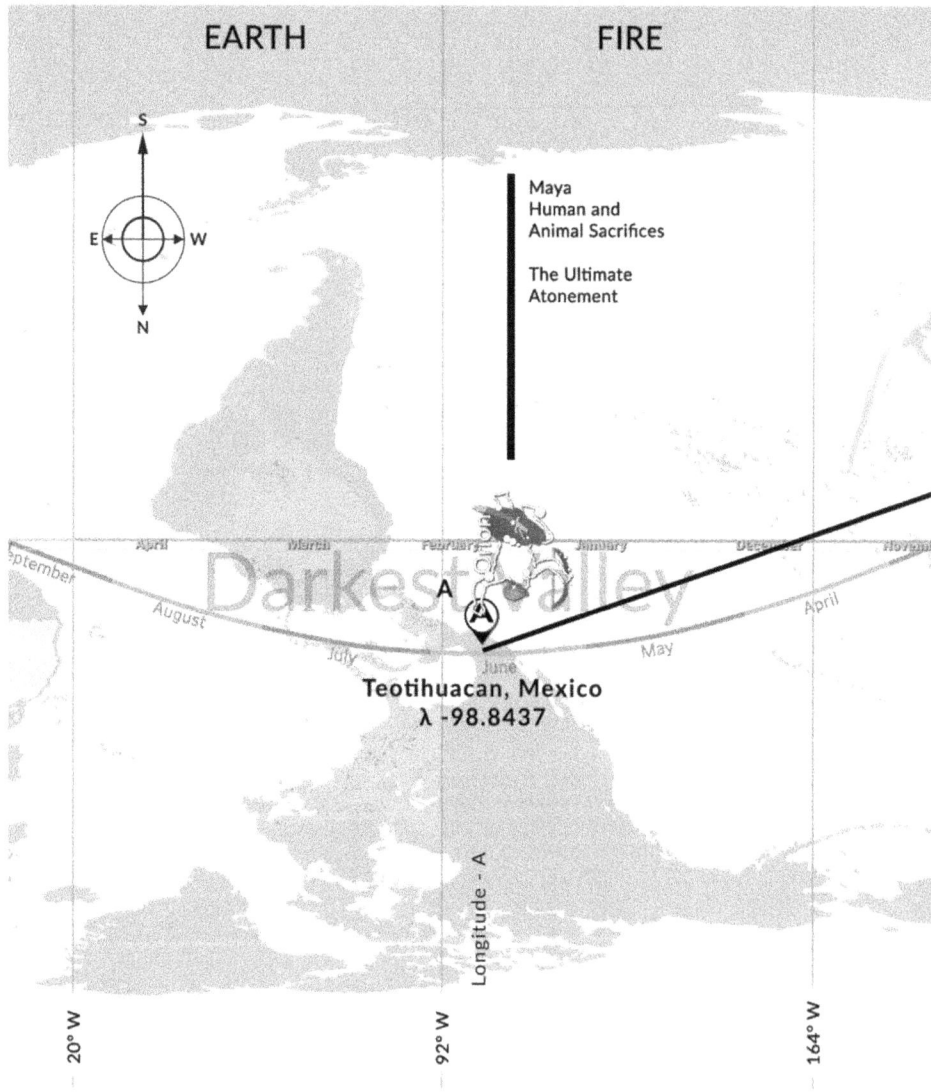

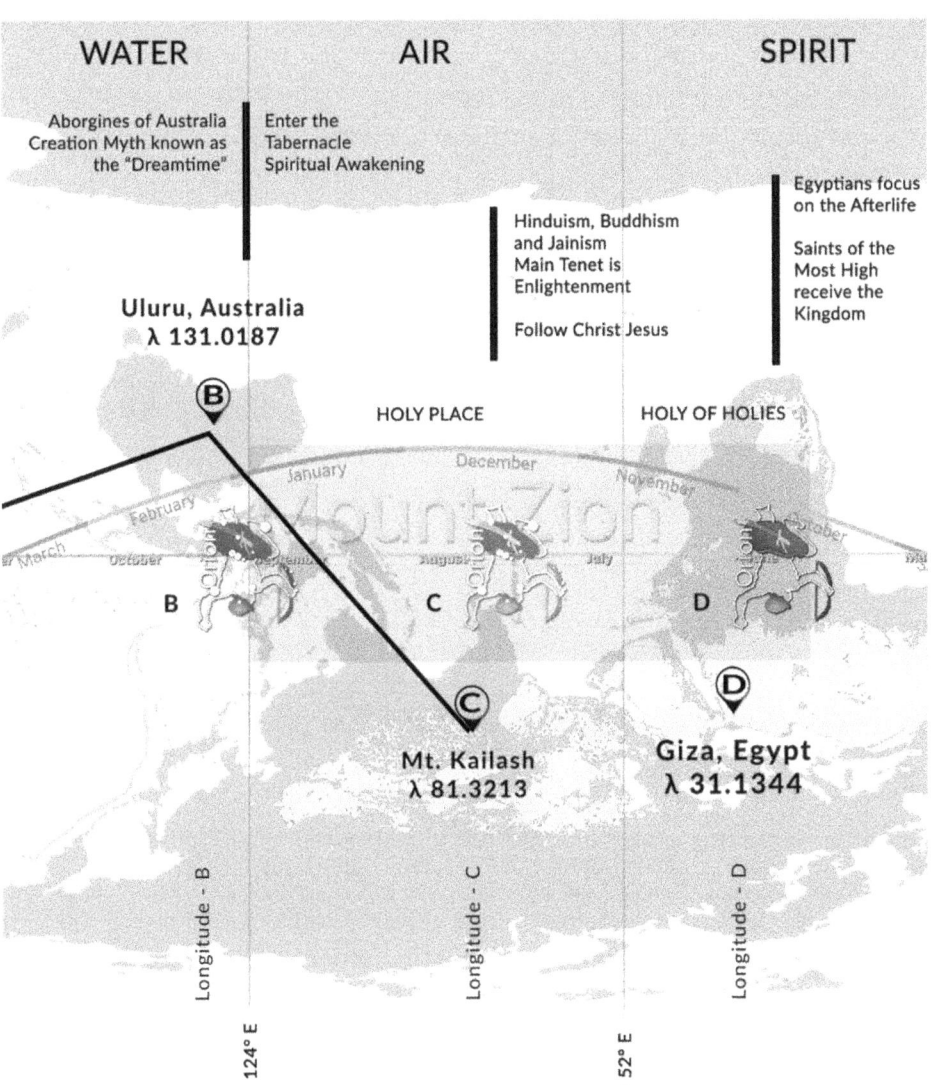

WATER

AIR

SPIRIT

Aborgines of Australia
Creation Myth known as
the "Dreamtime"

Enter the
Tabernacle
Spiritual Awakening

Egyptians focus
on the Afterlife

Hinduism, Buddhism
and Jainism
Main Tenet is
Enlightenment

Follow Christ Jesus

Saints of the
Most High
receive the
Kingdom

Uluru, Australia
λ 131.0187

HOLY PLACE

HOLY OF HOLIES

Mt. Kailash
λ 81.3213

Giza, Egypt
λ 31.1344

can illustrate the progression of the constellation Orion through its different stages, thereby delineating its spiritual journey.

Layout of the Spiritual Journey

The illustration presents a conceptual narrative of the spiritual journey of the Orion constellation, commencing at Teotihuacan. The celestial figure is depicted as a man; however, in this study, it is represented as a collective entity, specifically, the saints of the Most High. The three phases of the Orion constellation (points A, B, and C) illustrate the progression of spiritual life, traversing from the darkest point of the valley to reach the most brilliant point, full enlightenment. The depiction of the Orion constellation moving westward from Teotihuacan symbolizes the decision to leave the darkness and embrace the light. This notion is further reinforced by the belief that individuals who adhere to a faith in the Creator are meant to undertake this spiritual journey.

The layout of the illustration allows for the visualization of the concepts of Mount Zion and the darkest valley in terms of elevation. The depiction of Mount Zion symbolizes the declination of the Sun between the equator and the Tropic of Capricorn, while the darkest valley represents its declination between the equator and the Tropic of Cancer. This configuration is regarded as being fixed, akin to the initial association of celestial sky with the geography of the Earth in that Mount Zion aligns closely with the Eastern Hemisphere, and the darkest valley aligns closely with the Western Hemisphere. Due to the slight elliptical nature of the Earth's orbit around the Sun, the Southern Hemisphere experiences a greater number of days with shorter daylight hours between the March equinox and the September equinox. Consequently, the map is oriented with the Southern Hemisphere at the top, thereby illustrating the mountain of Mount Zion above the valley of the darkest valley.

The initial phase of the spiritual journey of the Orion constellation is associated with the brazen altar in conjunction with the Mesoamerican region where human and animal sacrifices were conducted. This phenomenon of human sacrifice observed among the Maya, Aztecs, and Toltecs was extraordinary in comparison to some non-Mesoamerican cultures, which may have engaged in it. The practice of human sacrifice was regarded as an integral aspect of their religious tradition. It was a systematic practice that likely persisted for over two millennia, spanning the period from the time of the Olmecs. Therefore, it can be argued that the initiation of this spiritual journey is the recognition of the necessity for a sacrifice.

The second phase of the spiritual journey of the Orion constellation is associated with the entrance of the tabernacle in conjunction with the mythology surrounding Uluru. The Aboriginal creation myth, which states that the spirit created the land and people, is known by two names: *The Dreaming* and *The Dreamtime*. This mythology is based on the concept of interconnectedness between all people and things, and the weaving together the spiritual and physical realms. The Orion constellation is depicted as departing the region associated with dreams, passing through the door of the tabernacle, and becoming spiritually conscious. In this way, the commencement of an individual's relationship with the Creator and their spiritual journey is symbolized by the act of entering the tabernacle.

It is only after an individual passes through the door of the tabernacle that they will encounter the path of enlightenment. The concept suggests that in order to transition out of the dream state, crossing the water element, an individual must have faith, as expressed in Hebrews 11:3, which is to understand that the invisible God created reality. The path to enlightenment remains imperceptible to those who are outside the tabernacle, as the path is symbolized by the light of the menorah and thus remains hidden within the tabernacle. This configuration suggests that the objective of the spiritual life is enlightenment, which can only be achieved by priests who serve God daily in the tabernacle by means of faith.

The pinnacle of the spiritual journey is perfection, a state characterized by the absence of falsehood, a quality exemplified by those referenced in Revelation 14:5. Additionally, Jesus instructs his disciples to "be perfect, just as your Father in heaven is perfect," as recorded in Matthew 5:48. This attainment in the state of perfection is depicted by the third position of the Orion constellation relative to the summit of Mount Zion and the menorah. It is important to note that the menorah functions as a symbol of the presence and guidance of God, as well as a representation of spiritual growth and power. In conclusion, the position of the constellation Orion at the brightest point in the Holy Place can be considered to represent an individual who has a profound love for the Creator.

Mount Kailash is regarded as a symbol of spiritual power and enlightenment in several religious traditions, including Hinduism, Buddhism, Jainism, and Bon. In the Buddhist and Hindu cosmology, Mount Kailash is regarded as the Axis Mundi, or the axis of the Earth, and the axis is regarded as a pathway through which an individual can ascend into the spiritual realm. It is noteworthy that no individual has ever physically reached the summit of Mount Kailash. This spiritual journey, as depicted by Mount Kailash in relation to the constellation Orion, is a path of ascent, where one can gain deeper insights and experience a more profound connection with God.

The fourth stage is associated with the throne of God in the Holy of Holies and the concept of the afterlife. The ancient Egyptians devoted a considerable amount of attention to it and even provided instructions on how to navigate it. The Book of the Dead, which has been preserved in tombs and on mummies, as well as in the Book of Gates, exemplifies their work in understanding the afterlife. Another of their mythological concepts is the Field of Reeds, which represents a heavenly paradise symbolizing a reflection of one's earthly life. Therefore, the fundamental objective of learning about the afterlife is to encourage individuals to live in a manner that is deemed worthy of eternal paradise, as their life will be evaluated in this context.

The scriptural passages from Daniel 7:18, 7:22, and 7:27 imply that the saints of the Most High will inherit a kingdom that will never pass away. The saints will have walked the path, illuminated by the word of God, thereby attaining their place of honor. According to Revelation 2:26, those who overcome and persevere in the works that Christ approves until the end of their life will be given power over the nations. They will be seated on the throne, as depicted by the constellation Orion within the spirit element, reigning with Christ. Therefore, the saints of the Most High, having embarked on the path that is guided by the word of God, will receive this inheritance of the kingdom of God through their relationship with Him.

The progression of these distinct cultures from east to west, along with their sacred sites, from the earth to the spirit element, provides an illustrative account of redemption, our relationship with God, and the afterlife. Each of these four ancient cultures perceived their respective geographical region as a comprehensive spiritual journey, with a central focus on their distinct phase. In this context, the distinct phases of the spiritual journey can be identified in relation to the geographical location of these cultures in relation to the Holy of Holies. The Earth is thus conceptualized as a courtyard with a tabernacle, which is based on the elemental pattern used for the celestial sky and the features of the Earth, as well as the location and ideologies of these cultures.

Time Starts at Teotihuacan

Teotihuacan is home to the Pyramid of the Sun, which is one of the largest structures in Mesoamerica. The name of the place translates as the place where time began. The Pyramid of the Sun presents the

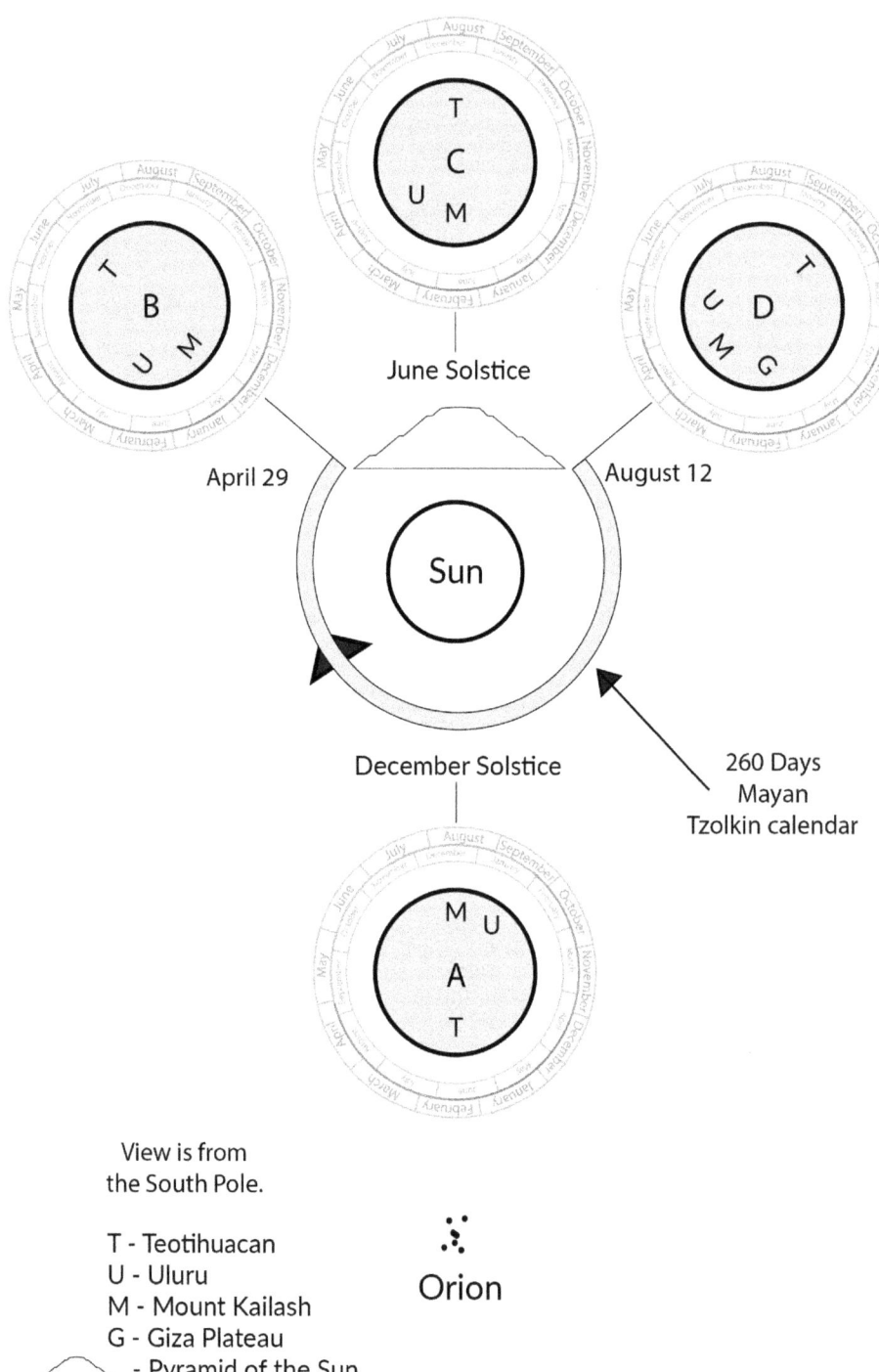

June Solstice

April 29

August 12

Sun

December Solstice

260 Days
Mayan
Tzolkin calendar

View is from
the South Pole.

T - Teotihuacan
U - Uluru
M - Mount Kailash
G - Giza Plateau
⌒ - Pyramid of the Sun

Orion

spiritual journey of the Orion constellation, wherein the constellation becomes invisible due to the Sun's position in the constellation between the months of May and July. Consequently, the location functions as the vantage point in the conceptual narrative of the spiritual journey of the Orion constellation in relation to the pyramid and the Sun.

The Pyramid of the Sun is associated with two sunset observations that occur at specific points in the course of a year. On April 29 and August 12, the pyramid is oriented such that it faces the sun at sunset. The two dates correspond to one-seventh of the circumference of the Earth's orbit before and after the June solstice. By utilizing the Sun, this pyramid allows for the progression of the Orion constellation from the time it enters the tabernacle to be traced until being seated on the throne. Therefore, the interplay of the Sun with the pyramid can be interpreted as a representation of an active spiritual life.

The alignment of these dates with the solstices serves to reinforce the correlation between astronomical observations and cultural traditions. In relation to the pattern, the position of the sun on April 29 is associated with Uluru and thus can correspond to the experience of entering through the door of the tabernacle, a spiritual awakening, and a transition from the earth to the spirit element. On the June solstice, the position of the sun, corresponding with Mount Kailash, is associated with the experience of enlightenment. The position of the sun on August 12 corresponds with Giza and is associated with the concept of the end, judgment, and resurrection. This analysis thus demonstrates the congruence between the dates exhibited by the Pyramid of the Sun and the pattern.

The Tzolkin is illustrated in relation to the Pyramid of the Sun, as the start and end of this calendar are shown to align with the two specific sunset observances. The Tzolkin is regarded as the oldest known calendar in Mesoamerica and the fundamental basis of Maya calendars. It consists of two hundred and sixty unique days, derived from the pairing of twenty named days and thirteen numbers. Due to its length, the Tzolkin will cycle repeatedly, irrespective of the time of the year.

Within the framework of this study, an interesting correlation can be observed where the sunset observances on April 29 and August 12 can correspond to the given spring and fall Hebrew observances. The evening of April 29 on the celestial calendar, corresponding to the second Passover, represents the final opportunity to accept the bride's price and thus gain entry into the tabernacle. The solar calendar date of August 12 corresponds to the day for the resurrection of Jesus, the eighteenth day of Abib, which begins on the evening of April 3 on the celestial calendar. The correlation between the spiritual journey and the Pyramid of the Sun is seen as commencing with a spiritual awakening, leading to the eventual rule with the eternal King of kings.

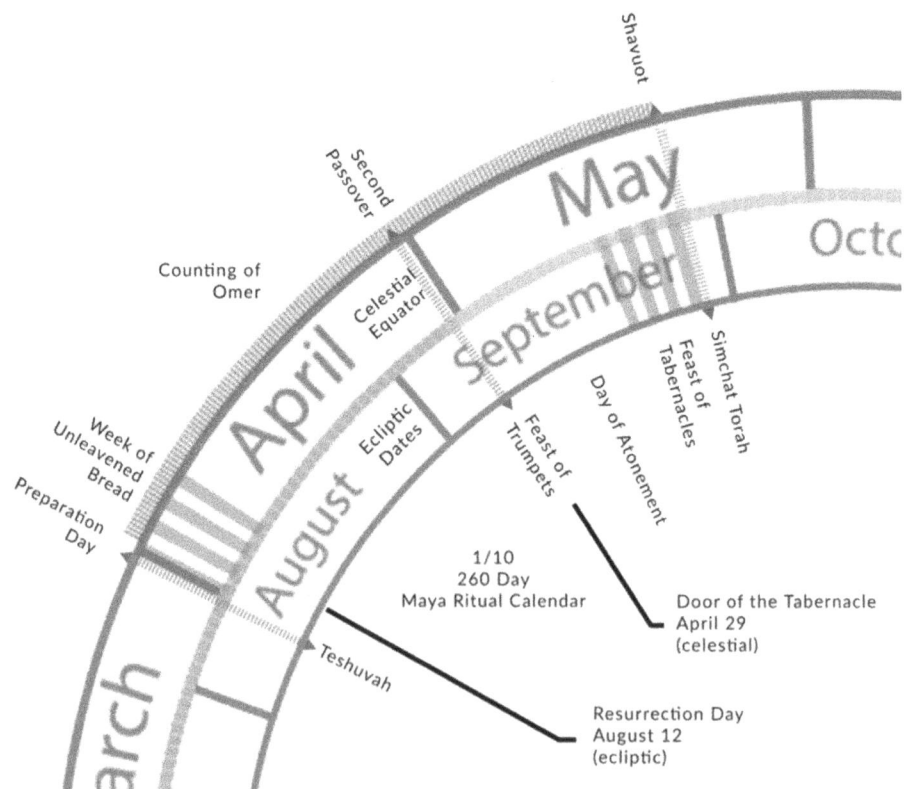

4

Atonement

S in is defined as any action or inaction that creates a separation of fellowship between an individual and God, regardless of whether such actions are deliberate or inadvertent. The atonement and reconciliation are provided by God; nevertheless, the restoration of the relationship with Him is contingent upon the willingness of the individual to return to God. Therefore, an individual who has committed an act of sin will remain in a state of sin until such time as they turn towards God and seek His guidance.

This process necessitates an honest introspective examination in which the individual acknowledges the impact of sin on their relationship with God. In instances where such actions are directed towards another individual, the relationship between the two parties is also affected. This realization represents the process of reestablishing a proper relationship with the Creator.

The tabernacle is a visual representation of the desire of God to be among His people and to engage in fellowship with humanity. It is important to note that God is love, and that those who transgress are effectively turning away from His love. The Creator provided the ultimate atonement to die for the ungodly, so that those who come to have faith in Him may experience His love. Therefore, the tabernacle serves as a teaching aid that instills respect for the authority of God, offers individuals liberation from the bondage of sin, and fosters the cultivation of a profound and loving relationship with God. All of which presents the concept of the restoration of all things.

For the nation of Israel, God had established procedures for the people of Israel to perform and observe in order to be seen as the people of God throughout the world. The earthly tabernacle was constructed according to a pattern intended to mirror that which is in heaven, and the ritual practices of the tabernacle were entrusted to the Levitical priesthood. Aaron, the older brother of Moses, served as the first high priest, and the position was then passed down through his descendants. In their capacity as high priests, they served as a mediator between the people and God, a role that entailed the ritual offering of sacrifices and the atonement for the sins of the people on the Day of Atonement. The earthly tabernacle thus reveals the manner in which humanity can engage with God, shadowing the heavenly tabernacle.

Day of Atonement on Display

The following illustration depicts the proceedings of the Day of Atonement for the bull, the Lord's goat, and the release of the scapegoat. The Day of Atonement is a solemn day, with the overarching objective being the atonement for the Levitical high priest and his family, as well as that for the people of the nation. The sequence of events that transpire on this day is illustrated by the constellations of Taurus, Capricorn, Eridanus, Ara, and Cygnus. In this manner, the function of the high priest within and around the tabernacle on the Day of Atonement can be illustrated by these constellations in conjunction with the revealed tabernacle. These configurations offer insights into the process of atonement, both for the individual and as a nation.

The Day of Atonement is associated with three altars, each of which is represented by the placement of the constellation Ara. The golden altar, also known as the altar of incense, is represented by the constellation Ara in the element of air, which aligns with the Holy Place. The brazen altar, represented by the constellation Ara in the fire element, is to have a fire burning continuously. The altar located outside the camp or city is represented by the constellation Ara in the earth element, in an area that is considered to be unclean. The function of these altars is therefore represented by the alignment of the constellation Ara with the corresponding elements.

Two of the three altars are described as having horns. The prominent horns of the constellation Taurus align with the constellation Ara for the brazen altar and the golden altar. In contrast, the altar situated outside the camp is constructed without horns. Moreover, the specific positioning of the altar outside the camp is not aligned with any placement of the horns of the constellation Taurus. It may, therefore, be inferred that the two altars were constructed with horns in mind, with the intention of reflecting the alignment between the constellation Ara and the celestial horns of Taurus.

The horns of the constellation Capricorn are associated with the concept of atonement in three distinct ways. Firstly, the horns of the constellation Capricorn are aligned with those of the Taurus constellation, which together would symbolize the mixed blood of the bull and the Lord's goat on the Day of Atonement. In the second instance, the horns of Capricorn are aligned with the wilderness as a scapegoat. In the third instance, the horns of Capricorn are aligned with the Northern Cross asterism and the altar located outside the city, representing the ultimate atonement of God as a goat. In light of these observations, it can be proposed that the configuration of the horns of Capricorn in relation to the heavenly tabernacle may be interpreted as a symbol representing the process of cleansing and removal of sin.

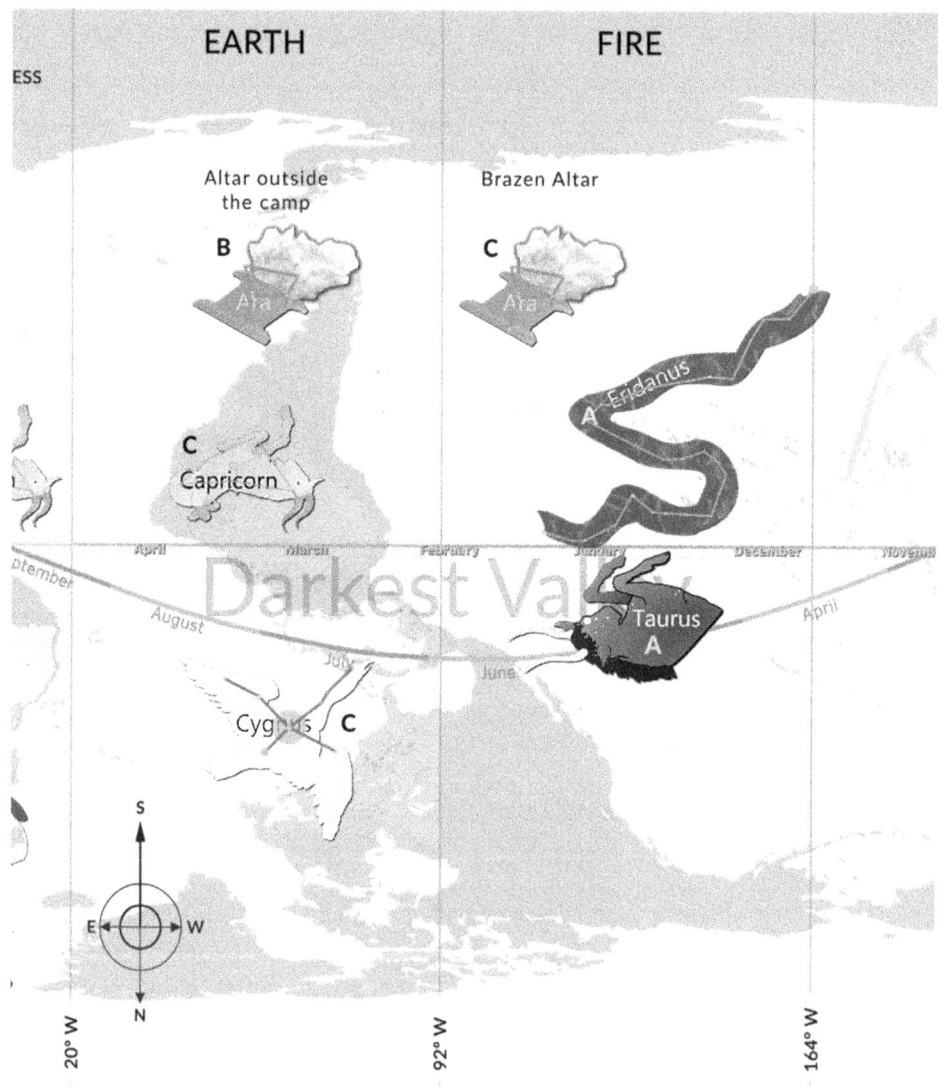

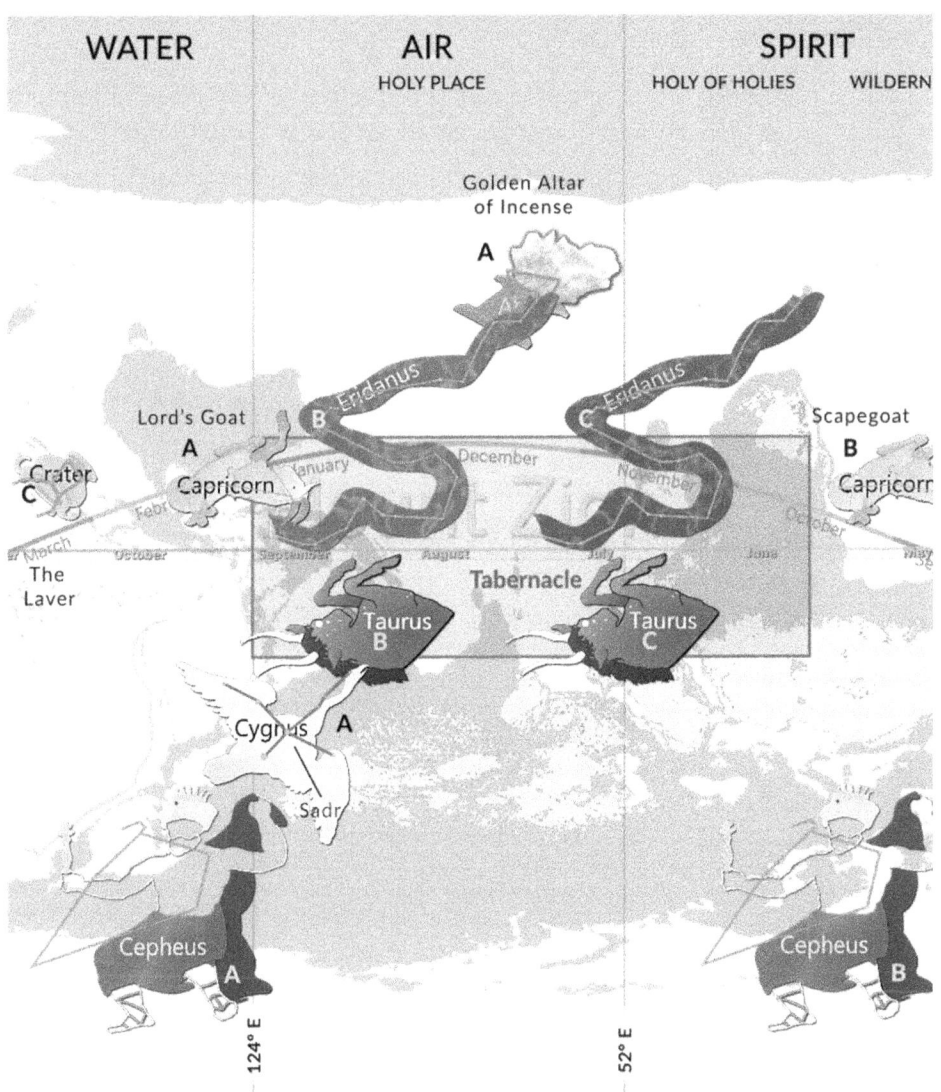

WATER

AIR
HOLY PLACE

SPIRIT
HOLY OF HOLIES   WILDERN

Golden Altar
of Incense

A

Eridanus

Eridanus

Lord's Goat

A

Capricorn

B

C

Scapegoat

B

Capricorn

Crater

C

January

December

November

October

March

October

September

August

July

June

May

The
Laver

Tabernacle

Taurus
B

Taurus
C

Cygnus   A

Sadr

Cepheus

A

Cepheus

B

124° E

52° E

The constellation of Eridanus symbolizes the redemptive scarlet thread and represents the application of shed blood for the purpose of atonement. Three locations are identified where blood is to be applied: before the Lord at the door of the tabernacle, on the horns of the golden altar, and before the mercy seat. The star Cursa represents the head of the river that receives the blood of the sacrifice, originating from the brazen altar. Achernar, the brightest star in the constellation, represents the mouth of the river and its location corresponds to the actual application of the blood. Therefore, the celestial river serves as an illustration of the principle that words reflect the condition of the heart, or what is in the head comes out of the mouth.

The Sin Offering

According to Leviticus 6:12-13, the priests are charged with the responsibility of maintaining the fire on the brazen altar and ensuring its continued existence. The brazen altar was to remain accessible at all times to the Israelites, who, having sinned were permitted to offer sacrifices in order to strengthen their relationship with God. It is important to highlight that while the sacrificial rituals of the Levitical priesthood allude to the cross, they do not signify the actual death of the ultimate atonement of God. The Levitical sacrifices are not intended to appease God; rather, they are designed to reveal God's love and compassion. Therefore, those who have repented and turned away from sin can always approach God.

As illustrated, the initial phase of the constellation Eridanus, which commences at the brazen altar, portrays the movement of blood from the constellation Taurus. According to Leviticus 4:6, the blood of the bull is to be sprinkled seven times before the Lord, symbolized by the constellation Cepheus. In this instance, the constellation Cepheus is depicted with its back to the door of the tabernacle, facing the priest who is sprinkling the blood in its direction. This application of the blood is illustrated by the mouth of the constellation Eridanus extending up to the border of the water element. The priest would perform this action prior to proceeding to the tabernacle.

The location for the sacrifice of the bull is always identified as the site of the brazen altar, which is also said to be before the entrance of the tabernacle, as indicated in Leviticus 4:18. The act of sacrifice, being performed at a distance from the laver, does not directly associate with the concept of the water element or faith. The blood functioned as a covering for their transgressions, while the act of faith is perceived as an individual taking a correct position in relation to God, involving trust and commitment. Therefore, the sin offering of the bull is subject to certain limitations, as evidenced by the absence of blood being applied within the water element or to the laver.

As the priest approaches the door of the tabernacle and the presence of the Lord, he is not permitted to bypass the laver. The element of water, delineated in the courtyard, is for those who live by faith and are dead to sin. Washing at the laver symbolizes the spiritual renewal necessary for approaching God. While the sin offering addresses the sin itself, the manner of faith in which one approaches the Lord is also significant. Therefore, after the sacrificial act for sins has been performed by the priest and the requisite faith has been demonstrated, he is then able to proceed with the process of purification.

The Bull and the Goats

The Day of Atonement is marked by the star Sadr, which is situated in the constellation Cygnus and is located at the intersection of the Northern Cross asterism. On this day, the blood from a bull and a goat was brought into the tabernacle for the purpose of cleansing and purification, as well as making atonement for the people. This reference is illustrated by the alignment of the Northern Cross asterism with the horns of the constellation Capricorn, which overlap the horns of the constellation Taurus. This configuration of the constellations is located just inside the entrance of the tabernacle.

Prior to the atonement for the people of Israel, the high priest is required to perform the ritual of atonement for himself and his family. This stipulation requires the sacrifice of a young bull that is free from defects, as specified in Leviticus 16:11. According to Leviticus 16:14, the high priest is to sprinkle the blood of the bull on the eastern side and in front of the throne of God. Following the completion of the atonement ritual, the high priest is then able to make atonement on behalf of the people.

The arrangement of the two Eridanus constellations within the tabernacle represents the path of the blood from the Northern Cross asterism to the Holy of Holies. The application of the blood in the Holy of Holies, symbolized by the mouth of the second constellation of Eridanus, is conducted by the high priest on the east side and in front of the mercy seat. The Ark of the Covenant is aligned with the constellation Cepheus in the spirit element, thereby associating the constellation with the figure known as the Ancient of Days, who dwells above the mercy seat. The application of the blood from the sin offering towards the mercy seat symbolizes the actual recognition of atonement for sin, as it satisfies the demands of God.

In the ritual of atonement for the people, two goats are presented to the high priest. According to Leviticus 16:8, the high priest then proceeds to cast lots in order to ascertain which goat is designated as the Lord's goat and which is to be designated as the scapegoat. The goat designated as the Lord's goat is utilized for the purposes of atonement for the people and the purification of the tabernacle. In contrast, the scapegoat serves as the means by which the collective sins of the people are removed from the presence of God. This process involves the sacrifice of the Lord's goat, followed by the release of the scapegoat into the wilderness.

The high priest then repeats the same process with the blood of the Lord's goat, in a manner identical to that which he did with the blood of the bull. The blood of both animals is then combined and applied, as illustrated by the initial constellation of Eridanus within the Holy Place, to the horns of the golden altar, which is symbolized by the alignment of the constellations of Ara and Taurus within the Holy Place of the tabernacle. This application to the golden altar is corroborated by the Mishna, which is regarded as an authoritative source of Jewish oral tradition, specifically in Yoma 58b. Therefore, the purification of the Holy Place and the altar is performed with a single application.

Upon completion of the atoning process for the Holy Place, the tabernacle of meeting, and the altar, the scapegoat is presented to the high priest. The high priest then places his hands upon the head of the scapegoat and confesses all sins, transgressions, and offenses committed by the Israelites. Following this, the scapegoat is led from the camp unharmed and released into the wilderness by a suitable man. As illustrated, the scapegoat is represented by the constellation Capricorn in the spirit element that is designated as the wilderness, having been separated from the camp. The removal of sins through the goat of departure enables God to dwell among the people, who are now regarded as pure and clean.

The Lord's Goat

According to Leviticus 16:27, the destruction of the body of the Lord's goat was to take place at the altar, located outside of the camp. The scriptural accounts presented in Hebrews 13:12 and Matthew 27:22 indicate that Jesus was also crucified and buried outside the city walls of Jerusalem. In the illustration presented previously, this event may be represented by the constellation Capricorn, positioned at the altar outside the camp, which also aligns with the Northern Cross asterism.

Therefore, a parallel can be drawn between the crucifixion of Jesus and the shed blood and destruction of the Lord's goat.

The act of atonement involving the Lord's goat and the scapegoat serves to illustrate the removal of the sin of the world from the presence of God, which Christ accomplished on the cross. By offering his life, Christ provided the means for humanity to be reconciled to God. Therefore, his selfless act, ordained by God, stands as a profound expression of His grace and mercy.

According to Hebrews 5:10, God designates Christ as a high priest according to the order of Melchizedek. In his role as high priest, he is thus able to atone for the sins of the people, as stated in Hebrews 2:17. It is noteworthy that, since he was without sin and did not have a family of his own, he was not required to offer the sacrifice of a young, unblemished bull before his death. According to Hebrews 9:24-26, Christ did not enter the Holy of Holies made by human hands; rather, he entered into heaven itself, in the presence of God, for all of humanity. Thus, Christ, in his role as the high priest, offers himself as the ultimate atonement of God, annulling the sins of the people.

Semicha

The following illustration depicts the constellation Orion positioned at the brazen altar, representing the saints of the Most High. The outstretched hand of the constellation Orion may be interpreted as a gesture of supplication, reaching out to align with the head of the constellation Taurus, the young, unblemished bull. The act of placing one's hands on the sacrifice and leaning one's weight on it signifies both an acknowledgment of sin and an acceptance of the sacrifice as a substitute for the individual, which in the Hebrew Bible is referred to as semicha. Therefore, through humility, acknowledging the need for God, the heart is at the same time transformed anew, in a position to seek wisdom and guidance from God.

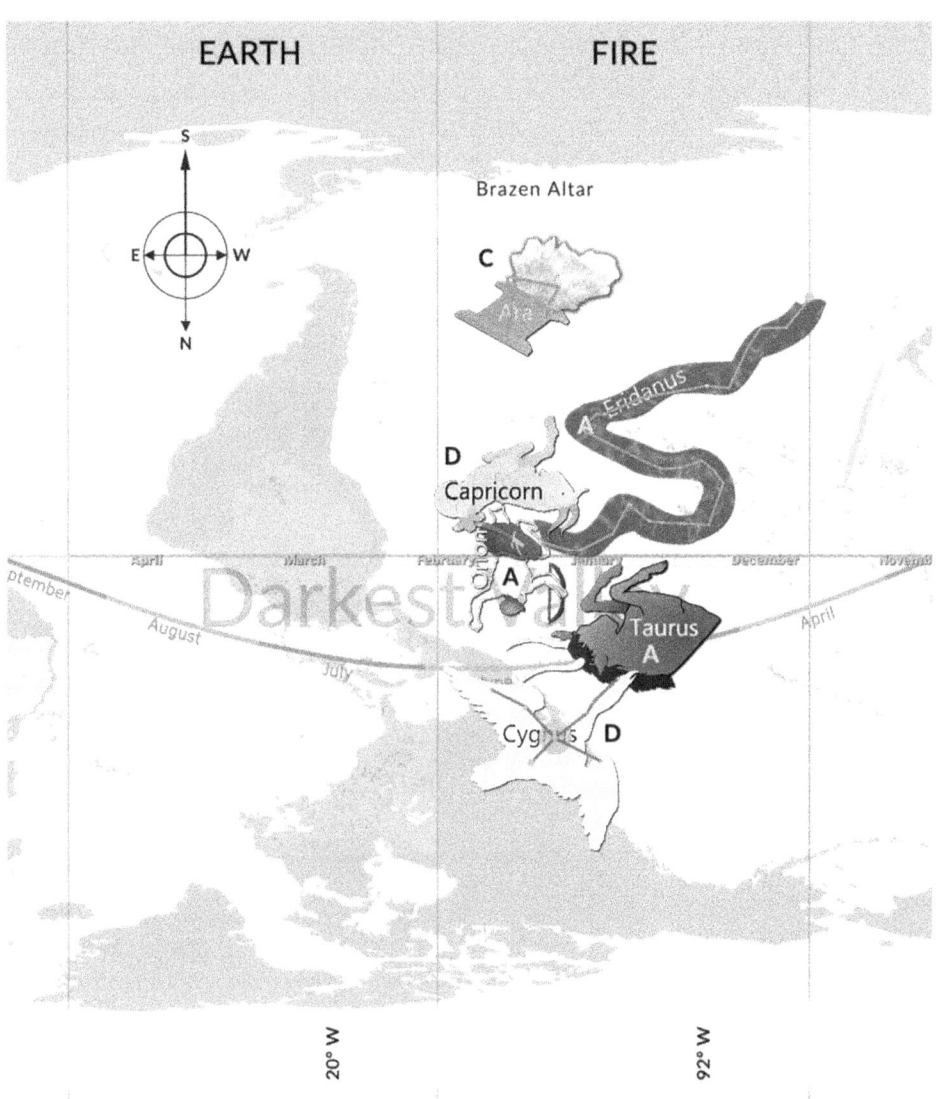

The rituals conducted at the brazen altar serve to illustrate the veracity of the cross. In this context, the role of Christ as the ultimate atonement of God entailed the expiation of the sin of the world, thereby drawing a parallel with the scapegoat after the cleansing of the tabernacle by the Lord's goat. The fourth instance of the constellations of Capricorn and Cygnus at the brazen altar symbolizes the fulfillment of the cross and signifies the acceptance of God of Jesus' death, as previously elaborated regarding the third instance of these constellations at the altar outside the camp. Therefore, the outstretched arm of the constellation Orion, positioned at the head of the constellation Capricorn, is a symbolic representation of the saints of the Most High, who identify with the atoning work of Christ.

5

Set Apart by God

For the Israelites, standing before the brazen altar was regarded as the first step in their approach to the presence of God. This ritual served to underscore the gravity of sin and the necessity of atonement through sacrifice. This pivotal moment is of critical importance, as it signifies a juncture at which individuals must reflect on the nature of their relationship with the Creator. Those who bear witness to this event are encouraged to perceive this initial step of justification and redemption as an act of honoring God and as a means of spiritual renewal through faith. Therefore, the decision of an individual to pursue a personal relationship with the Creator is a prerequisite for being set apart for Him.

In a manner consistent with the complete surrender of Jesus to the will and plan of God, it is incumbent upon those who place their trust in God to do the same. It is essential to demonstrate love for the Creator with one's entire being, encompassing the heart, soul, and strength. As stated in Matthew 5:14-16, those who adhere to the teachings of the word of God are expected to embody these qualities in their actions, allowing others to observe their virtuous conduct and, as a result, glorify the Creator. In this regard, the life and teachings of Jesus Christ serve as a model for those who have faith in the Creator.

Spiritual Apostasy

In his first epistle to the Corinthians, Paul makes an observation that the message of the cross is a stumbling block for those who are perishing. This concept can be illustrated through the constellation Virgo, depicted in a fallen state after tripping over the narrative of the cross symbolized by the brazen altar. Furthermore, Jesus refers to himself as a stumbling stone, suggesting that individuals who pursue righteousness through their own endeavors will ultimately lead to their own downfall. In this context, the constellation Virgo is understood to represent the great city of Babylon, which is described as a rebellious harlot against God, who does not pursue righteousness by faith. In this way, the great city of Babylon, along with its inhabitants, distracts people from the truth of Christ and is therefore in conflict with the saving grace of God.

It is possible for individuals to become immersed in a state of spiritual darkness without being aware of it. Such individuals may continue to conform to the prevailing social norms of everyday life without being aware of the deterioration of their own spiritual condition. Additionally, those who are reluctant to establish a relationship with God are also considered to be apostates. Therefore, a lack of interest in God and His word inevitably leads to individuals being deceived and accepting false doctrines.

The devil, as the adversary, seeks to deceive people through the tactics of false prophets and false christs. Paul likely refers to the results of their actions as the "falling away" in 2 Thessalonians 2:3 to denote a significant number of individuals who have turned away from the faith in the living God, having instead adopted erroneous doctrines. Moreover, the harlot and those associated with the great city seek to

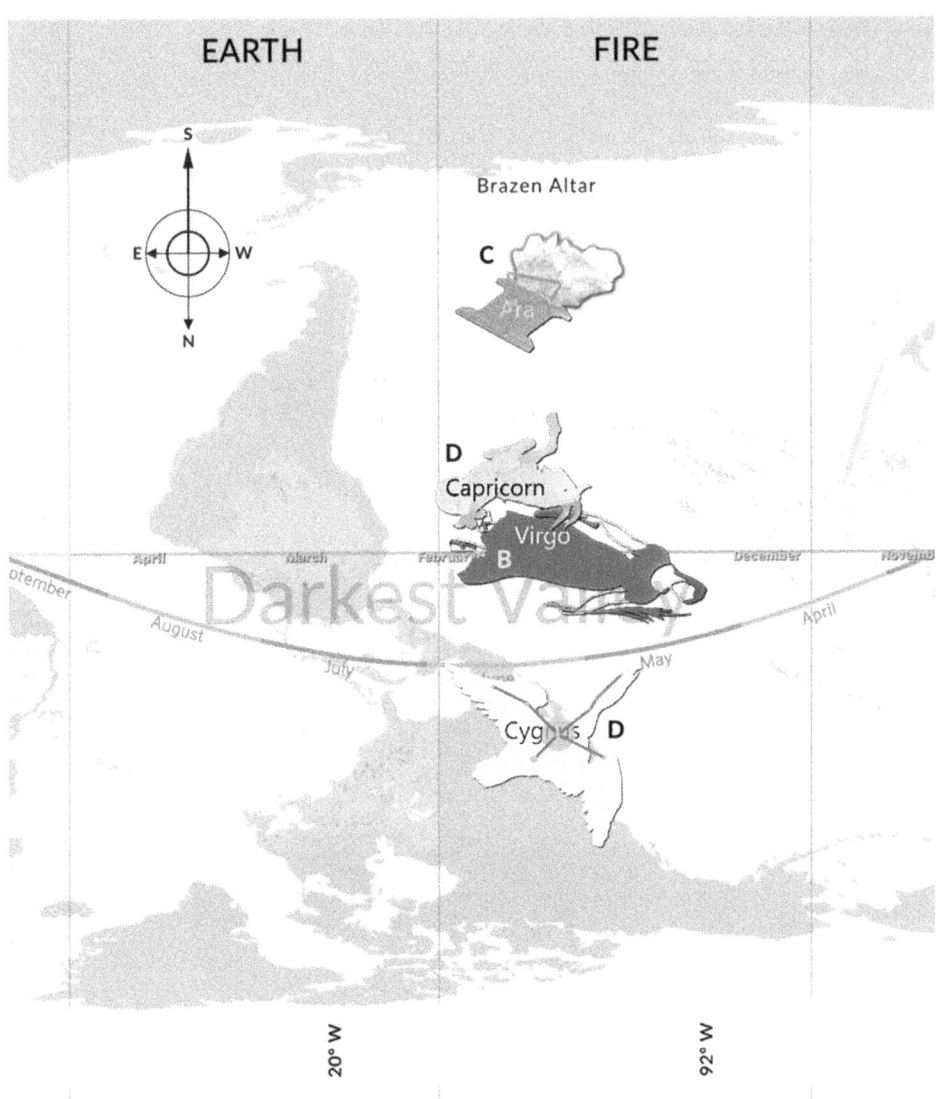

insult and offend those justified by faith who have accepted the message of the cross. In point of fact, there is success in their effects, signifying a pervasive decline in the love for God.

The time of the falling away is referred to as the great apostasy and is also antithetical to the day of Teshuvah. This moment is associated with the location of the brazen altar and the date of February 7 on the celestial calendar. The designated date corresponds to the day opposite that of Teshuvah, which is the day when one is to return to God. In accordance with this analysis, the opposing themes are situated at the opposite points on the calendar.

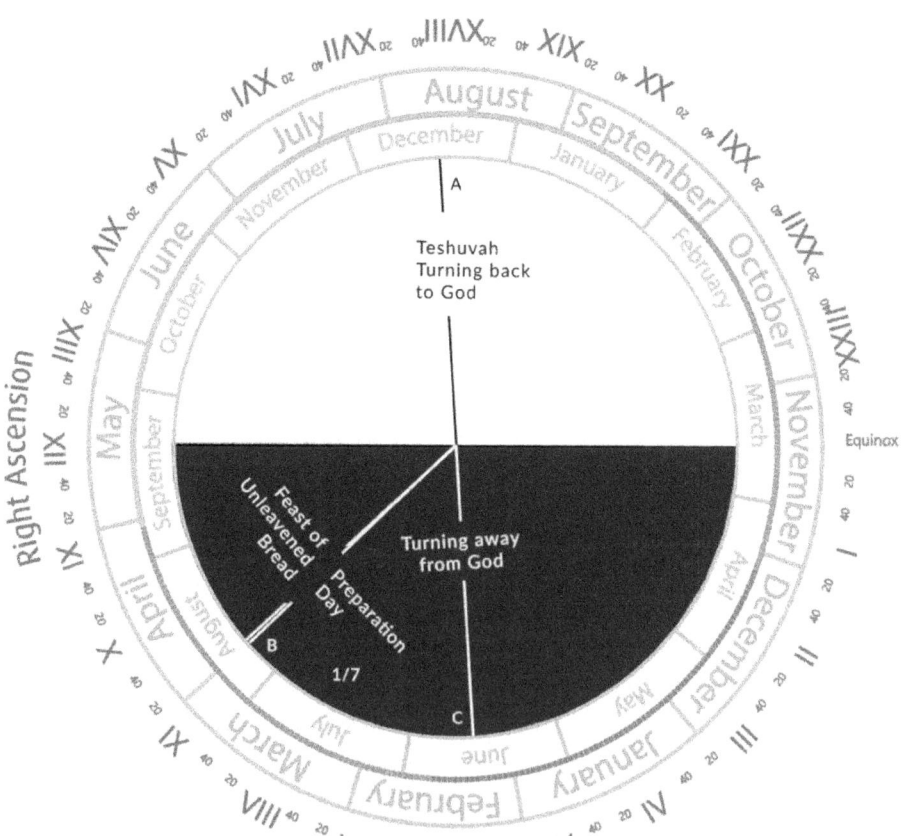

The accompanying illustration delineates the day of Teshuvah opposite the day of the falling away, demonstrating that both points of reference can correspond to the day of preparation in terms of the pattern. Preparation day is recognized as a pivotal juncture in which a significant decision is to be made regarding the bride's price and the acceptance of the bridegroom. It becomes evident that a clear distinction emerges between individuals who are eligible to partake in the Week of Unleavened Bread and those who do not acknowledge or have faith in the Creator. Thus, those who turn to God and participate in the Week of Unleavened Bread recognize the significance of living a sin-free life in their relationship with God.

The Days of the Lord

The Feast of Unleavened Bread is observed on the fifteenth day of the month of Abib according to the Hebrew calendar. This feast day is considered as a holy day, signifying liberation from an immoral world, destruction, and bondage. In Luke 17:26-30, a future day of the Lord is likened to the biblical accounts of Noah entering the ark and Lot leaving Sodom. Moreover, this date marks the beginning of the Hebrew exodus from Egypt. Accordingly, this holy day will similarly signify a future day when God will separate His people from the nations.

Prior to the great flood, the tenth plague of Egypt, and the destruction of Sodom and Gomorrah, God made a distinction between those who were His people and those who were wicked. Each of these events can be demonstrated to have occurred on the Feast of Unleavened Bread. In the context of these events, the preceding day, preparation day, is associated with a decision that is likely to have been formulated by an individual over an extended period. Therefore, it follows that God is able to distinguish between those who choose to adhere to His commandments and those who have fallen away.

In the account of Noah, the biblical narrative implies that all the animals were gathered on board the ark prior to the tenth day of the second month. Noah enters the ark, and God closes the door. According to Genesis 7:11, the rain began seven days later, on the seventeenth day of the second month. It is noteworthy that the months and days are recorded differently at the time of the flood, yet the day the door is closed may align with the beginning of the Feast of Unleavened Bread, a hypothesis explored under the subchapter titled *Calendar Reasonings*. Considering these factors, the seven days between the door of the ark being closed and the onset of the rain can correspond with the Week of Unleavened Bread.

The narrative of Lot and the destruction of Sodom exhibits parallels with the account of the first Passover and the Feast of Unleavened Bread. In this narrative, Lot, the nephew of Abraham, observes two angels entering the gates of Sodom at sunset. He is concerned for their safety and requests that they seek refuge in his home for the night. Upon their arrival, he prepares unleavened bread and a feast for them. The mention of unleavened bread can be correlated with the hasty departure of the Israelites during the Feast of Unleavened Bread, as evidenced by the early morning departure of Lot and his family.

In Genesis 19:4-5, the men of the city, comprising both young and old, approached Lot's house that night with the intention of engaging in carnal acts with the angels. In response, Lot proposed his daughters instead. However, the men rejected this compromise and sought to inflict harm upon him and his guests. The angels then intervened on behalf of Lot and his family by closing the door and blinding the men. As a result, the men of the city were unable to ascertain the location of the door, became weary, and discontinued their search.

In each of these instances, the door is secured from potential harm, which also alludes to the first Passover meal. The Israelites applied the blood of lambs to the top and sides of the doorposts as a means of protection from the arrival of the destroying angel, as documented in

Exodus 12:6-13. The Israelites were further instructed that no part of the Passover should be taken outside the home or shared with strangers or uncircumcised individuals. This directive can be interpreted as a metaphor for the day of Jesus' burial, when his tomb was sealed with a large stone and guarded by Roman soldiers to prevent his body from being taken. These examples illustrate the distinction between those who partake in the Passover meal, for whom God's protection is extended, and those who do not partake in the meal and are not under His protection.

Path of Enlightenment Begins

One aspect of the spiritual life can be defined as a state of enlightenment, which is understood as a consequence of a relationship with the Creator, along with His word and His spirit. This state of enlightenment can be defined as a condition of being in which the individual is aware of their existence beyond the limitations of the physical body and the mind. This state is characterized by an individual's engagement with the world while not being preoccupied with worldly concerns that would distract from a spiritual perspective.

Spiritual enlightenment for those who believe in the Creator is to have the word of God serve as an authoritative source of guidance, correction, and wisdom. The concept is that we should strive to become like Christ, who was a stranger in this world, as described in John 14:15-21. The message conveyed in Matthew 16:24-25 is illustrated by the constellation Orion, which is shown entering the tabernacle and taking up the cross, which is represented by the Northern Cross asterism in the constellation Cygnus. One who denies himself and follows Christ could be said to have left the outer courtyard and entered the tabernacle. The act of entering the tabernacle thus signifies a transition to a spiritual existence, lived from the divine perspective.

In the Holy Place, the menorah illuminates the path that priests

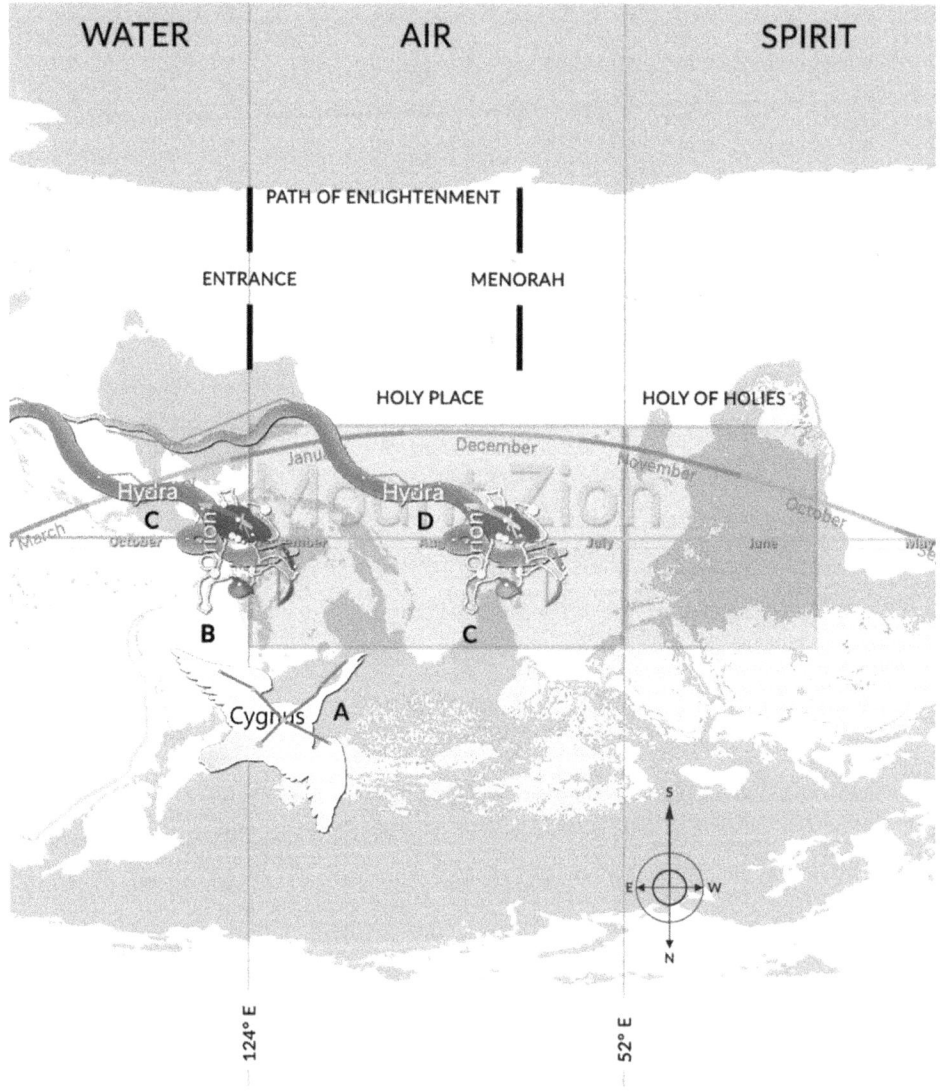

are to follow, thereby symbolizing the divine light of the glory of God. When the sun, along the ecliptic, is positioned above the head of the constellation Orion, it is understood to represent the saints of the Most High having entered and remaining within the tabernacle. Within the context of spirituality, the entry of the saint into the tabernacle as a priest signifies a spiritual journey of learning and following the guidance of the Holy Spirit. Therefore, when a priest is in the tabernacle, they are considered to be in the presence of God, as symbolized by the light of the menorah.

An additional component of this conceptual framework of the path of enlightenment within the Holy Place of the tabernacle is the serpent, which is represented by the two instances of the constellation Hydra. The nature of the serpent can be understood to represent spiritual discernment and the development of a keen sense of spiritual awareness, as well as the ability to recognize the tactics of Satan and avoid his snares. This concept is grounded in the phrase "wise as serpents," as found in Matthew 10:16, in which Jesus provides guidance to his disciples on how to navigate a challenging world. This path within the Holy Place corresponds with the constellation Orion, reaching the pinnacle of enlightenment at the menorah, which is symbolized by the sun and its alignment with Mount Kailash.

Calendar Reasonings

The illustration provides a potential framework for understanding the accounting of time for the great flood within the context of the ancient Egyptian civil calendar. The Egyptian civil calendar consists of twelve months of thirty days each, with an additional five intercalary days appended at the end. This calendar is based on the first sighting of Sirius, which is in the constellation Canis Major, when the sun is positioned just below the eastern horizon. This heliacal rising of Sirius not only marks the first day of the calendar, but also serves to signal the impending flood season along the Nile River for the ancient Egyptians. Thus, the new year was marked by the evacuation of the floodplain, in anticipation of the subsequent rise of the river.

The objective of implementing this calendar system is to establish an association between the date on which the door of the ark was closed and the Feast of Unleavened Bread, as presented in this study. The star Sirius is aligned with July 1 on the solar calendar, which could have been its heliacal rising at that time, and February 21 is the date on the celestial calendar. The study indicates that the fortieth day after this latter date is the tenth day of the second month of the year, or

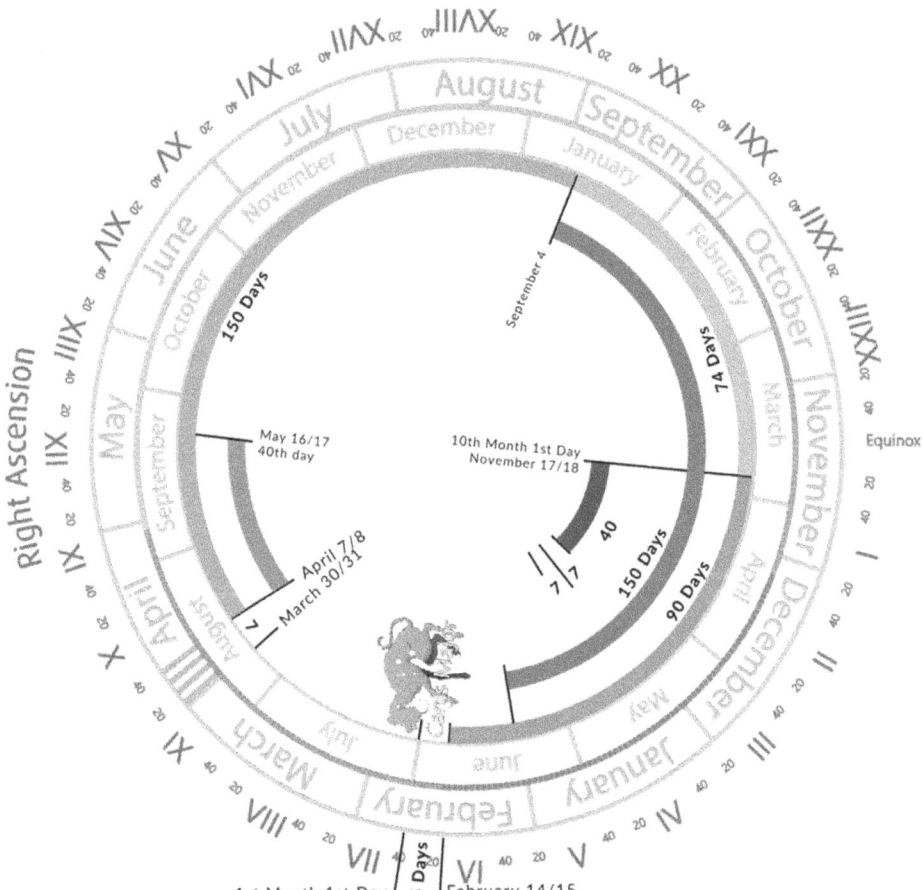

April 1, which corresponds with the date of the Feast of Unleavened Bread. While there is no means to prove this hypothesis with absolute certainty, the potential alignment of the calendars with the narrative is nevertheless intriguing.

Opposite Review and Preview

This study also explores the notion that the depiction of a constellation as being identified with Teotihuacan and Mount Kailash can present an antithetical idea. The alignment of a constellation with the revealed tabernacle and other constellations, as well as areas designated as Mount Zion and the darkest valley, serve to further enhance the theme of opposites. This concept can be likened to the effects of the seasons, such as summer and winter, which exert contrasting impacts on nature. Therefore, the contrasting arrangement of constellations in these illustrations provides a clearer understanding of their unique characteristics and applications in the relation to God.

The opposing positions of the constellation Cepheus are associated with the Lord. In the illustrations, the initial placement is before the tabernacle, symbolizing the way, the truth, and the life. In the opposite placement, the constellation represents the second coming of the Lord, who brings judgment with the sword that proceeds from his mouth. In one sense, the Lord is inviting everyone to follow him in order to grow spiritually; in another, he is preparing to battle those who would not in order to set up the kingdom of God on the earth.

As illustrated, the constellation Virgo is depicted as falling over the message of the cross at the brazen altar. One of the themes of the constellation appears to be related to the concept of descent. In the initial placement, the constellation Virgo is understood to represent the heavenly Jerusalem, which is depicted as descending from heaven to earth. In the opposite placement, the constellation can be interpreted as representing Babylon, which is depicted as being cast into the sea and sinking like a burnt mountain, as described in the second trumpet. In this scenario, heavenly Jerusalem is inhabited by saints, while the great city of Babylon is populated by apostates.

The star Alpheratz, situated in the constellation Andromeda, is positioned in the forehead of the woman. In the initial position, the star is situated in the area designated as the darkest valley and is interpreted as representing the mark of the beast. Those who accept the mark will experience torment and a desire to end their life during the fifth trumpet, and later will face torment with fire and brimstone. In the opposite position, the star is situated in the area designated as Mount Zion, symbolizing the remnant who return to Jerusalem with everlasting joy on their foreheads. These contrasting depictions represent the stark difference between those who experience joy and those who experience anguish.

The golden altar of incense and the altar of burnt offerings are positioned in direct opposition to each other, according to the pattern. The brazen altar is associated with sin and the necessity for justice and righteousness, whereas the golden altar represents the sweet and fragrant aspect of the desire for intimate communion with God. At the brazen altar, the coal, representing the consuming nature of the holiness of God, is brought to the golden altar to ignite the incense, which represents the prayers of the saints, as described in Revelation 5:8. The purifying nature of these burning embers, when added to the prayers of the saints, facilitates their ascent to God, as represented by the smoke rising with their prayers before Him. The application of the embers thus underscores the notion that atonement, in that an individual seeks forgiveness for their sins, is necessary before prayers will be heard by God.

Sadr, a star located at the intersection of the Northern Cross asterism, is associated with the Day of Atonement. On this day, rituals involving the sacrifice of a bull and a goat took place, with the goat, designated as the Lord's goat, contrasting the sacrifice of Christ outside the city. The blood of the bull and the Lord's goat covered sin, and cleansed the tabernacle, a ritual that had to be repeated yearly. In contrast, the sacrifice of God's ultimate atonement permanently atones for sin and cleanses the temple in heaven. Thus, the annual sacrifice of the bull and the Lord's goat on the Day of Atonement can be regarded as a shadow of the sacrifice of God's ultimate atonement.

6
Kingdoms of the Courtyard

In the books of Daniel and Revelation, the Scriptures mention eight epochs relating to the Gentile kingdoms and the great city of Babylon. These entities represent those who are apostate, or referred to as Gentiles, and as such are mere observers of the activities taking place in the outer courtyard. Their lack of spiritual conviction and thus estrangement from the Creator results in their confinement between the eastern gate of the courtyard and the area designated by the water element. Despite the possibility of approaching the brazen altar and even offering a sin-offering for atonement, it remains impossible to cross the area represented by water without faith. Consequently, the kingdoms represented by the Gentiles and the apostates are confined to and represented within this particular area of the courtyard.

According to Revelation 11:1b-2, the holy city and the outer courtyard will be trodden underfoot by the Gentiles for forty-two lunar months, or approximately one thousand two hundred and forty-one days. The period of forty-two lunar months is represented by the areal combination of the elements of earth and fire designated in the outer courtyard. The total span of the combined area, which is one

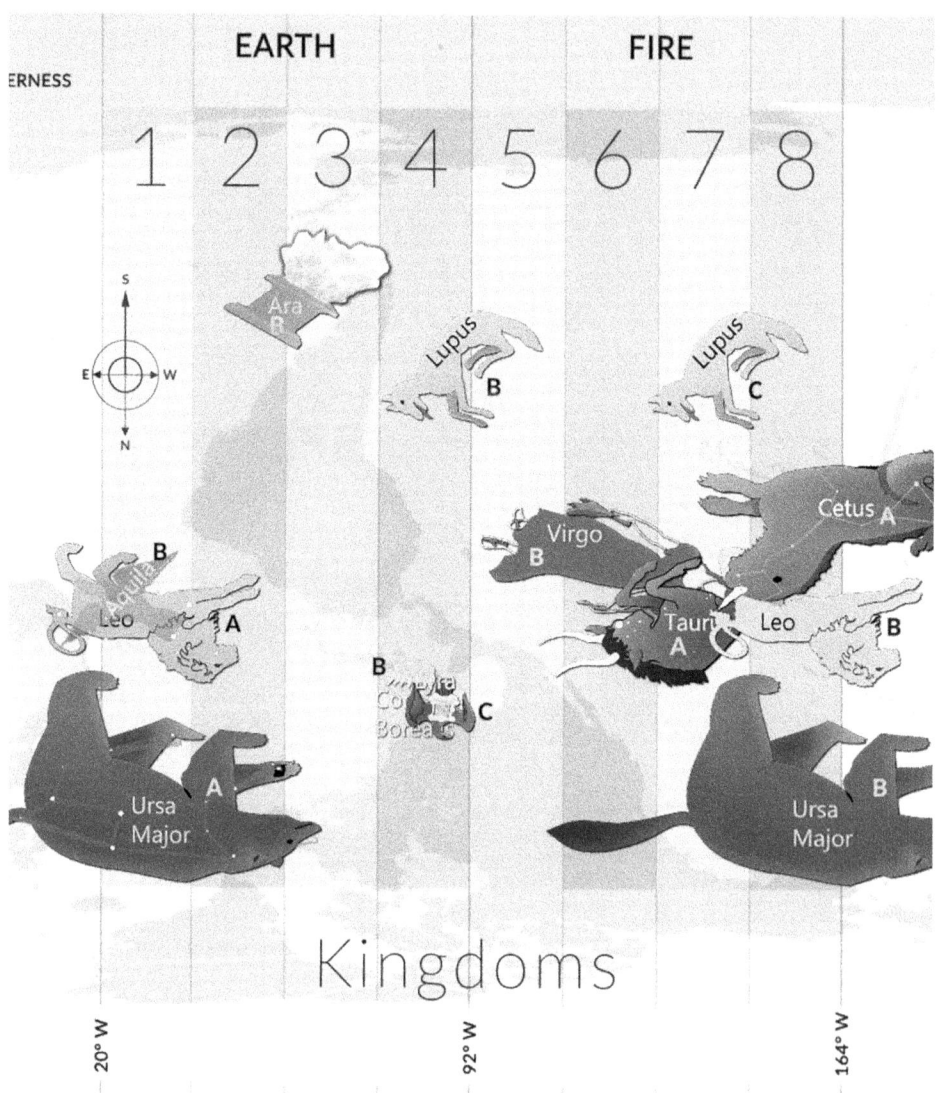

hundred and forty-six days, is equivalent to forty-two lunar months when coupled with an additional three years, one thousand and ninety-five days. It can therefore be concluded that the tenure of the Gentiles is identified within the specific confines of the outer courtyard, both in terms of time and conceptualization.

In the illustration, the area delineated as being trodden underfoot by the Gentiles is equally partitioned into eight segments, each assigned a numerical designation. The following table catalogs eight distinct kingdoms associated with the outer courtyard, accompanied by their respective constellation composition and numerical representation. The kingdoms are presented in order of their appearance in Scripture, from east to west. In this manner, the numerical designation increases from the gate of the courtyard, with each segment corresponding to the number associated with the narrative of the kingdoms.

Segment	Kingdoms	Number Correlation
1	Leo - Aquila	one set of eagle's wings, heart
2	Leo	stands on two feet
3	Ursa Major	three ribs in mouth
4	Lupus - Lyra	four-headed leopard, four wings
5	Taurus (ten kings)	five times each horn
6	Virgo (Harlot)	five kingdoms have fallen
7	Cetus	seven-headed beast
8	Cetus, Leo, Ursa Major, Lupus, and Taurus	eighth and of the seven

These kingdoms can be correlated with specific constellations, which, when depicted overlapping a numerical boundary, can illustrate the concept of transformation or transition. This concept is exemplified by several key events in scripture, including the metamorphosis of the first beast, the trampling of the harlot by the fourth beast, and the resurrection of the beast. Additionally, the seventh chapter of the Book of Daniel provides a detailed description of the ascent of the little horn from behind the fourth kingdom, which is illustrated as coming up behind the ten kings, corresponding to the numerical representation of the fifth segment. Therefore, an understanding of numerical references provides a foundational framework for a systematic account of the succession of nations.

An additional aspect of these kingdoms is presented in the second chapter of the Book of Daniel. In this chapter, King Nebuchadnezzar experiences a dream in which he sees a great figure. This image is composed of a variety of materials representing different nations throughout history: gold, silver, bronze, iron, and clay. It is noteworthy that these same materials are typically found in the fabrication of idols. The dream concludes with the image being crushed by a stone, signifying its ultimate destruction.

In the event that these metals are obtained as spoils of war, they are not to be incorporated into the treasury of the Lord until they have been melted by fire, as indicated in Numbers 31:22-23 and Joshua 6:19. Similarly, an individual who places their trust in the Lord God for salvation can be likened to molten metal, undergoing a profound and positive transformation, becoming a valuable asset for the tabernacle. This transformation is described in John 3:5 as occurring when an individual is born of water and the spirit. Therefore, those who have been redeemed are expected to conduct their lives in accordance with the will of God, refraining from engaging in the practices of the ungodly.

The beasts that emerge from the great sea as described in the books of Daniel and Revelation are not explicitly identified as specific nations or kingdoms. Instead, they are regarded as symbolic representations of powerful kingdoms. The sequential order in which they emerge from the area of the courtyard designated as the water element is the same as illustrated. Furthermore, the placement of these beasts in the courtyard indicates that they are not associated with God. Consequently, the emphasis of the scriptures is on the role and characteristics of these beasts and their confrontation with God, who will usher in His kingdom in their place.

The Lion's Metamorphosis

The first beast to emerge from the great sea is portrayed as a lion with the wings of an eagle. The majestic winged lion, which may exhibit similarities to griffins and winged sphinxes, can be interpreted as a representation of these guardians of sacred places and as a symbol of divine power. In this manner, the kingdom is endowed with qualities of strength and wisdom. As illustrated, the beast may also be depicted as a guardian against any attempt to approach the tabernacle and the Holy of Holies from the west. In consideration of these observations, it can be proposed that this kingdom may perceive its duty as aligned with a higher power or divine cause.

However, a significant transformation occurs as the kingdom loses its winged identity, which reflects a loss of honor, and is forced to stand on two feet like a human. In the first segment, there is a pronounced focus on the winged lion, which is represented by the conjunction of the constellations of Leo and Aquila. The second segment represents the transformation and directs attention to the outstretched forelegs of the constellation Leo. Consequently, the first beast transforms into a second kingdom, which is distinct from the first, as outlined in the framework of the eight segments of the courtyard.

Moreover, the progression of the kingdom to the second segment results in the loss of the heart, which is then replaced with a heart of a man. The star Regulus, which is situated in close proximity to the boundary between the first and second segments of the courtyard, is representative of the heart of the lion. It is important to note, however, that this star is located within the first segment. Consequently, the metamorphosis in the form of the beast signifies a shift in the disposition of its population.

This profound transformation may be compared to the moment when the eyes of Adam and the woman were opened, enabling them to perceive a new perspective on life. As a consequence of the transgression of Adam, God banishes him and Eve from the Garden of Eden. When applied to the beast, its transformation gives rise to new moral codes, philosophies, and belief systems that challenge the teachings of God. Therefore, it can be concluded that the populace of this kingdom would perceive the response from God to their sin as at odds with their own expectations.

The Three Ribs

The third segment of the courtyard depicts the second beast to emerge from the great sea, with an emphasis on its mouth. The beast is represented as a bear, which is symbolized by the constellation Ursa Major, and it has three ribs in its mouth. The populace of this kingdom is directed by the three ribs to consume much flesh from the altar located outside the camp, which is represented by the constellation Ara. The cultural practices of this kingdom are designed to maintain a state of sin among the people, as evidenced by the consumption of the sacrifices, which were deemed so offensive that they had to be burned outside the camp. Therefore, the cultural norms of this kingdom are structured in a manner that perpetuates sin among the population, thereby creating a spiritual disconnect between the people and God.

The three ribs can be associated with the three categories of sin described in 1 John 2:16, namely the lust of the flesh, the lust of the eyes, and the pride of life. These categories of sin are exemplified in the temptation of the woman in the Garden of Eden, when she sees the fruit of the tree of the knowledge of good and evil. She discerns that the fruit of this tree is palatable, aesthetically pleasing, and desirable. Similarly, the bear is influenced by the command of the ribs and thus decides to consume sin. In this way, the ribs exert control over the kingdom by instilling a proclivity for sin in its people.

These categories of sin can also be correlated with the three temptations that Jesus successfully overcame after his forty days in the wilderness. The first temptation is to transform stones into bread to satisfy his hunger, a factor that potentially influenced the actions of the woman and the bear. The second temptation involved the allure of prestige outside the framework of the divine plan, in which the tempter omitted certain words from Psalm 91:11-12. In the third temptation, the devil showed Jesus all the kingdoms of the world and their glory, offering to give them to him in exchange for worship. Despite the tangible allure of these enticements, Jesus does not allow himself to be influenced by the persuasive messages of the devil, thereby maintaining his relationship with the Creator.

The Judgmental Leopard

The third beast to emerge from the great sea is located in the fourth segment of the courtyard. The kingdom is represented by the numerical representation of the segment, which is described as having four heads and four wings of a bird on its back. The celestial composition of the beast is formed by the constellation Lupus with the wings of the constellation Lyra. While the constellation Lupus is conventionally represented as a wolf, the Arabic title signifies a leopard or panther. Therefore, it can be concluded that the placement of the constellation Lupus within the courtyard, along with the reference to its name, serve to indicate that it accurately symbolizes the third beast from the sea.

According to Daniel 7:6, this kingdom is given dominion. In the illustration, the head of the constellation Lupus is aligned with the crown, the constellation Corona Borealis, and the serpent, the

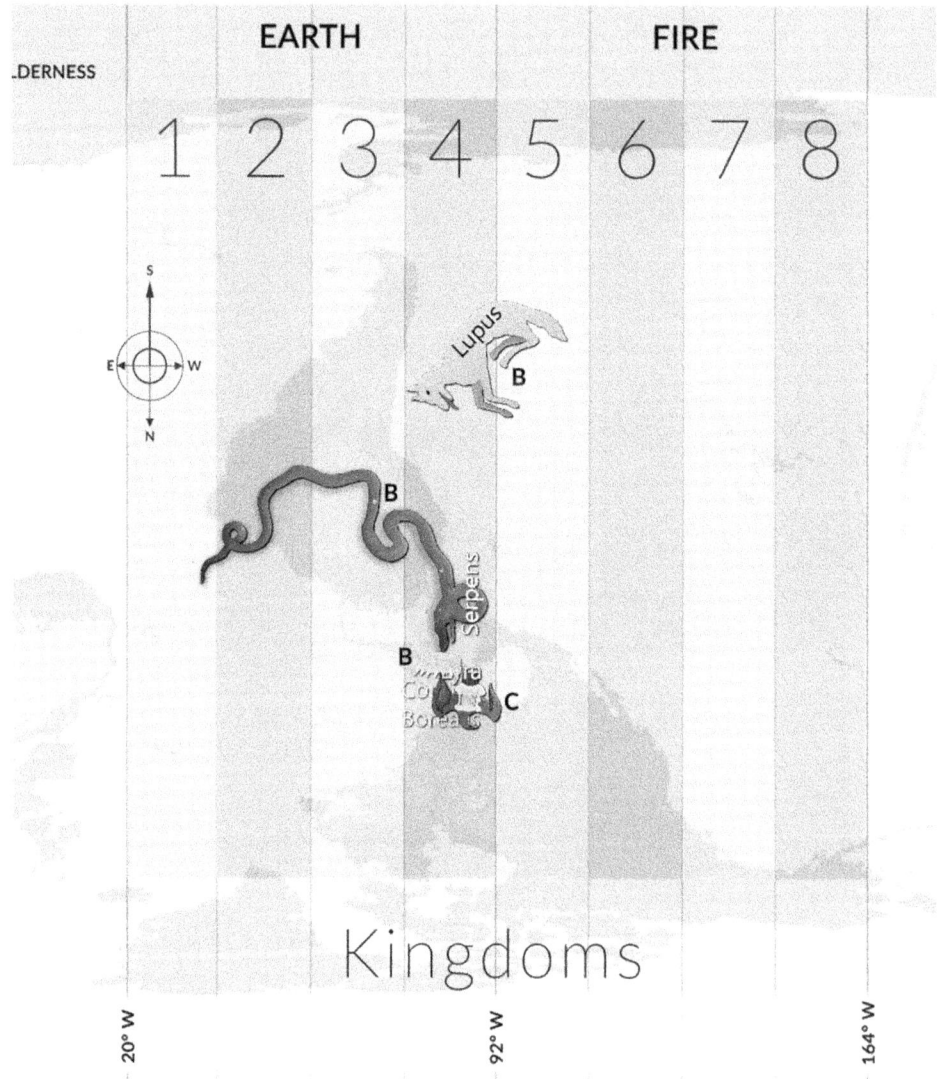

constellation Serpens. This configuration can be interpreted as a kingdom that has been granted dominion by the serpent for its benefit. Therefore, the populace of this kingdom conducts itself in accordance with this arrangement.

The leopard is regarded as an extremely dangerous animal, primarily due to its ferocity. The leopard is always watchful, surveilling the surrounding population, and prepared to swiftly attack those who are weak, ignorant, or who reject wisdom. The idiom *a leopard cannot change its spots* suggests that the nature of this animal is unchangeable. Consequently, the population of the leopard kingdom is inclined to engage in discrimination, assuming the roles of both accuser and judge.

The Confederacy

The fourth beast to emerge from the great sea commences in the fifth segment of the outer courtyard. The kingdom is identified as a confederacy of ten kings, symbolized by the two horns of the constellation Taurus. The numerical representation of the fifth segment is expressed as a multiplication factor, whereby the number of horns is related to the number of kings. It is important to note that the horns have not yet received their kingdom; rather, they will become kings at the onset of the seventh segment. Consequently, the ten horns will become kings with the beast of the seventh segment.

As described in Daniel 7:7, the activities of the ten kings commence with their assumption of kingship. The ten horns are granted authority for one hour by the serpent, as indicated by the alignment with the constellations Serpens and Corona Borealis in the seventh segment. Moreover, this segment emphasizes that they will reign with the seven-headed beast, symbolized by the constellation Cetus, at the time the crown is given to them. In this way, their role in relation to the beast will be pivotal in the subjugation of the entire earth when the appropriate time arrives.

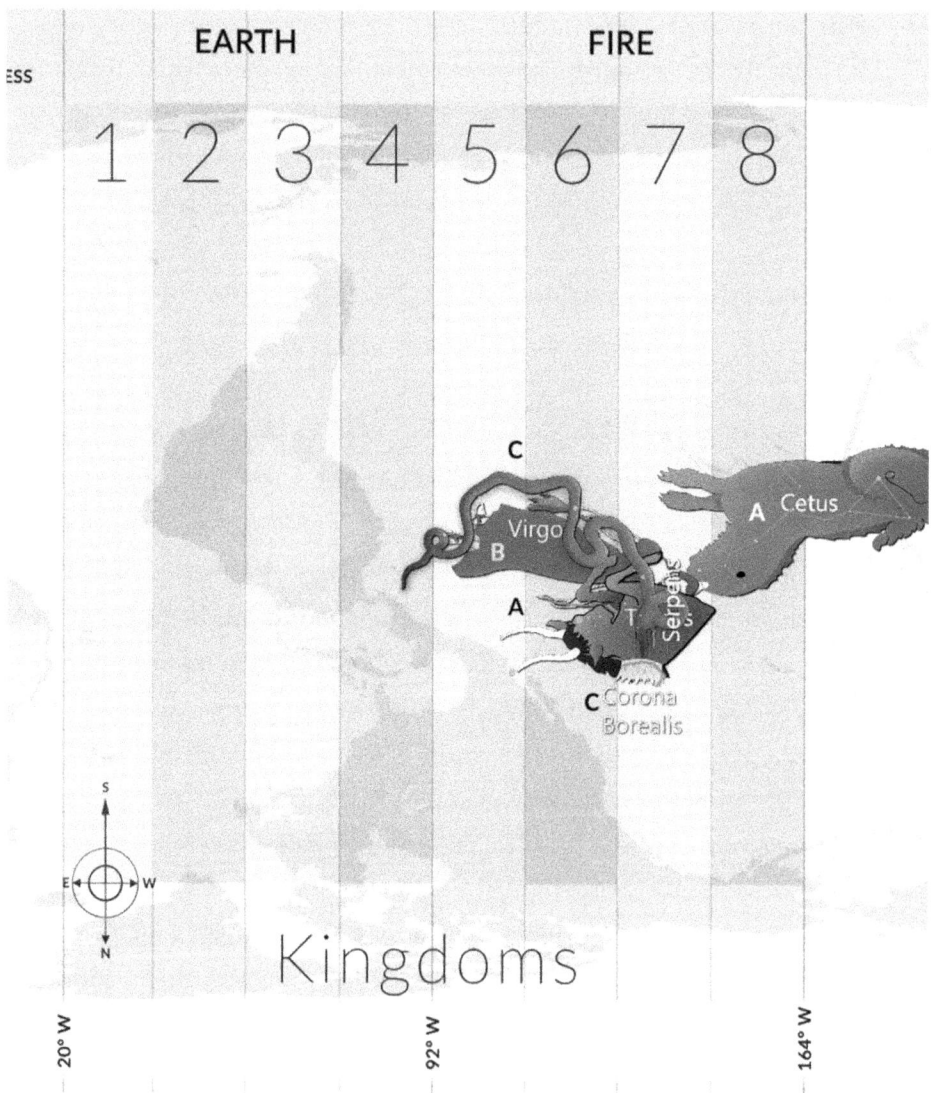

At that juncture, the hooves of the fourth beast will crush the earth and trample the residue, as indicated in Daniel 7:7 and 7:23. Moreover, Revelation 17:16-17 indicates that the kings will trample down the great city of Babylon, thereby fulfilling the purpose of God. Therefore, the great city exists prior to the ten horns becoming kings, thereby establishing their purpose in her destruction.

In Exodus 21:28, it is written that if a bull gores a man or woman to death, the animal must be stoned to death. This kingdom, symbolized by the bull, does not acknowledge the Creator, yet through divine providence will destroy the great city. The brutal atrocities committed by this beast are illustrated by its hooves trampling the constellation Virgo. According to Daniel 2:44-45, the establishment of the kingdom of God will occur during the period of these kings. Therefore, the kingdoms, including the ten horns, will be destroyed by a kingdom likened to a stone cut out of a mountain without human hands.

Breeched in the Matrix

The womb of the constellation Virgo is of particular emphasis with regard to the sixth segment of the courtyard. This specific instance of the constellation Virgo is emblematic of Babylon the Great, the Mother of Harlots. The fallen nature of the great city is attributed to apostasy, symbolized by the number 666, which corresponds to the number of the segment. The repetition of the number six serves to reinforce its significance, signifying the arrogance of the self-made woman who subjugates others through her opposition to the truth. Therefore, the great city and those who are inside the city are described as unfaithful to God, holding fast to spiritual corruption.

The apparent disinterest of the populace in reconciliation with God is indicative of their position. The great city is characterized by apostasy, which is part of a broader societal movement that is rejecting belief in the Creator. In Romans 9:21-22, the verses draw a comparison of those who engage in harlotry to dishonorable clay vessels that are not in the hands of the potter and are ready to be destroyed. The populace of the great city will not comply with the divine plan of God nor with the fourth beast from the great sea after being trampled. Consequently, the behavior of the great city implies a rationale that is distinct from the objectives of the other kingdoms and God.

Prior to the ten horns being granted authority as kings, a voice from heaven issues a warning to the people of the great city to flee from her. According to Revelation 18:4-5, the population is advised to evacuate in order to avoid participation in her sins and the repercussions of her plagues. In 1 Thessalonians chapter five, Paul explains that those who live in a state of spiritual darkness will be unable to perceive the Day of the Lord until it is too late. He further states that this day will arrive unexpectedly, like a thief in the night or the pangs of labor for a woman in childbirth, and will bring about sudden destruction. From a spiritual perspective, the people will have to choose to live in the light and emerge from the matrix of Babylon.

For those who elect to remain in the great city, this moment is of critical importance. These individuals, akin to the narrative of Ephraim in Hosea 13:12–13, are regarded as being breeched in the womb of a dying woman. The situation is of a life-or-death nature, and a turnaround cannot be achieved within the metaphorical womb unless there is first a turnabout to God. Ultimately, divine judgment will cause the great city significant distress, resulting in her destruction. Consequently, the inhabitants of Babylon will face death, mourning, and famine when the great city perishes, akin to an unborn child when its mother perishes.

Seven Mountains and Kings

In this study, the kings referenced in Revelation 17:10 represent the eight segments of the outer courtyard. An angel states that there are seven kings, of which five have fallen. Following the fall of the great city, the sixth king, the people of the prince to come, the seventh king, is said to briefly rule. The arrival of the man of lawlessness is the eighth and of the seven.

The transition from the sixth to the seventh segment of the courtyard is marked by the granting of authority to the ten kings with the beast for one hour against Babylon the Great. In Revelation 17:7-8a, the scarlet beast is described as having seven heads, which corresponds to the numerical reference of the seventh segment of the outer courtyard and is represented by the constellation Cetus. The alliance between the ten kings and the beast contributes to the description of its horns. Collectively, the beast and the ten kings play a crucial role in the plan of God to bring judgment, resulting in the swift overthrow and destruction of the great city.

The Eighth

In the thirteenth chapter of Revelation, the eighth is introduced as it emerges from the great sea. Following the decapitation of one of its heads at the conclusion of the seventh segment, the transformed kingdom is observed to be resurrected, its outward appearance having been transformed at the onset of the eighth segment. The beast is described in this text as having seven heads and ten horns, with ten crowns on its head. Moreover, as indicated in Daniel 7:8, the first three horns are uprooted, which corresponds with the first three beasts that had emerged from the great sea and are now depicted in the segments associated with the seventh and the eighth. At this juncture, the beast is comprised of all the kingdoms that preceded it.

The beast can also be illustrated with the celestial representations from each kingdom within the seventh and eighth segments. The kingdom is described as a leopard, which is symbolized by the constellation Lupus. Furthermore, the beast is depicted with feet like

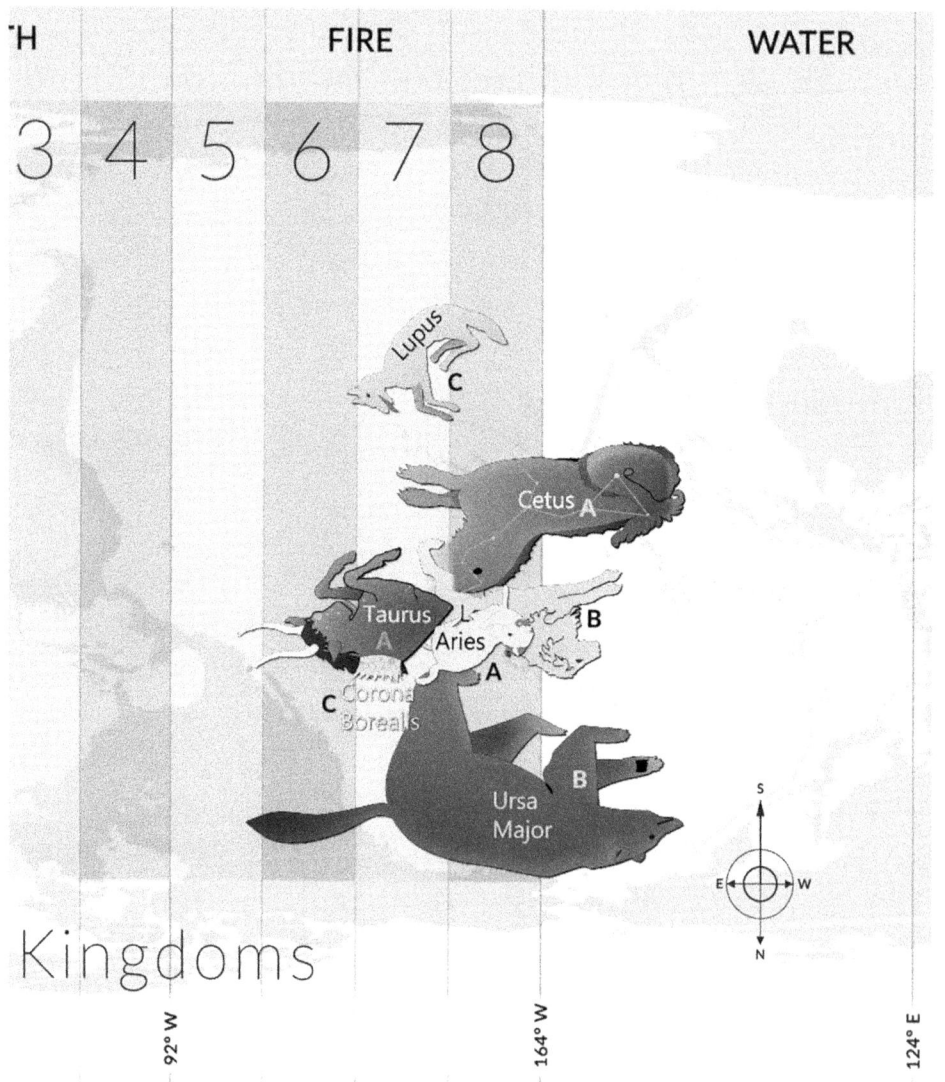

those of a bear and a mouth like that of a lion, which correspond to the constellations Ursa Major and Leo, respectively. As indicated in Revelation 17:13 and Daniel 7:24, the ten kings symbolized by the Taurus constellation relinquish their authority to the beast. Therefore, this beast assumes dominion over all the kingdoms.

According to Revelation 13:7 and 17:14, the beast wages war against the saints and the Lamb of God. This war is illustrated in the eighth segment of the courtyard, along with the Lamb, which is symbolized by the constellation Aries. The Lamb will emerge triumphant over the kingdom and dominion of the beast. Therefore, those who remain faithful to the Lamb of God will also attain victory, wherein the saints of the Most High will receive an everlasting kingdom.

7

The Seals

In the right hand of Him, who is seated on the throne, there is a scroll described as being inscribed on both sides and to which seven seals are attached. According to Revelation 5:3, no individual in heaven, on earth, or under the earth is deemed worthy to open the scroll. The scroll will remain unopened as God awaits the fulfillment of His promise, as outlined in Genesis 3:15, which is to crush the head of Satan. In this manner, the seed of the woman, along with God's absolute necessity for the ultimate atonement, establishes the uniqueness of the individual who will open the scroll.

In John 1:29, John the Baptist identifies Jesus of Nazareth as the Lamb of God, who takes away the sin of the world. The Lamb of God is regarded as the ultimate atonement of God, and as such, is deemed worthy to receive the scroll from Him who sits on the throne. According to Revelation 13:8, the Lamb of God was predestined since the foundation of the world to accomplish the work of redemption through his death. Therefore, it can be concluded that the Creator determined the precise moment at which the Lamb of God would complete the work of the cross.

The contents of the scroll are instrumental in the eventual establishment of the kingdom of God on Earth, which the saints of the Most High will inherit. Prior to its establishment, those who persist in the great apostasy and those who engage in warfare against the saints will be subject to divine judgment, in an attempt to prompt them to repent and enter into a relationship with God. At the conclusion of the great tribulation, the Son of Man will differentiate between individuals based on their affiliation with the kingdom to which they belong. Those who maintain a relationship with God will be granted entry into the kingdom of God, while those who have persisted in apostasy or sought to harm the saints will be removed from the Earth.

Outline of the Seven Seals		
1	White horse, crown	Revelation 6:1-2
2	Great sword	Revelation 6:3-4
3	Day's wage for barley and wheat	Revelation 6:5-6
4	Death & Hades kill fourth of the earth	Revelation 6:7-8
5	Dead in the Lord receive robes	Revelation 6:9-11
6	They hide from the face of Him	Revelation 6:12-17
7	Silence	Revelation 8:1

Events Surrounding the Millennial Reign of Christ		
1	White horse, many crowns	Revelation 19:11-14
2	From His mouth is a sharp sword	Revelation 19:15-16
3	Flesh, the great feast of God	Revelation 19:17-18
4	Lord kills in the Armageddon battle	Revelation 19:19-20:3
5	Resurrection of the dead in Christ	Revelation 20:4-6
6	Heaven and earth flee from His face	Revelation 20:7-15
7	Old pass away, new heaven and earth	Revelation 21

The two tables present a parallel between the narrative of the seven seals, which provides an overview of the events that will transpire during the tribulation period, and the passages in Revelation, chapters nineteen through twenty-two. The first table delineates the seals, which can be conceptualized in alignment with the sequence of events surrounding the return of the Son of Man and his millennial reign, as presented in the second table. The elaboration of the parallels is structured to align with the enumeration of the seals. This comparison reveals that the seal judgments of God and the events associated with the return and reign of the Lord are not simultaneous occurrences.

The seven seals are depicted on the eastern side of the brazen altar, with the focal point being the day after the great apostasy. The day associated with the great apostasy corresponds with the illustration at the point of the great city stumbling over the narrative of the cross. The brazen altar, as delineated in the narrative, functions as a divide between those who choose to live in sin and those who seek to cultivate a relationship with God, akin to the day of preparation. The opening of the seals is a response to the great apostasy, which occurs much like the beginning of the Feast of Unleavened Bread following the day of preparation. Therefore, the seven seals will be opened immediately following the day marking the point of the great falling away, with the objective of prompting individuals to engage in repentance.

True and False Messiahs

Following the opening of the first seal by the Lamb of God, John is prompted by the voice of one of the four living creatures to "Come and see." John then beholds a white horse and its rider, symbolized by the constellation Sagittarius. The rider is depicted holding a bow and wearing a crown, which is represented by the constellation Corona Borealis. The horseman represents the man of lawlessness, the false messiah, whose goal is to subjugate and unite the peoples of all nations

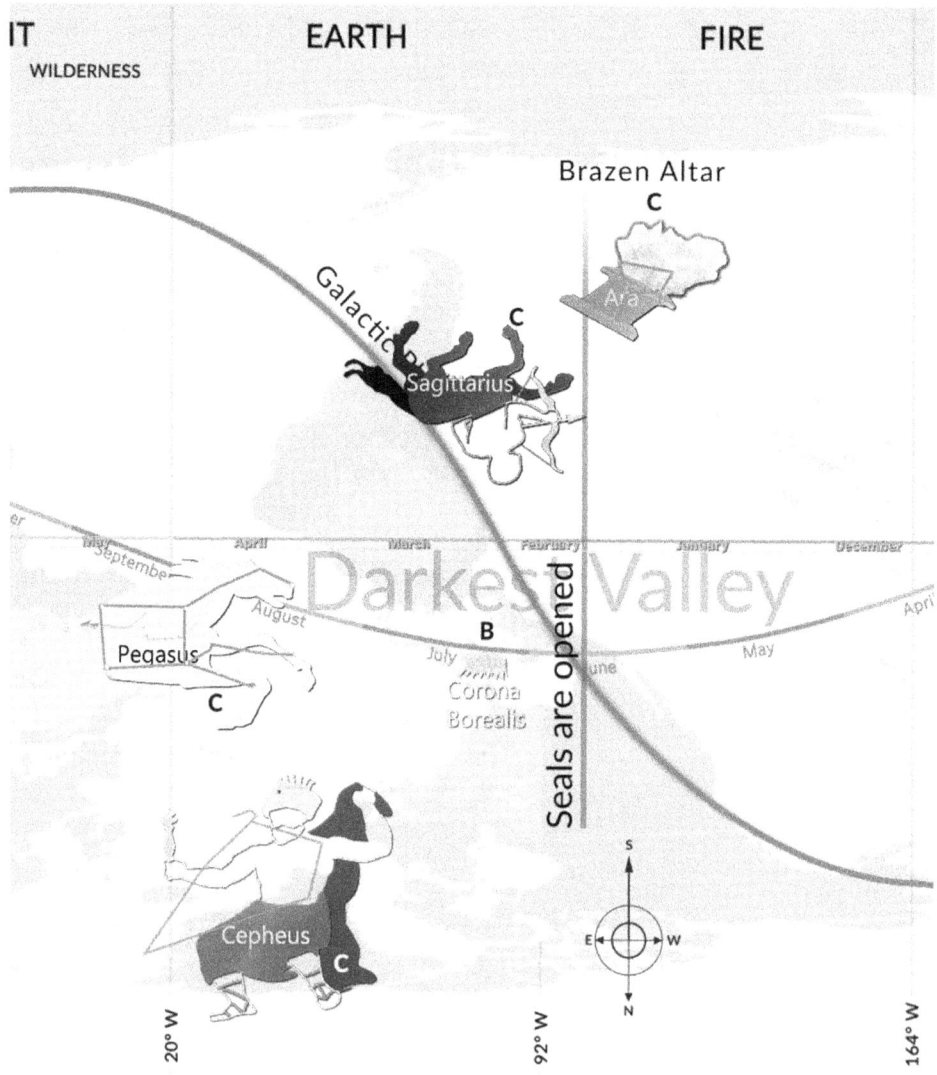

in order to be worshiped by them as a deity. The opening of the first seal, therefore, indicates the last days of the end of the age.

According to Revelation 13:8, the false messiah gains significant influence in his rise to power, and the text indicates that individuals whose names are not recorded in the Lamb's Book of Life will engage in the worship of both the beast from the sea and the dragon, who bestowed authority upon him. The false messiah is not aligned with the truth and receives the kingdoms of the world from the devil, which the true messiah rejected when he was tempted after forty days in the wilderness. Consequently, those whose names are not inscribed in the Lamb's Book of Life will align themselves with the tenets espoused by the false messiah, who seeks to glorify himself.

The illustration provides a comparison between the two events: the arrival of the first horseman at the onset of the great tribulation and that of the true messiah, which is to occur at the conclusion of the great tribulation. In Revelation 19:11-14, the true messiah is described as "Faithful and True," in marked contrast to the first horseman, who subjugates the people and holds to a false ideology. The true messiah is represented by the constellation Cepheus and depicted as transitioning between the elements of spirit and earth on a white horse, symbolized by the constellation Pegasus. The arrival of the second coming of the Son of Man, the true messiah, signifies the imminent establishment of the kingdom of God on Earth, thereby bringing to a conclusion the times of the Gentiles.

War of Words

Following the opening of the second seal, John is encouraged by the second living creature to "Come and see," and a fiery red horse appears. The horse and rider are represented by the constellation Centaurus. The horseman is granted the power to remove peace from the earth and is provided with a great sword, symbolized by the sword asterism in the

constellation Orion. The actions of the horseman will create a socially toxic environment on a global scale, thereby prompting people around the world to take matters into their own hands. Such actions will be irrespective of whether they are ethical or unethical, and whether the target of their action is directed against an individual or a group.

The great sword can be understood as rhetoric that employs sharp and divisive language, thereby inciting social unrest. The second horseman will persuade and deliberately cultivate moral decay and corruption at all levels of society. The mouth, which is likened to a sword or a cause of division, is given to the beast from the sea and enables it to speak blasphemous words against God. This rider will wield his sword to persuade people to become indifferent to the truth, in a manner consistent with his own actions and attitudes. Thus, the actions of this rider will lead to a worldwide decline in respect for the rule of law.

However, when the Lord comes to establish his dominion, he will bring about the end to the establishment of the beast from the sea. He will strike the nations with a sharp, double-edged sword that proceeds from his mouth, and he will trample them underfoot in the winepress of God's wrath. As referenced in Revelation 19:15-16, the robe and the thigh of the Lord bear the name "KING OF KINGS AND LORD OF LORDS." The title *King of kings* is associated with the leg of the constellation Cepheus in the earth element, while the title *Lord of lords* corresponds to his other leg in the spirit element. This designation implies that all kingdoms are subjected to his rule upon his arrival.

Flesh and Bread

Following the opening of the third seal by the Lamb of God, John is prompted by the third living creature to "Come and see," which results in the revelation of a black horse. In the illustration, the horse is represented by the constellation Sagittarius. The rider is depicted with

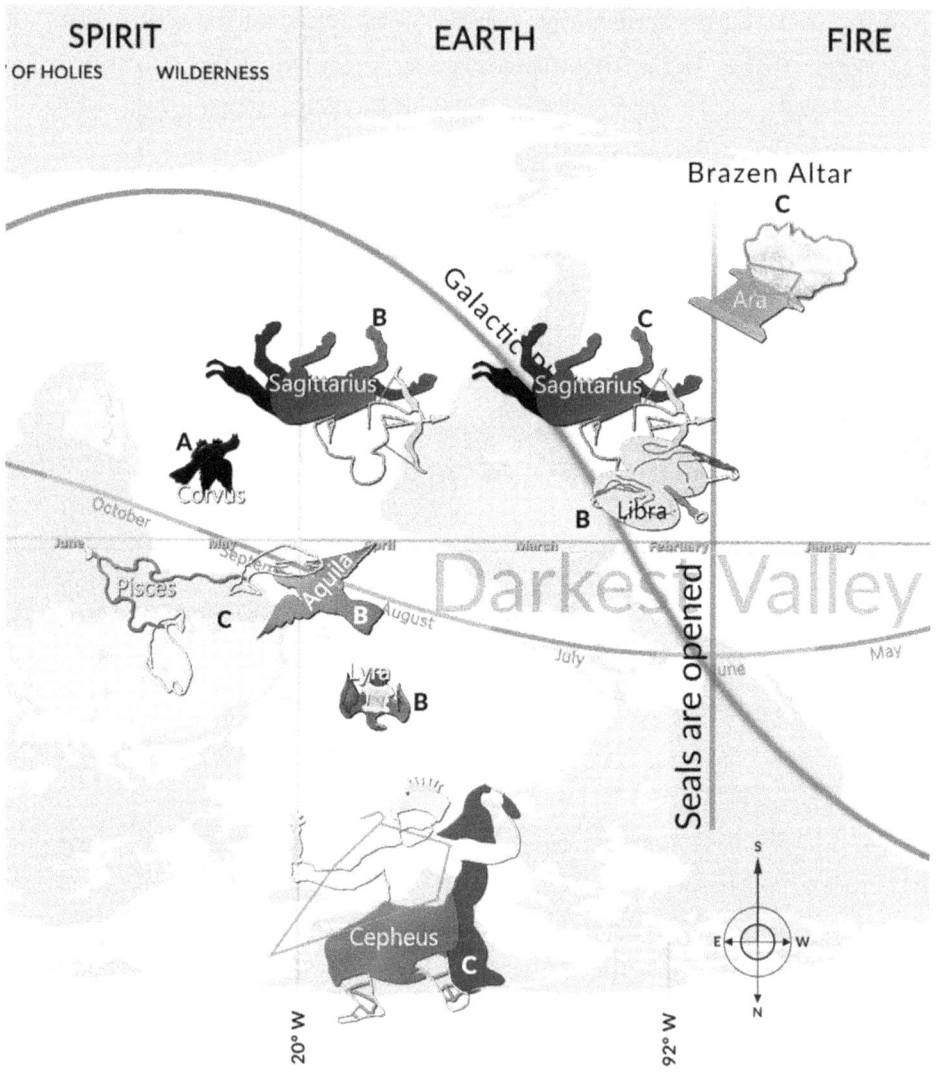

a pair of scales, which are represented by the constellation Libra. The conventional representation of the scales symbolizes the principles of fairness and justice, whereby the measure one buys or sells is ultimately determined by the demands of the marketplace. In this particular instance, the scales serve to reinforce the desired outcome of the one who has provided the rider with his mission.

In Revelation 6:6, John reports hearing what seems to be a voice emanating from the midst of the four living creatures saying, "A quart of wheat for a denarius, and three quarts of barley for a denarius, and do not harm the oil or the wine." The directives are addressed to the horseman and stipulate the quantity of wheat and barley that may be purchased. The allusion to oil and wine supplies indicates that they should not be subject to artificial control. The daily allotment of grain is utilized for the production of bread, thereby fulfilling both the daily physical needs and, by analogy, the spiritual needs of the individual. Therefore, the rider simply weighs the quantity of grain against the established daily wage standard.

According to Revelation 13:16-17, the verses state that the image of the beast will make it impossible for an individual to engage in buying or selling unless they possess either the mark, the name of the beast, or the number of his name. Those who chose not to adhere to this stipulation are subject to a state of physical privation. Conversely, the act of purchasing grain on a daily basis by those who fulfill this requirement can be viewed as equivalent to their daily act in the worship of the beast and the dragon. Those who obtain their sustenance from the image of the beast are in stark contrast to those who, according to John 6:53-58, are strengthened by consuming the flesh of Christ, the bread of heaven, on a daily basis. Therefore, individuals engaged in transactions for the procurement of grain are in a state of spiritual privation due to their lack of faith in the Creator.

Revelation 19:17-19 describes the return of the Son of Man, at which point an angel issues an invitation to the birds that fly in the midst of heaven to gather for the great supper of God. One of the two fishes that form the constellation Pisces is situated in the darkest valley, which represents the souls of the fallen, regardless of their social status. The constellation Sagittarius, which is aligned with the constellation Cepheus, is understood to represent the horses and the horsemen who have engaged in combat against the spirit and the righteousness of God. The fallen souls, horsemen, and horses will be consumed by the birds, as illustrated by the constellations of Corvus, Aquila, and Lyra. In this manner, the erroneous teachings of false teachers and false prophets will be eradicated from the earth, as symbolized by the consumption of their flesh by the birds.

Wake-Up Call

Following the opening of the fourth seal by the Lamb of God, John is prompted by the fourth living creature to "Come and see." John observes a pale or yellowish-green horse, represented by the constellation Centaurus. The rider represents the personification of Death, which is symbolized by the star Lesath, which corresponds to the stinger in the constellation Scorpio, which is depicted riding above the horse. In close proximity is Hades, the underworld, which is mythologically linked to Antares, which corresponds to the heart of the constellation Scorpio. Thus, the personification of Death is closely followed by the location associated with the dead.

The rider is granted the authority to kill a quarter of the unbelieving inhabitants of the earth through various means, including the sword, famine, widespread death, and wild animals. These same plagues are also referenced in Ezekiel 14:12-23, where God sought to eliminate the wicked from Jerusalem and the land. The purpose of this action is to serve as a cautionary example for others, so that they may witness the devastation and be prompted to turn back to God. It is important to

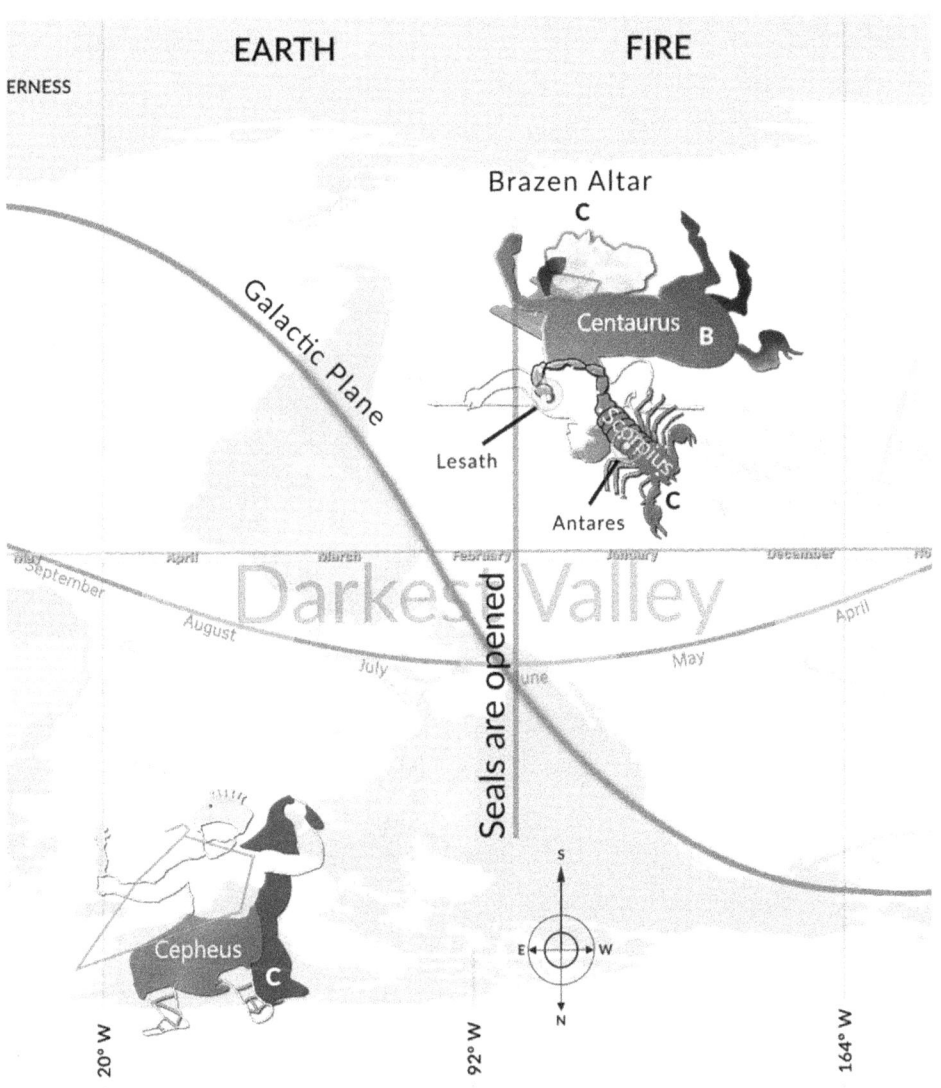

note that, as evidenced by this seal and Revelation 20:13, those who perish as a consequence of the fourth seal will not have had their names inscribed in the book of life. This substantial and significant loss of life serves as an urgent wake-up call to those who are at risk of being excluded from the kingdom of God.

This event can be compared to the period during the time of Noah and Lot, when only a minority of the people were considered righteous. Those whose names are inscribed in the Lamb's Book of Life will refuse to venerate the beast, despite the intention of the beast to kill with the sword the saints who do not worship the image of the beast. The saints are expected to bear witness before kings and rulers, with the assurance that those who kill with the sword will themselves be killed with the sword. Accordingly, the saints are expected to serve as ambassadors of the kingdom of God, as the gospel will have been proclaimed throughout all nations.

The concept of Death, which is followed by Hades, contrasts with the death of the saints, who have maintained the commandments of God and the faith of Jesus. For the faithful, the fruits of their labor are to inevitably follow them in death, suggesting that they will attain eternal rest. Therefore, it becomes imperative for the saints of the Most High to exercise patience, even in the face of death. According to 1 Corinthians 15:58, the faithful have the assurance that their endeavors in the service of the Lord will not be in vain. Thus, it is a matter of faith for them that their efforts will be rewarded in the future and that they will have peace in the Lord.

Remembered and Rewarded

After the Lamb of God opened the fifth seal, John observes the martyrs for the word of God beneath the brazen altar. In this particular instance, as illustrated, the constellation Orion, which is representative of the saints of the Most High, is also representative of the martyrs who are

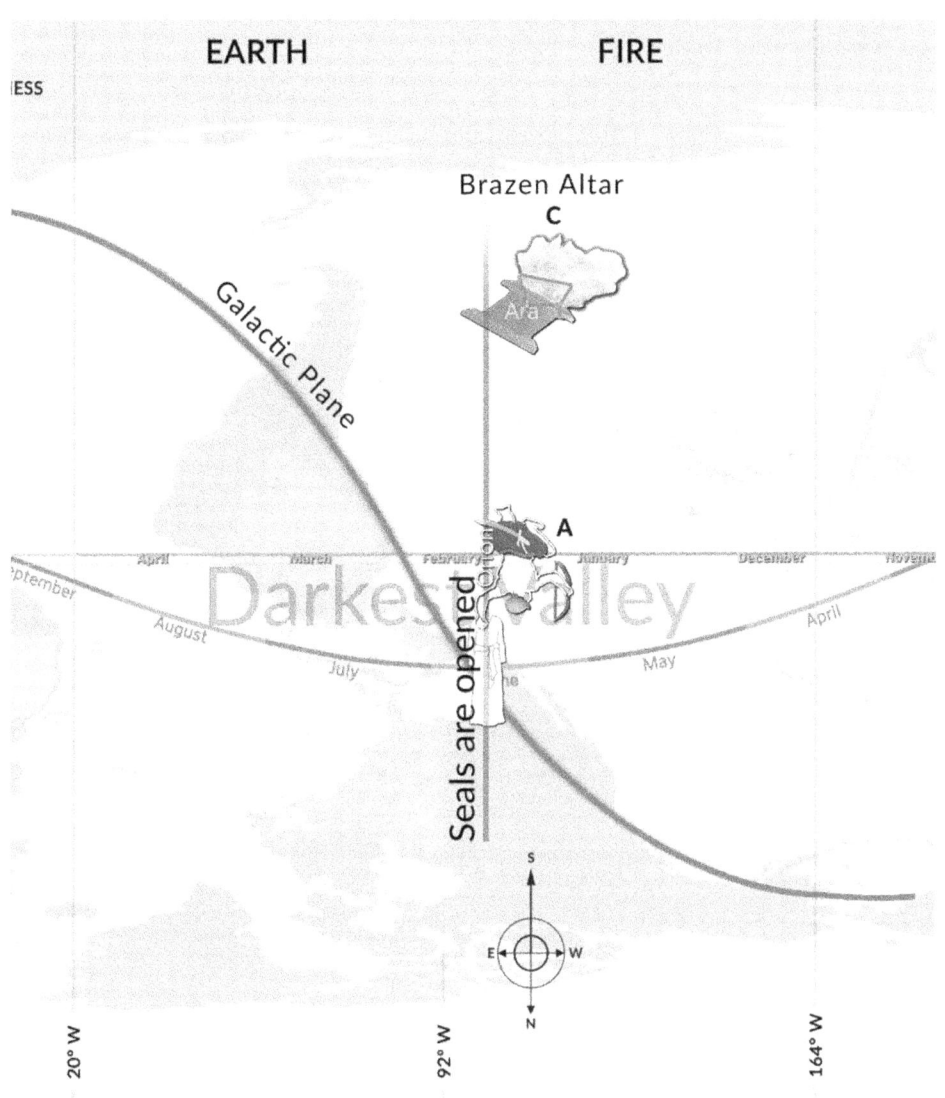

situated beneath the foot of the brazen altar. This location is the place where the blood of the Levitical sacrifices was poured out following atonement involving an animal. Those who are subjected to tribulation and killed for the sake of the name of the Lord become martyrs who, figuratively speaking, are killed at the altar. These individuals hold fast to the cross of Christ, which symbolizes the atoning work for salvation, and their blood metaphorically enters the earth at that location, symbolizing their sacrifice.

In Revelation 6:9-11, it is written that the martyrs are each given a white robe and will rest until the number of their fellow servants and brethren who die as they did is complete. The robes can be regarded as a tangible symbol of recognition for their service to God. The duration of their period of waiting is the same as the length of time that the saints are delivered into the hands of the beast. As indicated in Daniel 12:3, the surviving saints are to instruct others in the worship of God and to purify themselves until the time of the end. It is therefore important that the martyrs rest and remain patient until the process is complete.

In this context, the robes symbolize eternal security. The martyrs will experience resurrection and participate in the millennial reign as priests of God and of Christ, as indicated in Revelation 20:4-6. John observes that the martyrs did not receive the mark of the beast nor engage in its worship. As a result of their faithfulness, an eternal relationship is established between the Messiah, who serves as the head of the kingdom of God, and the martyrs, who are designated as heirs to the kingdom.

Islands and Mountains

John then proceeds to delineate the sequence of events that will transpire after the tribulation period, following the opening of the sixth seal. As indicated by the references in the first five seals, in which the effects are experienced throughout the tribulation, such as the patience of the martyrs, and the horseman being granted to take peace from the earth, the sixth seal focuses on the coming of the Son of Man. As delineated in Matthew 24:29-31, a parallel is established between the celestial events and the role of the Son of Man in saving the remnant, which is described as the sending out of his angels and the gathering of his elect. Although the sixth seal is opened at the beginning of the tribulation, the events described in it indicate the aftermath of the seventh bowl judgment.

The act of pouring out of the seventh bowl, which represents the final judgment during the tribulation, can be described as the collapse of the walls of a city by the greatest earthquake in human history. In this scenario, the hailstones, which descend as if they were stone fragments, will weigh as much as a talent. The populace will seek refuge in caves and among the rocks of the mountains, as if an army were poised to scale the debris of the city walls and annihilate them. In that moment, when the pouring out of the seventh bowl is complete, they will begin to question which of them will be able to endure it. The people of the earth will come to a realization that the day of the wrath of God is imminent and that escape is impossible.

At this juncture, the great city is subdivided into three parts, which is illustrated by the alignment of three distinct feminine constellations: Virgo, Cassiopeia, and Andromeda. The positioning of the feet of the three feminine constellations within the fire element can be interpreted as a representation of accountability. This notion aligns with the idiom to *hold someone's feet to the fire*, which implies that individuals are responsible for their own actions. It can be suggested that the divisions reflect three aspects of the great city, as depicted by the constellations of Virgo, Cassiopeia, and Andromeda: Babylon, the harlot, and those who take the mark of the beast, respectively. Therefore, those who are apostate, have taken the mark of the beast, or have engaged in war against the saints will be held accountable for their actions.

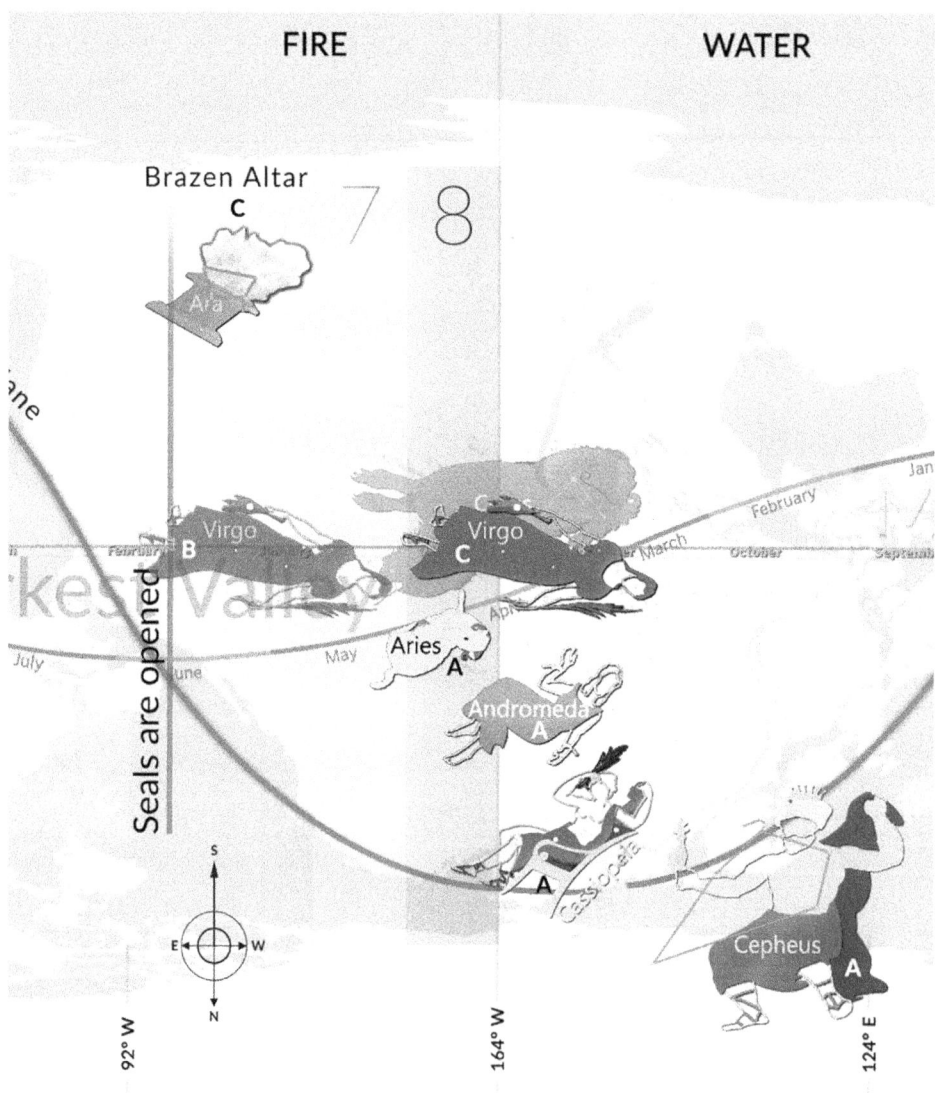

A distinction is established between the defeat of the beast and the defeat of the dragon, which occurs a thousand years later, with respect to the outcome before the face of the One who is seated on the throne. Following the defeat of the beast, every island will flee, and the mountains will be no more. In Revelation 20:11, when the dragon is ultimately defeated, the earth and heaven will flee. This indicates that the beast is associated with the islands and the mountains, whereas the dragon is linked to the earth and heaven. The defeat of the beast will lead to the establishment of the kingdom of God, and the defeat of the dragon will result in the creation of a new heaven and new earth.

Silence

Prior to the opening of the seventh seal, John describes two events in which individuals are separated according to their relationship with God. The initial separation is that of the tribes of Israel and pertains to the one hundred and forty-four thousand servants of God who will be sealed on their foreheads with the Father's name. The subsequent group comprises the vast multitude who are able to stand before the throne and before the Lamb. The ability to stand is related to the question posed at the conclusion of the sixth seal by individuals situated in the valley of Megiddo. Therefore, the separation of the faithful from the apostates, as well as those who have sought to inflict harm upon the saints, will occur following the events of the sixth seal.

Upon his return, the Son of Man will preside over the judgment of the nations, which excludes the saints of the Most High, when he separates the sheep from the goats. This moment represents an answer to the prayers offered by the saints, which are aided in part by the intercession of an angel at the golden altar of incense. In this context, the angel holds a golden censer and is provided with much incense, which allows for the smoke from the incense to ascend with the prayers of the saints before God. It is noteworthy that the final prayer in the

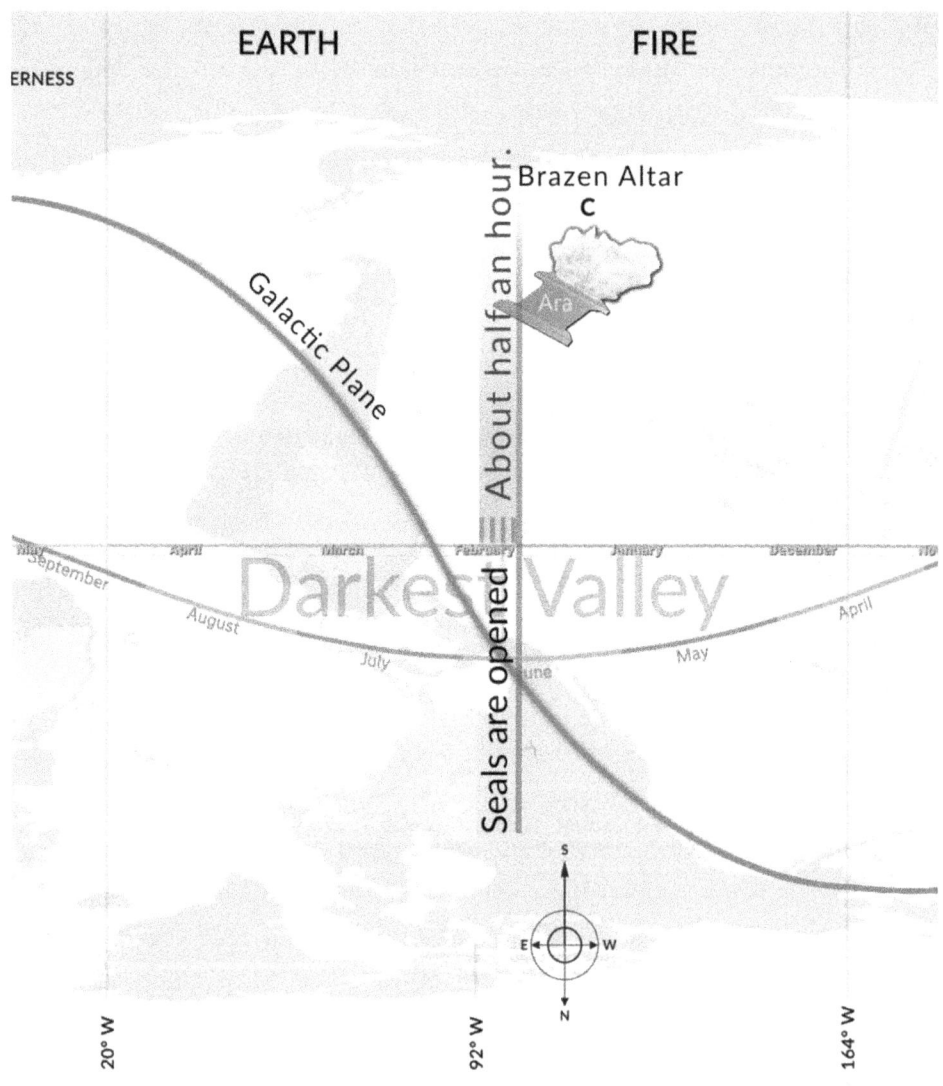

Bible, found in Revelation 22:20, reflects this desire for the return of Jesus. Accordingly, the saints are to prepare themselves in anticipation of his return so that they may enter the kingdom of God and participate in it.

Following the opening of the seventh seal, a period of approximately thirty minutes will elapse during which the heavens will be silent. This duration is based on the right ascension from the opening of the seals to the border of the earth and fire elements, and thus is illustrated as spanning between seven and eight days with regard to the celestial calendar. During this interval, seven angels will position themselves before the throne of God. Each of them will be provided with a trumpet and will await their signal to sound.

Subsequently, the angel will fill the golden censer with fire and cast it upon the earth, thereby initiating divine judgment. This event corresponds with the fire from heaven at the conclusion of the millennial reign of Christ, which will consume the army of the dragon as it surrounds the camp of the saints. At this juncture, the dragon is definitively vanquished, and a final judgment will be conducted at the great white throne. The seventh seal is therefore associated with separation, which ushers in an everlasting time of peace.

8
First Six Trumpets

The sounding of the first six trumpets serves to convey the authority and power of God, with the objective of awakening the conscience of those who have turned away from the Lord. It is, however, important to note that the far-reaching ramifications of each trumpet will challenge or affect all individuals in one way or another. Those who have placed their trust in the Lord God may derive solace from the knowledge that He will not abandon or forsake them. In contrast, those who have rejected the guidance of the Good Shepherd, Christ, may find themselves in a situation where death is a real possibility. In light of the foregoing, those who have elected to reside in a state of spiritual darkness are being prompted to reconsider their position with the sounding of each trumpet.

The following illustration delineates the sequence of the first six trumpets as they appear within the context of the darkest valley. Each bracket is designated with a trumpet, and they constitute a series in which one trumpet follows another. After a period of approximately half an hour of silence, the golden censer is thrown to the earth, and this action is then followed by the sound of the first trumpet. As

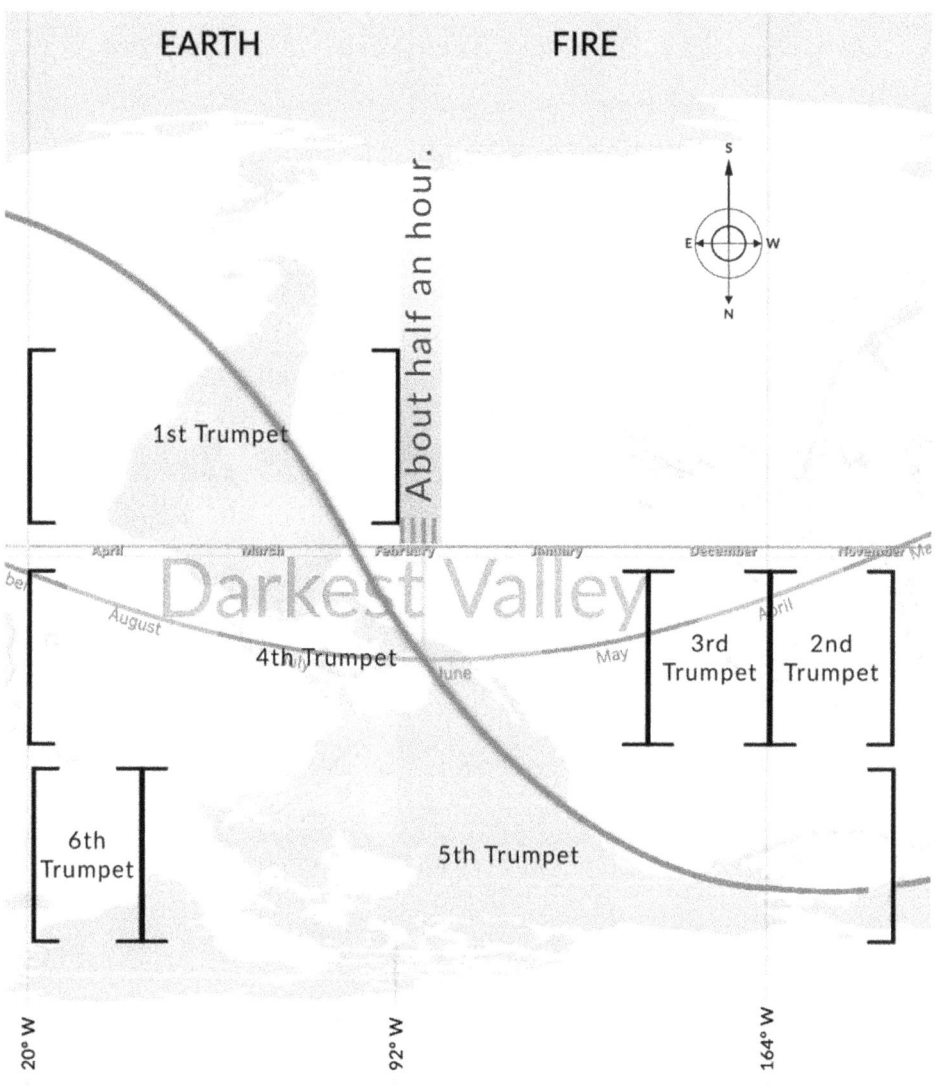

with the illustrations of the opening of the seals, the impact of the trumpets is represented within the designated brackets by the respective constellations, their association with the elements, and the span of time. Consequently, the celestial figures and elemental emphasis associated with each judgment can be identified in their respective area and are illustrated in the context of the darkest valley.

The first six trumpets evoke imagery of destruction, with multiple references to the devastation being inflicted in relation to thirds. The initial three trumpets inflict damage on one-third of the trees, one-third of the creatures that inhabit the sea, and one-third of the rivers and springs, respectively, thereby collectively impacting one-third of the circumference of the Earth. The effects of the fourth trumpet are observed to encompass one-third of the circumference of the Earth in relation to the affected portion of the night sky. The sounding of the fifth trumpet marks the beginning of the first of the three woes, whereas the sounding of the sixth trumpet leads to the death of one-third of the world's population. In conclusion, the cumulative impact of the destruction brought about by the sounding of these trumpets is a third, affecting the Earth, the night sky, and humanity.

	Trumpets	Exodus
1	All Grass Burned	Departing Egypt for the Desert
2	Burning Mountain in the Sea	Egyptian Military Loss
3	Rivers / Springs Made Bitter	Bitter Water at Marah
4	Sun, Moon, Stars Struck	Third of the Year from Shavuot
5	Locust Torment	Construction of the Tabernacle
6	A Third of Humanity Killed	Death Penalty for Military Men

The table demonstrates the correlation between the tribulation associated with the first six trumpets and the Exodus, when the Israelites embarked on their journey to the land of promise for the first time. The sequence of the trumpets can be interpreted as corresponding to the sequence of events in their journey, as observed through an evaluative process. In this context, God provides the multitude with the necessary resources for survival. Nevertheless, many failed to maintain their faith in the plan of God, a scenario that will be repeated in the tribulation period. Therefore, the sounding of the first six trumpets is a reference to the initial journey to the land of promise, which began on the day the Israelites departed from Egypt and should have ended with their entry into the land.

Enter the Wilderness

The events that transpire following the sounding of the first trumpet are delineated in Revelation 8:7. The green grass and one-third of the trees are described as being burned up due to a combination of hail and fire mixed with blood that is hurled upon the earth. In the illustration, the element of earth is interpreted as a representation of the totality of the green grass. The Northern Cross asterism, situated at the altar outside the camp, corresponds to one of the three positions of the constellation Cygnus, thereby symbolizing one-third of the trees that are burned up. Therefore, the sounding of the first trumpet is indicative of an event of global significance pertaining to the environment.

The Northern Cross asterism, in this instance, which symbolizes the cross in the crucifixion of Christ, can also represent the affected trees referenced in the first trumpet. It is noteworthy that there are scriptural references that correlate the cross with a tree in the crucifixion of Jesus. These references include the passages of Acts 5:30 and 1 Peter 2:24. Consequently, in this particular instance, the Northern Cross asterism may be associated with the trees that will be burned up.

In the context of this trumpet correlating to the Exodus, the sounding of the first trumpet would be associated with the departure of the Israelites from Egypt on the Feast of Unleavened Bread. As

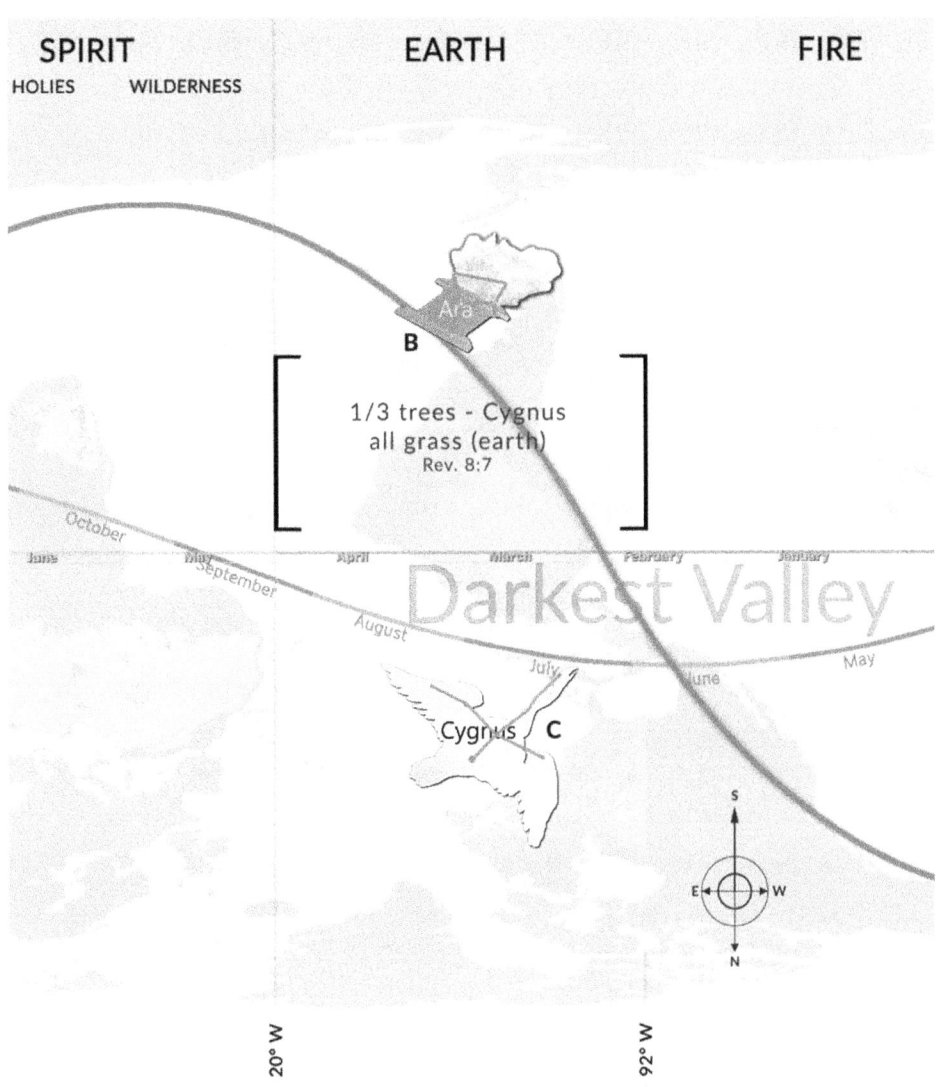

the Israelites ventured into the wilderness, they encountered an arid environment devoid of vegetation and a scarcity of trees. At this point in the narrative, the Israelites have not yet crossed the *yam suph*, which is interpreted from the Hebrew as a sea of reeds. Therefore, it can be suggested that the reference to the burning of the grass and the trees is not an abrupt one, but rather one that will occur relatively quickly.

Burning Mountain

The second trumpet sounds, and John describes something that resembles a great mountain ablaze with fire, which is then hurled into the sea. This event results in one-third of the sea becoming blood, and the affected area is illustrated between the border of the water and fire elements and extending to the edge of the darkest valley. The delineation of this area equates to twenty-four days and a third of a day, or one-third of the water element. In light of these considerations, the point of origin for the darkest valley, as applied in this study, is delineated by the extent to which the water element is affected.

The southern fish constellation, Piscis Austrinus, and the constellation Pisces collectively represent the three fishes in the water element. The fish in Pisces facing north symbolizes one-third of the living creatures in the sea that perish as a result of the aforementioned event. Moreover, the constellation Argo Navis is positioned over the region of the water element that has been impacted, and the location of this particular ship constellation represents one-third of the total number of ships that will be destroyed. As a result, this judgment affects both what lies beneath and above the surface of the sea.

A correlation can be drawn between the sounding of the second trumpet and the destruction of the Egyptian army. In this instance, the great city of Babylon is represented as a mountain that has been set ablaze and will sink into the waters on which she sits. The great city is referred to spiritually as Egypt, which experienced a military loss at the

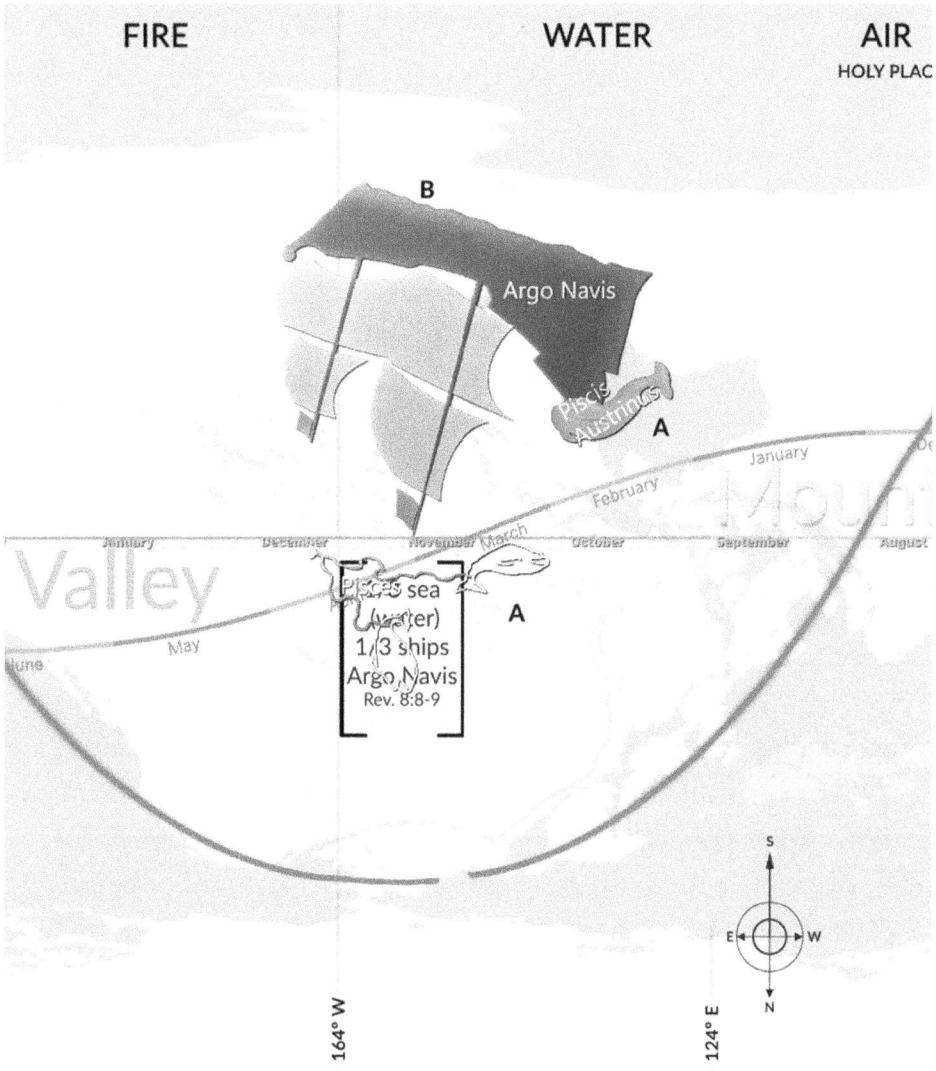

sea of reeds, and as Sodom, which was completely destroyed in part by fire. Therefore, the portrayal of Babylon as a great burning mountain hurled into the sea can be understood to signify that she will suffer an overwhelming military defeat and complete destruction.

The Burning Torch

According to Revelation 8:10-11, the third trumpet sounds, and a great star, burning like a torch, falls on a third of the rivers and on the springs of water, which makes the waters bitter. This event follows the destruction of Babylon and will result in significant losses due to the bitterness among the people. This social context bears a striking resemblance to the one described in the third chapter of Lamentations, which was written in the aftermath of the fall of Jerusalem in 586 BCE. This comparison suggests the emergence of a sentiment of bitterness, stemming from the perception that God is indifferent to their cause and has not intervened.

In the illustration, the constellation Eridanus represents one-third of the ribbon-shaped bodies of water that have been polluted by the great star. The influence of the constellation Cetus, which emerges from the sea and delineates the affected area of the third trumpet, is representative of the pollution. The area of impact spans twenty-four days and one-third of a day, which corresponds to one-third of the fire element, as measured from the border with the water element. Consequently, the constellation Cetus is regarded as an instrument of the divine wrath of God, resulting in the rivers and springs of water becoming bitter.

The experience of bitterness can be likened to the circumstances described in the Exodus narrative, specifically the incident at Marah and the notion that the people were not able to return to Egypt, and in this future case, to Jerusalem. After a period of three days spent wandering the wilderness of Shur without locating a source of water,

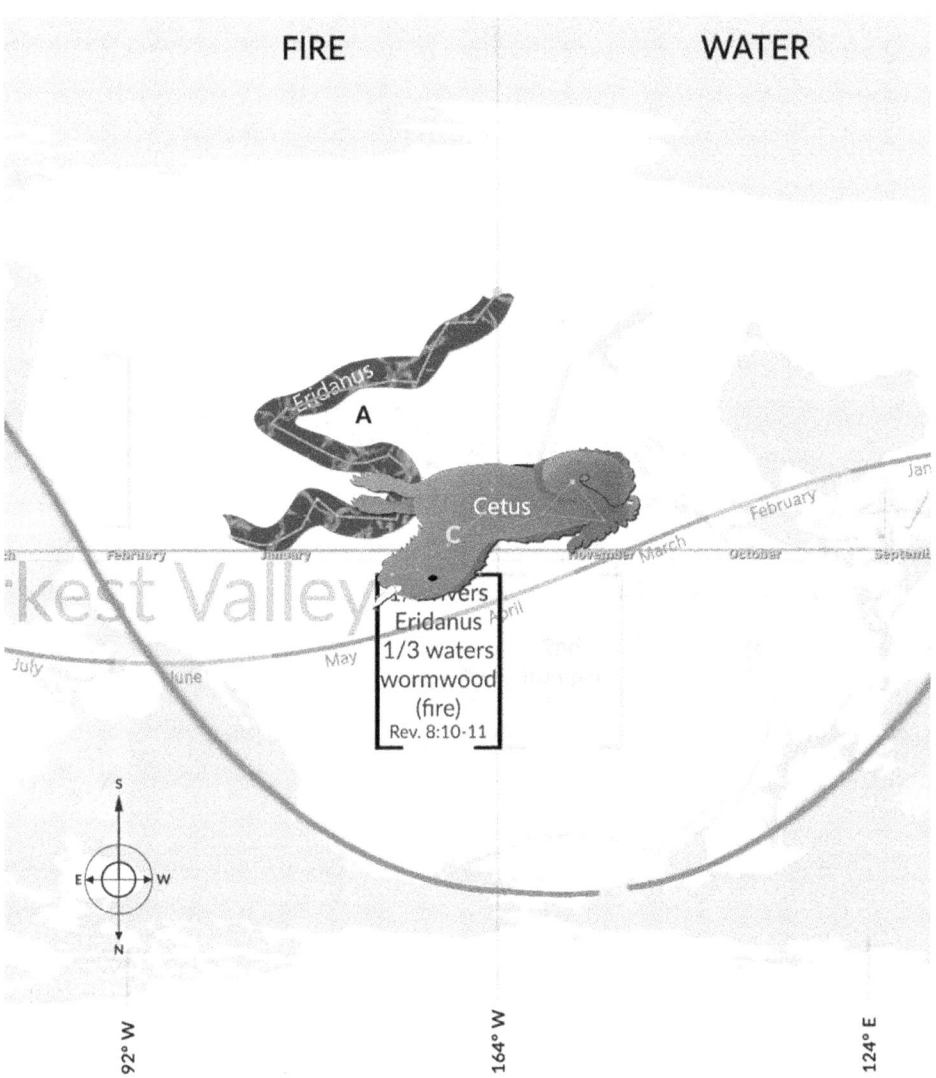

FIRE

WATER

Eridanus

A

Cetus

C

1/3 rivers
Eridanus
1/3 waters
wormwood
(fire)
Rev. 8:10-11

92° W

164° W

124° E

the Israelites arrive at Marah, where they discover a water source that was too bitter to drink. Moses prayed to God, and God provided a solution to make the water sweet. Despite having drinkable water, those who had previously complained will not turn to God and place their trust in Him. Similarly, as a result of the third trumpet, many will not seek God due to the bitterness of the situation and perish.

Influence of the Dragon

Upon the sounding of the fourth trumpet, a third of the celestial bodies will be darkened. The constellation Draco, representing the dragon, delineates the region of the night sky where the Sun and Moon are obscured from the Earth. In terms of right ascension, this constellation spans approximately one-third of the celestial sky. Within the outer courtyard, the constellation Draco corresponds to the area where one-third of the stars are hurled to the earth by the tail of the dragon, as described in Revelation 12:4. Therefore, the constellation Draco symbolizes the darkening influence in that region of the celestial sky.

The impact of the fourth trumpet is illustrated as encompassing approximately one-third of a year, or one hundred and twenty-one days and two-thirds of a day. An analogy can thus be drawn between this duration and the journey of the Israelites between the festival of Shavuot and the Day of Atonement. The interval between these two Hebrew observances amounts to approximately one hundred and twenty-two days. When these factors are taken into consideration, this period of time, as observed in relation to the two observances, begins with the celebration of the harvest and culminates in the reconciliation of the people to God.

The festival of Shavuot commemorates the moment when the Israelites accepted the words of the Lord and the Book of the Covenant. Subsequently, Moses proceeds to sprinkle the blood of the peace offerings upon the people, as detailed in Exodus 24:8. Conversely, the

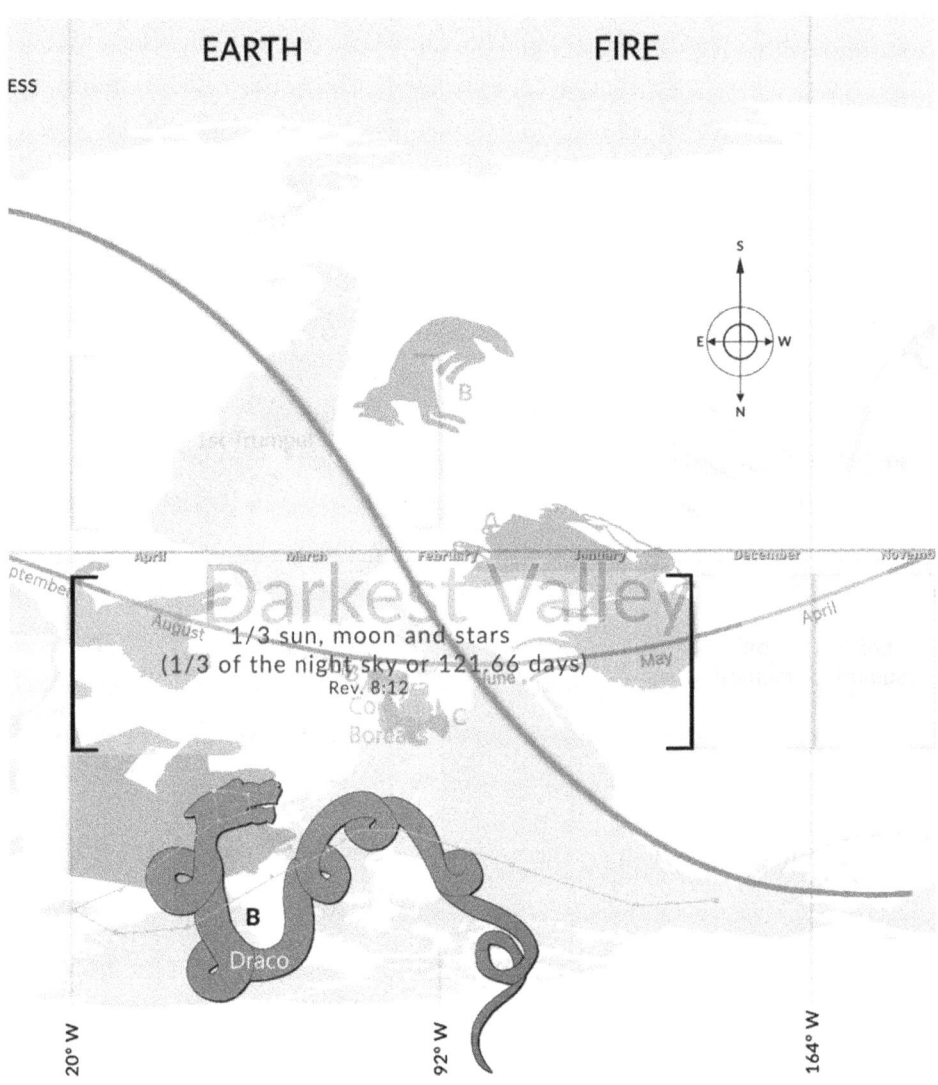

darkening of the celestial bodies can be correlated with the uprooting of the first three horns, the fall of Babylon, and the ten kings relinquishing their authority to the beast. In conclusion, the sounding of the fourth trumpet can be seen to allude to the establishment of the eighth beast.

The Day of Atonement thus establishes a separation between two distinct nations: the kingdom of God, which is represented by the chosen people of the Almighty, and the kingdom in which the populace does not belong to the Creator. In the Exodus narrative, the Israelites observe the Day of Atonement for the first time and engage in a ritual of atonement for the collective sins of the people. This spiritual cleansing can be likened to the practice of a ritual bath of the bride, a customary practice in the Jewish tradition that occurs prior to the wedding feast. It can be suggested that in the chronology of the establishment of the nation of Israel on the Day of Atonement, when those who are not humble will be cut off from the people of God, is a relevant factor in the formation of a nation under the rule of God. Therefore, those who are cut off from the people of God are in alignment with the dragon and the establishment of a nation under the rule of the beast.

Abaddon and the Temple

The sounding of the fifth trumpet is followed by a star that has fallen to the earth and has been given the key to the shaft of the bottomless pit. The shaft of the bottomless pit is situated opposite the door to the tabernacle, according to the celestial calendar. The location of the shaft opposite the tabernacle, which is a symbol of the pathway to life, suggests that those in the bottomless pit are spiritually dead. This dynamic therefore gives rise to a confrontation between two groups: the spiritually dead and the apostates.

According to the text, an army of locusts as well as Abaddon, who is described as the king of the army of locusts and the bottomless pit, are released from the bottomless pit. The word Abaddon is derived

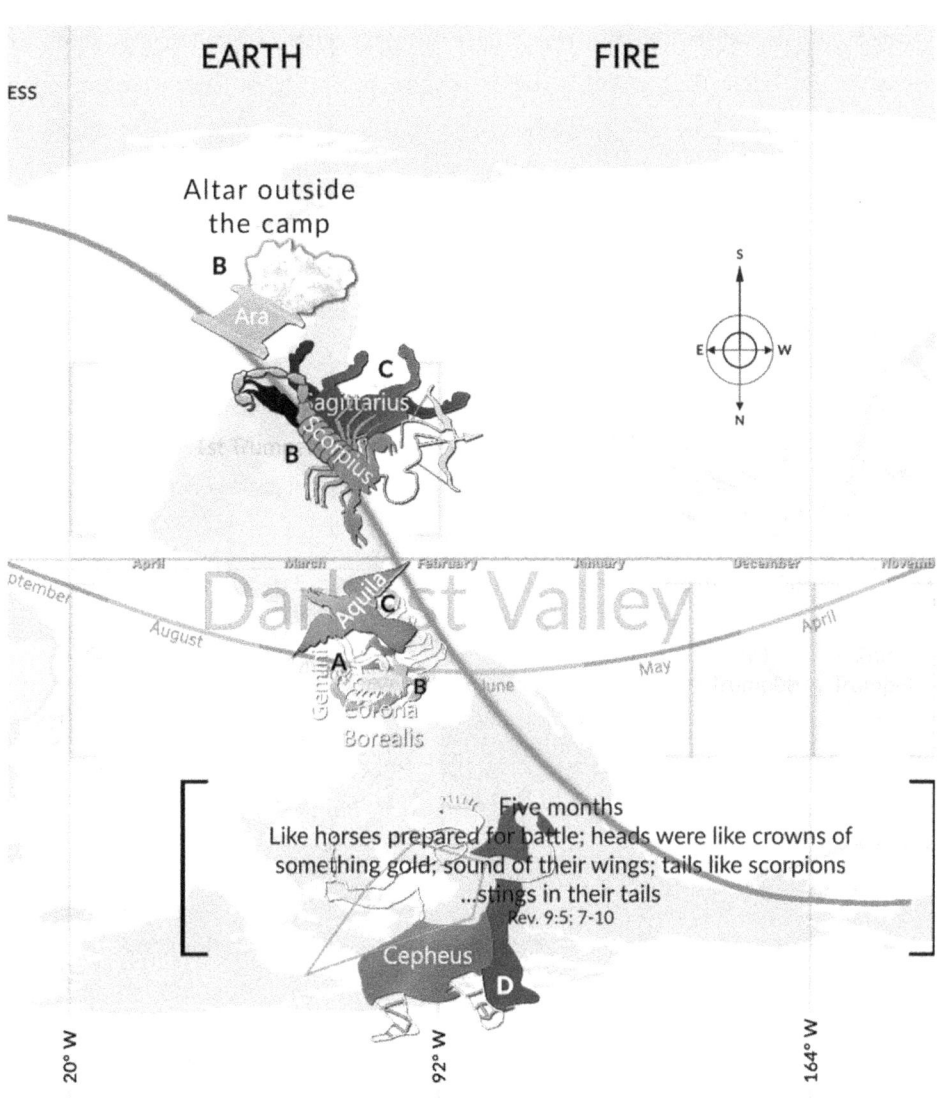

EARTH   FIRE

ESS

Altar outside
the camp

B

Ara

C

Sagittarius

Scorpius

B

April   March   February   January   December   November

ptember

August

Gemini   Aquila   C

A

B

Corona

Borealis

May   April

June

[
Five months
Like horses prepared for battle; heads were like crowns of
something gold; sound of their wings; tails like scorpions
...stings in their tails
Rev. 9:5; 7-10
]

Cepheus

D

20° W   92° W   164° W

from the Hebrew term for a place of destruction or desolation. The illustration depicts the locusts departing the altar outside the camp, with the constellation Cepheus symbolizing the king who presides over them. It is noteworthy that the function of the altar is to consume and destroy all that is deemed cursed or sinful. Therefore, the reference to Abaddon can be interpreted as the place associated with the altar outside the camp as well as a figure associated with destruction.

These locusts are empowered to inflict pain and suffering upon those who lack the seal of the living God for a period of approximately one hundred and forty-eight days, or five lunar months. This study proposes a connection between the seals with the Father's name and the tribes of Israel, thereby establishing that individuals afflicted by the locust are exclusively of Israelite lineage. Consequently, the locusts will cause despair and diminish the quality of life among the descendants of the Israelites who lack the seal of the living God.

In his account, John provides a detailed description of the appearance of the locust as they emerge. These beings are characterized as having the shape of horses and bearing something golden on their heads that resembles a crown. Their faces are likened to those of men, while their hair is described as being similar to that of women. Furthermore, they are described as being winged and possessing tails with stingers that are similar to those of scorpions.

As illustrated, the locusts are depicted departing from the altar outside the camp, which is represented by the constellation Ara. The shape of the locust is like the constellation Sagittarius, which is a depicted as a horse ready for battle. The constellation Corona Borealis is associated with the crown on their head, while the constellation Scorpio is linked to the scorpion tails and the constellation Aquila is connected to the wings. Furthermore, the Gemini constellation symbolizes the integration of masculine and feminine attributes, as evidenced by the facial features of the locust. When these constellations are considered collectively, their configuration forms the description of the locust depicted at the base of the altar.

During the Exodus, the command to depart from Mount Sinai can be likened to the emergence of the locusts. The Lord reveals to Moses of His intention to expel the Canaanite, Amorite, Hittite, Perizzite, Hivite, and Jebusite from the land. On days when a cloud enveloped the tabernacle, signifying the glory of the Lord within it, the Israelites were to remain encamped. Conversely, when the cloud lifted, they were permitted to travel. This image, therefore, appears to show the advance of the people when the cloud lifted as from the rising of smoke.

Casualties of Spiritual Warfare

The sixth trumpet sounds, and John hears a voice emanating from the four horns of the golden altar. The voice issues an order for the sixth angel to release the four angels that are currently held at the river Euphrates. The four angels are symbolized by the four brightest stars in the Southern Cross asterism, a smaller star grouping in the Crux constellation. According to Revelation 9:15-19, the four angels are prepared for the hour, day, month, and year to slay one-third of humanity. In essence, the four angels are tasked with carrying out a death sentence upon humanity within the specified time frame.

The four angels are accompanied by an army of horsemen, symbolized by the constellation Centaurus. It is noteworthy that during the composition of Revelation, the constellation Centaurus included the stars that are currently regarded as part of the Crux constellation. In light of this information, the angels and horsemen are depicted as departing together from the river Euphrates, which is represented by the constellation Eridanus. Although the angels and the horsemen are referenced as distinct entities, they are unified by a singular purpose.

In Revelation 9:16, it is stated that the number of the army of the horsemen, which is released at the river Euphrates, is two myriads of myriads. The heads of the horses are described as resembling those of lions, while their tails are depicted as serpents with heads, represented by the constellation Hydra. The tails of the horses can cause harm, but they are also capable of killing with fire, smoke, and brimstone that comes out of their mouths. Therefore, it can be concluded that a significant number of horsemen will be needed to fulfill the purpose of God's divine wrath at this time.

The three plagues of fire, smoke, and brimstone are represented by the colors of fire, hyacinth, and sulfur on the breastplates worn by the horsemen. These colors symbolize the purification offerings made at the brazen altar. As illustrated, this altar, the constellation Ara, from which smoke rises, is depicted on the breast of the constellation Centaurus. The purification of sulfur, the burning fire, and the rising smoke are therefore associated with the actions of the horsemen, who are removing those who continue to live in sin.

The deaths of one-third of the global population can correspond to the death sentence that God imposed on the Israelites after ten of the twelve spies rejected His plan for their future. The objections raised by the dissenting spies were based on their perception and attraction to the wealth and strength of the people, which led the leaders of Israel to be persuaded by these accounts as reasons to avoid the conquest of the land. The people were so convinced of these stories that they called for Moses, Aaron, and the two spies to be stoned. In response, God prohibited them from entering the land of promise and decreed that they would perish in the wilderness.

The death sentence, as decreed by God, was applied to all individuals of military age, defined as those aged twenty years or older, and who had been numbered according to Numbers 1:1-3. This directive did not apply to the two spies, women, Levitical priests, or individuals not included in the census. It can be reasonably deduced that the probable outcome of this proclamation is the death of approximately one-third

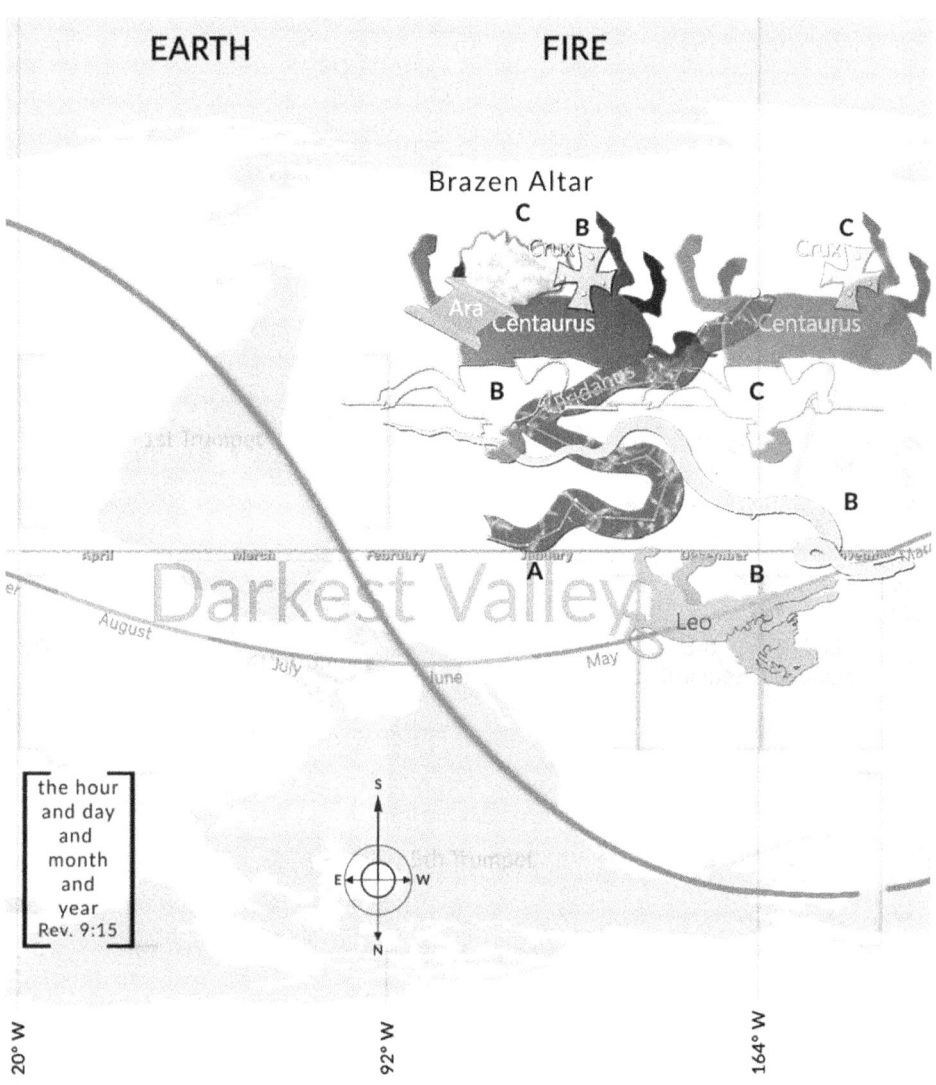

of the Israelites. This figure can thus be considered the equivalent to the outcome of the sounding of the sixth trumpet for the global population.

About Time

The fifth and sixth trumpets provide insight into the projected duration of the two plagues. The fifth trumpet is associated with a period of approximately one hundred and forty-eight days, which corresponds to five lunar months. In regard to the sixth trumpet, John indicates that the angels were prepared for a specific period of time, namely the hour, day, month, and year. The length of this period is approximately thirteen lunar months and one day, or approximately three hundred and eighty-six days, as delineated in the Hebrew calendar. The sum of the two trumpet periods is thus approximately five hundred and thirty-four days.

The number of days for the two trumpets may be interpreted as representing a period of time, in the phrase "time, times, and half a time," referenced in Daniel 12:7. This calculation suggests that the period of times is equivalent to one thousand and sixty-eight days, while half a time spans two hundred and sixty-seven days. The proposed combined period of times and half a time corresponds to the specified duration mentioned in Daniel 12:12, which is one thousand three hundred and thirty-five days. According to this verse, those who wait until the completion of those days will be blessed. Therefore, the total duration of the fifth and sixth trumpets as time is consistent with the chronology presented in Daniel chapter twelve.

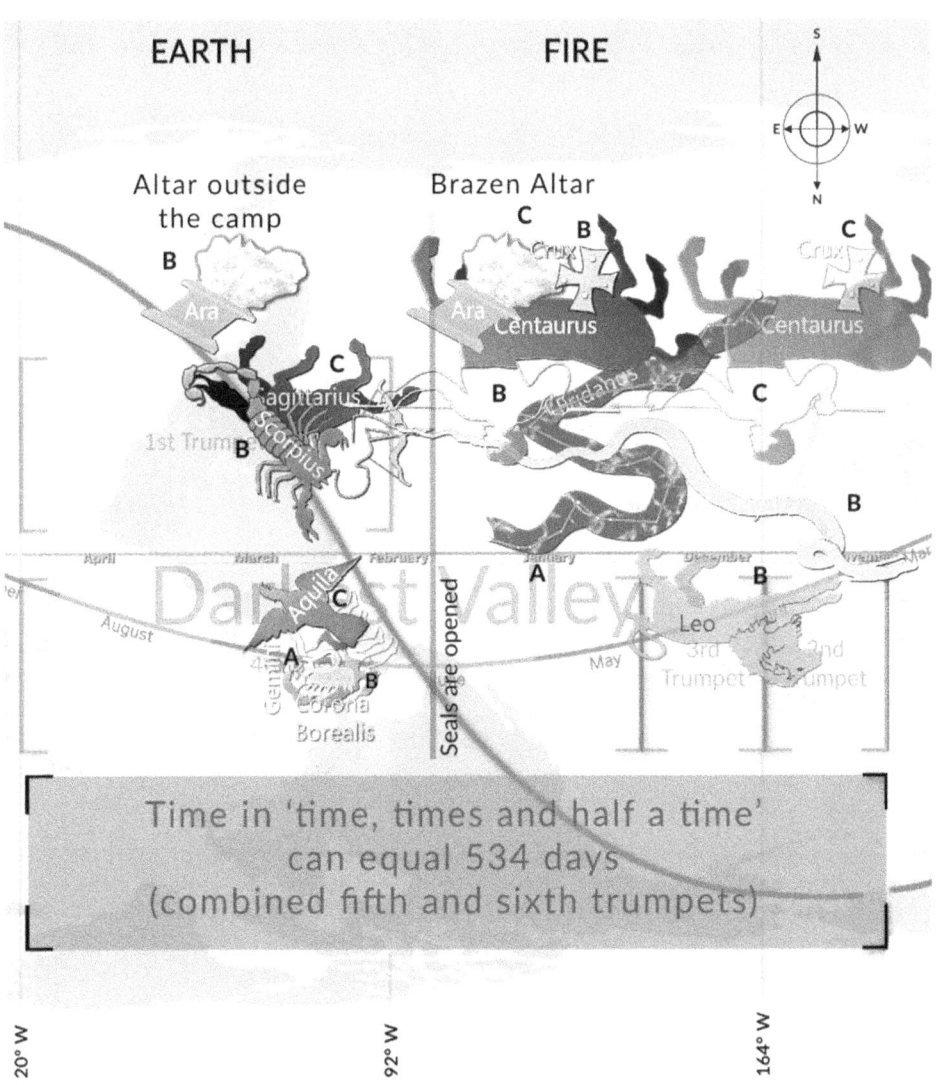

9

Situational Aspects

Following the events of the fourth trumpet, John sees an angel flying through the midst of heaven, saying "Woe, woe, woe to the inhabitants of the earth." The first woe is associated with the fifth trumpet and the release of an army of locusts by a star that has previously fallen, which will occur after the dragon gives his authority to the beast from the sea. The second woe, in relation to the sixth trumpet, culminates with one-third of the population having been killed. Those who persist in the worship of idols will face the third and final woe. Therefore, the declaration of the angel is directed towards those who venerate the beast and the dragon.

Prior to the sounding of the seventh trumpet, John observes a mighty angel of God descending to Earth, holding a small book in his hand. The angel swears by the Creator of heaven and earth, as well as of the sea, and all that is within them, that there shall be no further delay. He then proceeds to state that the mystery of God, as revealed through His servants and prophets, would reach its conclusion, according to Revelation 10:7. Therefore, prior to the mystery of God being finished, the events of the second woe must be completed.

Until that time comes, there exists an ongoing separation between those who are holy and righteous, who continue to praise God, and those who are filthy and unjust, who do not seek Him. While the spirit of God endeavors to draw humanity to God, it is important to mention that no individual is compelled by God to turn to Him against their own volition. While all of humanity is extended the opportunity to be a part of the kingdom of God, the choice to fellowship with God ultimately rests with the individual.

Following the pronouncement by the angel that there would be no further delay, John is instructed by a voice from heaven to take the book from the angel and eat it. After eating the book, the angel directs John to prophesy anew regarding the people, nations, tongues, and kings, as stated in Revelation 10:8-11. John is thus given further insights into the situational aspects associated with the end times and the last judgments.

Signs in the Heavens

According to Revelation chapter twelve, John observes a great sign in heaven. In this sign, he sees a woman in labor, on the verge of childbirth. The woman is portrayed as the constellation Virgo, which in this instance is within the spirit element. As illustrated, the feet of the constellation are positioned in the Holy of Holies. Therefore, the woman can be regarded as virtuous and morally perfect.

The woman is regarded as the daughter of Zion and is clothed with the sun. This reference to the sun can be understood to signify the apparent path of the sun along the constellation Virgo, and it can also be likened to the cloak of zeal worn by God, as referenced in Psalm 104:2 and Isaiah 59:17. The moon is positioned beneath her feet and the twelve stars encircle her head, symbolizing that she walks in the light and is mindful of the living God. Therefore, her outward beauty is considered a reflection of her inner relationship with God.

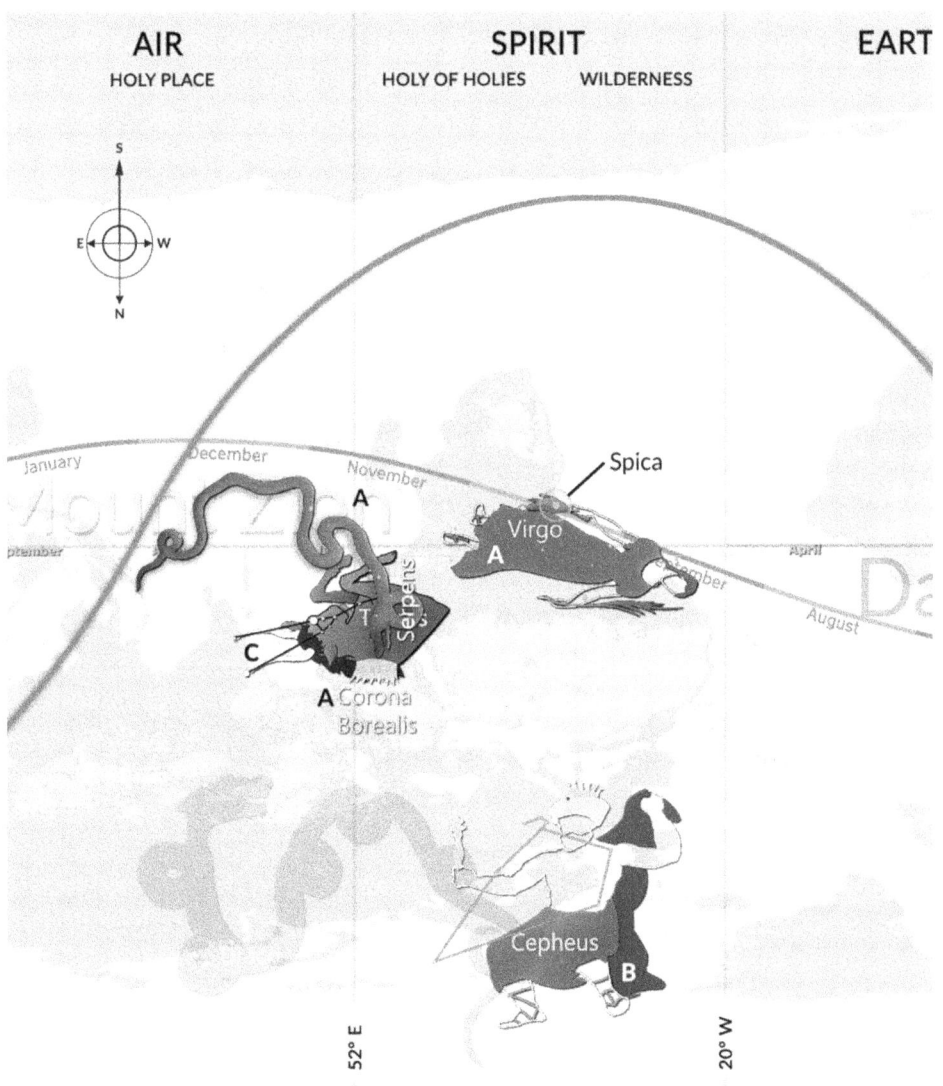

Another sign appears in heaven before her: a great red dragon that has cast a third of the stars of heaven to the earth. The great red dragon, as described in Revelation 12:3, is characterized by its seven heads, seven crowns, and ten horns, and rules by deception over the kingdoms of the world. The dragon is illustrated by the alignment of the constellations Taurus and Serpens, while the constellation Corona Borealis represents the seven crowns that adorn its head. The numerical traits are associated with the appearance of the eighth beast in the outer courtyard and represent all the nations that were given to the beast. The numerical delineation of the dragon corresponds to its perceived power in the world, which is limited to the eight segments of the courtyard.

This celestial imagery is interpreted as an attempt to prevent the realization of the first promise, as given in Genesis 3:15. According to this promise, God says that the seed of the woman will crush the head of the serpent. The correlation of the two great signs indicates that the dragon awaits the birth of the child, poised to devour the child at the very start of his life. This action by the dragon, therefore, represents a challenge to the fulfillment of the first promise.

The ear of wheat carried by the constellation Virgo contains a seed, the star Spica, which its Hebrew name translates to branch. The ear of wheat is a symbol of the cyclical nature of life, death, and rebirth. In the context of the branch metaphor, the male child is interpreted as the offspring of righteousness that the Lord will raise up for David, as referenced in Jeremiah 23:5. The branch aligns with the constellation Cepheus, the Ancient of Days and His throne, and will be taken up to God and His throne, as stated in Revelation 12:5. The male child, representing the lineage of David, will return to the Earth and govern as king, with justice and righteousness.

Actions of the Dragon

In Revelation 12:7, shortly after the ascension of the male child, a war

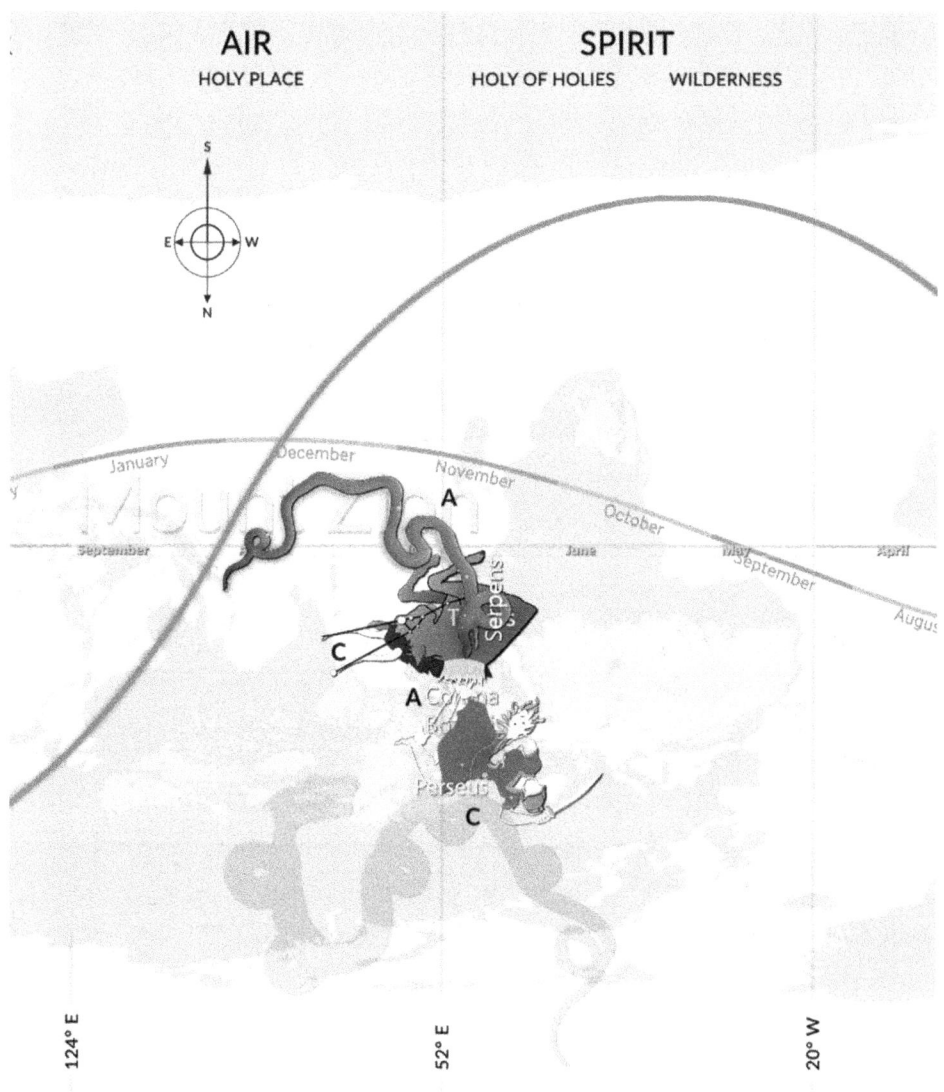

breaks out in heaven. This confrontation is depicted as a battle between the archangel Michael and his angels on one side and the dragon and his angels on the other. The illustration portrays the constellation Perseus as the archangel Michael, who is depicted engaging in combat with the great red dragon. This act of desperation on the part of Satan signifies his attempt to maintain his presence in the heavens by any means necessary. The attempted coup d'etat by the great red dragon, therefore, is an effort to dethrone the male child.

The outcome of this heavenly war is the defeat and subsequent expulsion from heaven of the dragon and his angels. This event occurs prior to the conclusion of the one thousand two hundred and sixty-day period of the woman being in the wilderness, as delineated in Revelation 12:6. It is noteworthy that this expulsion will also occur shortly before the midpoint of the seventieth week, as referenced in the book of Daniel chapter nine, which marks the start of the period known as the great tribulation. At this juncture, Satan and his activities in heaven will have been brought to an end.

The Two Witnesses

In Revelation 11:4, John gives an account of two witnesses, who stand before the Lord of the whole earth. These anointed ones are symbolized by the constellation Gemini in the water element, while the Lord of the whole earth is represented by the constellation Cepheus. According to Zechariah chapter four, the vision of Zechariah includes two olive branches, which are also referred to as the sons of oil, standing beside the Lord, which can be depicted as an alignment of the constellations of Gemini and Cepheus. The anointed ones serve God as instruments of His will, providing spiritual guidance and testimony.

In the illustration, the two witnesses are positioned between the entrance of the tabernacle and the darkest valley, where they bear witness to the Lord. Their message appears to align with the notion

that in order to depart from the darkest valley, an individual must first wash at the laver, which requires faith. This washing is essential for attaining spiritual purity, which is necessary for serving God and for distinguishing oneself from the nations in the outer courtyard. The depiction of the two witnesses in a state of spiritual purity is, therefore, intended to motivate others to do the same.

The path is delineated by the Big Dipper, a seven-star asterism in the Ursa Major constellation. In various cultures, this grouping of seven fixed stars has been interpreted as an image of a plow, an open farm wagon drawn by oxen or horses, or the foreleg of an ox or bull. The Big Dipper was believed to serve as a celestial guide, metaphorically signifying a stairway to heaven, due to its consistent visibility throughout the year for those in the Northern Hemisphere. The earliest known reference to this asterism as a plow dates back to the ancient Roman period, prior to the ministry of Jesus. Therefore, it is reasonable to interpret the Big Dipper as a celestial sign that guides individuals towards spiritual purity and immorality.

The two witnesses, in conjunction with this instance of the celestial plow, can be interpreted as a reference to the plowing of a narrow trench for the planting and watering of seeds. This narrow path is similar to the menorah in the tabernacle, which serves to illuminate the path of enlightenment. It is noteworthy that the arrangement of the seven candles on the menorah, as given in Numbers 8:2, is such that its light is directed to shine in front of it. In this context, the two witnesses function as a beacon of guidance and illumination, akin to the source and light of a menorah, guiding individuals toward understanding and spiritual awakening.

Ministry of the Two Witnesses

After God had sentenced the men of military age to death, an event during the Exodus which this study correlates with the sixth trumpet, only two people would have seen the land of promise. According to Numbers 14:36-38, the ten spies who gave a bad report died as a result of a plague. As the Israelites wandered the wilderness for an additional thirty-eight years, only Joshua and Caleb had explored the land of promise. It stands to reason that, as witnesses of the land of promise, they would endeavor to communicate with those who had rebelled in order to bring them around to the plan of God.

In a similar manner, during the great tribulation, the ministry of the two witnesses would occur at a time when one-third of the population would perish and the nations would trample on the holy city. According to Revelation 11:3, the two witnesses engage in prophecy for a period of one thousand two hundred and sixty days, while clothed in sackcloth. In the following verse, the two witnesses are described as olive trees and lampstands, thereby symbolizing their role in illuminating the path for the peoples, nations, tongues, and kings to seek God. The function of their ministry is thus characterized as a witness, for the people of the world to turn to God, which in turn will cause those who do so to wear sackcloth spiritually.

The two anointed ones are capable of demonstrating considerable power against those who would seek to cause them harm. This power is evidenced by the occurrence of fire, drought, and plagues, which can be administered as often as desired. Their ministry is depicted as having an impact to the same extent as the first six trumpets, affecting the earth, the sea, the rivers, and the heavens, as stated in Revelation 11:6. These plagues are meant to cause a spiritual introspection within the peoples, nations, tongues, and kings so that they will forsake sin and choose righteousness by turning to God.

The plagues that the two witnesses are empowered to unleash are similar in nature to the following: Elijah proclaimed to Ahab that rain would not fall in the land unless he gave the command for it to do so. Moses demonstrated the ability to control the waters and to strike the earth with various plagues. Moreover, the two witnesses can be likened to Joshua the high priest and Zerubbabel, the governor of Judah, who returned from Babylon with a remnant of the people and proceeded to rebuild the temple with great dedication. The fire that emanates from their mouths represents the word of God, and those who intend to harm them are akin to wood that God will judge, condemn, and burn, as stated in Jeremiah 5:14.

The illustration delineates the correlation between the extent of the trumpet judgments and the darkest valley, as well as the duration of

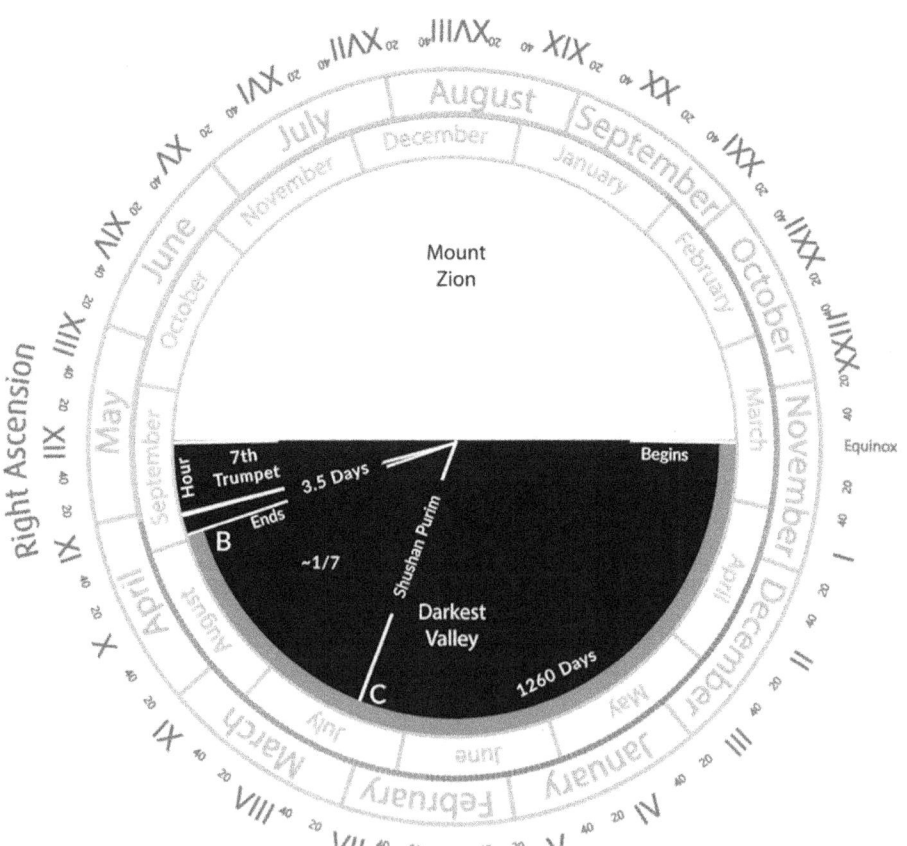

the ministry of the two witnesses. The ministry of the two witnesses is shown to begin at approximately the same point in time as the transition to the darkest valley around the March equinox. Upon the conclusion of their ministry, they will be killed by the beast that comes up out of the bottomless pit. The bodies will remain unburied and in the streets for a period of three and a half days. Therefore, the complete timeline of the two witnesses spans nearly one thousand two hundred and sixty-four days.

In commemoration of the death of the two witnesses, those who dwell on the earth will engage in activities similar to those observed during the celebration of Shushan Purim. This festival is observed exclusively in Jerusalem on the day following Purim and commemorates the Jewish victory at Shushan over Haman. During this celebration, it is customary to exchange gifts. Therefore, the triumph of the beast over the two witnesses is regarded as a victory to be celebrated by those who dwell on the earth.

The two witnesses will be brought back to life and ascend to heaven following a period in which they were dead for three and a half days. In that same hour, a great earthquake will claim the lives of seven thousand people, a number that may be indicative of the last of those who will die as a result of the sounding of the sixth trumpet. Those who survive will offer praise to the God of heaven. At this juncture, the second woe is complete.

The wicked are cognizant of their role in the destruction of the earth through bloodshed, yet they persist in their actions, unwilling to be held responsible for their actions. According to Revelation 11:5, all those complicit in the death of the two witnesses are to be killed and cast into the lake of fire alongside the beast from the sea. The death of the two witnesses brings into play the principle outlined in Deuteronomy 17:6, which stipulates that those who merit death will be put to death because of the testimony of two or more witnesses.

Thus, the third woe that follows signifies that the wicked, knowing the end is imminent, will fight against the Lord until the very end.

Equinoctial Perspective

The chronologies of the two witnesses and the first departure of the woman into the wilderness span a period of one thousand two hundred and sixty days, with an additional three and a half days being appended to the period of the two witnesses as part of their narrative. This difference in the length of time allows for the delineation of the

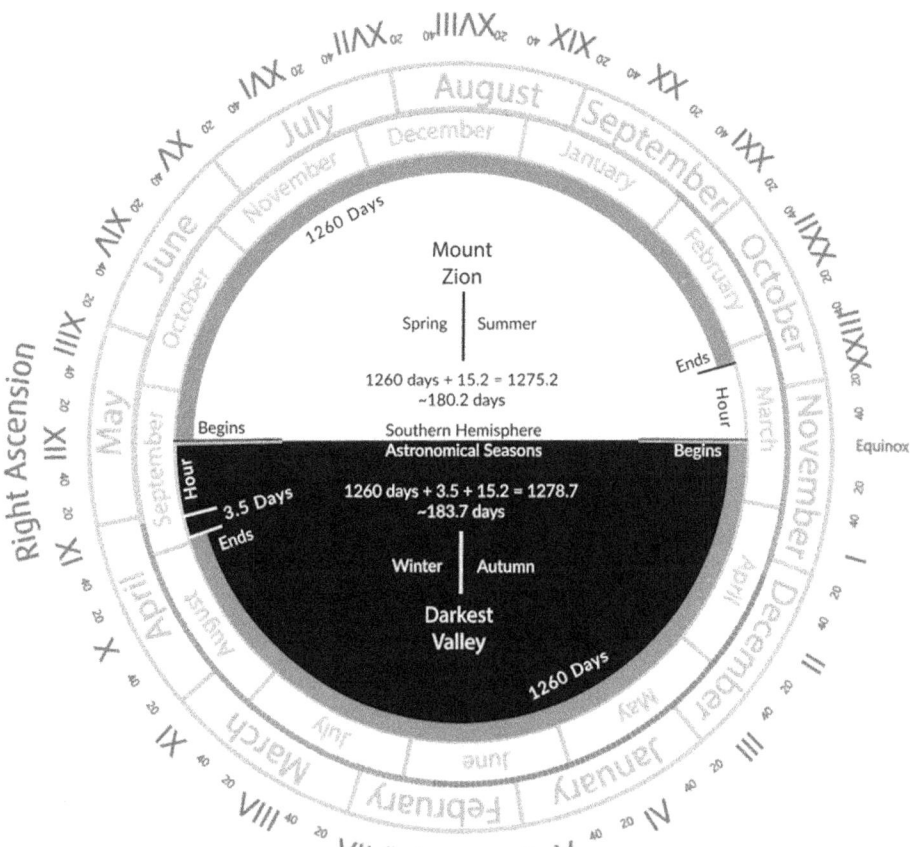

two time periods to appear in opposition to each other, aligning with different seasons. As illustrated, the darkest valley corresponds to the seasons of winter and autumn, while Mount Zion corresponds to the seasons of spring and summer, as the seasons pertain to the southern hemisphere. Thus, the ministry of the two witnesses corresponds to the darkest valley, and the first departure of the woman into the wilderness corresponds to Mount Zion.

As a result, the two chronologies are shown to begin at opposite equinoctial points and end approximately fifteen to sixteen days prior to their respective opposite beginning equinoctial points. The fifteen- to sixteen-day periods can be measured in terms of right ascension and thus can be referenced as one hour. In this manner, the period following the return of the woman from the wilderness corresponds to the fall of Babylon, while the period following the ministry of the two witnesses aligns with the third woe. Therefore, it can be reasonably inferred that the two equinoctial points mark the conclusion of God's judgments, whether it is against the great city or the beast from the sea.

Coordinating with the Ascension

The ascent of the male child to God and to His throne serves as the catalyst for the beginning of the seventieth week, as outlined in Daniel 9:24-27. According to Acts 1:2-3, the ascension of Jesus is said to occur on the fortieth day following his resurrection. When this reference is considered in conjunction with the dates utilized in this study, the ascension is shown to potentially occur on May 13, according to the celestial calendar. This date corresponds to the transition from the darkest valley to Mount Zion on the September equinox. Therefore, this interpretation associates the ascension of Jesus with the ascent to Mount Zion.

The table presents a list of various events that may occur in proximity to the equinoxes, corresponding with the dates of the celestial calendar.

The ascent of Mount Zion is associated with the first day of the seven-day observance of the Feast of Tabernacles, also known as the Feast of Booths. This observance acknowledges the provision and protection of God during the journey of the Israelites through the wilderness. The correlation between the solar and celestial calendars indicates that the first day of the Feast of Tabernacles is May 14, which begins on May 13. Therefore, the ascent of the male child also signifies the departure of the woman, who acknowledges her reliance on God.

Celestial Calendar			Observances
April	4	Day 1	Resurrection of Jesus
May	13	Day 40	Ascension of Jesus
		9:25 A. M.	Woman goes into the Wilderness, Feast of Tabernacles (May 13/14)
November	10	10:00 A. M.	Begins Ministry of Two Witnesses 1260 days - (1095 days or 3 years) + 3.5 days = 168.5 days
April	27	10:00 P. M.	Ascension of the Two Witnesses
	28		The third woe begins (~15.2 days)
May	13		The third woe concludes

In conclusion, the woman departs for the wilderness following the ascension of the male child to heaven, which leads to war in heaven between the great red dragon and the archangel Michael. The devil and his angels are cast out of heaven, and the woman returns from the wilderness. It is at this juncture that the one-hour judgment against the great city begins. The great city is destroyed by the midpoint of the seventieth week, which also marks the beginning of the ministry of the two witnesses. Thus, the war in heaven between God and the devil is associated with Mount Zion, while the war on earth between God and the devil is associated with the darkest valley.

10
Fall in the Week

One of the seven angels, who had the seven bowls, informs John of the impending judgment of the great harlot. The condemnation is attributed to apostasy, as evidenced by her claim of being a self-made woman and her apparent unwillingness to repent and return to God. She is convinced that she is deserving of God's blessings despite her involvement in activities that are morally questionable. The wrath of God is declared to befall her as a result of her perception regarding her role in the world as being of greater importance than her conduct respectful to the Creator.

The self-perception of the great harlot is shaped by her immoral behavior, which leads her to believe that she is esteemed among the nations. The harlot's rejection of the notion of the second coming of Christ underscores her aspiration to maintain her status as a world leader. Furthermore, she fails to acknowledge the Messiah as the high priest, opting instead to serve in the role of the high priestess with her drink offering. Therefore, as a religious system that worships idols and engages in unethical practices, her actions are in direct opposition to the will of the Creator and His Christ.

The great harlot is associated with Babylon and is identified as the mother of harlots. This description of her, in addition to her being the mother of the abominations of the earth, is expressed on her forehead, as described in Revelation 17:5. The wording is in stark contrast to the inscription on the seal of the high priest, which bears the words "HOLINESS TO THE LORD," as referenced in Exodus 28:36-38. The latter inscription is displayed on a gold plate attached to the turban of the high priest and positioned on his forehead. In this way, the Lord underscores the characterization of the great city as a place filled with abominations and unclean rituals.

Strategic Subjugation

The great harlot is described in Revelation 17:1-2 and 18:7 as sitting like a queen, seated on the many waters, prior to experiencing the judgment of God. The constellation Cassiopeia is associated with the figure of the great harlot, which in this instance is depicted as a queen sitting in her chair within the water element. As stated in Revelation 17:15, the many waters symbolize the peoples, multitudes, nations, and tongues. This depiction suggests that the influence of the great harlot is felt throughout the world.

The constellations of Cassiopeia, Crater, and Pisces align to present the inhabitants of the earth partaking of the wine of her fornication. The constellation Pisces, specifically the fish oriented northwards in the darkest valley, is representative of the kings of the earth, with whom the great harlot engages in fornication. Additionally, Revelation 18:3 and 18:19 state that mariners and the merchants of the earth, as illustrated by the constellation Argo Navis, have become wealthy due to the abundance of her luxury. Therefore, the judgment of the harlot will also have a profound impact on the kings and merchants of the earth.

According to Revelation 17:3, John is carried away by the angel in the Spirit into the wilderness and observes a woman seated on a scarlet

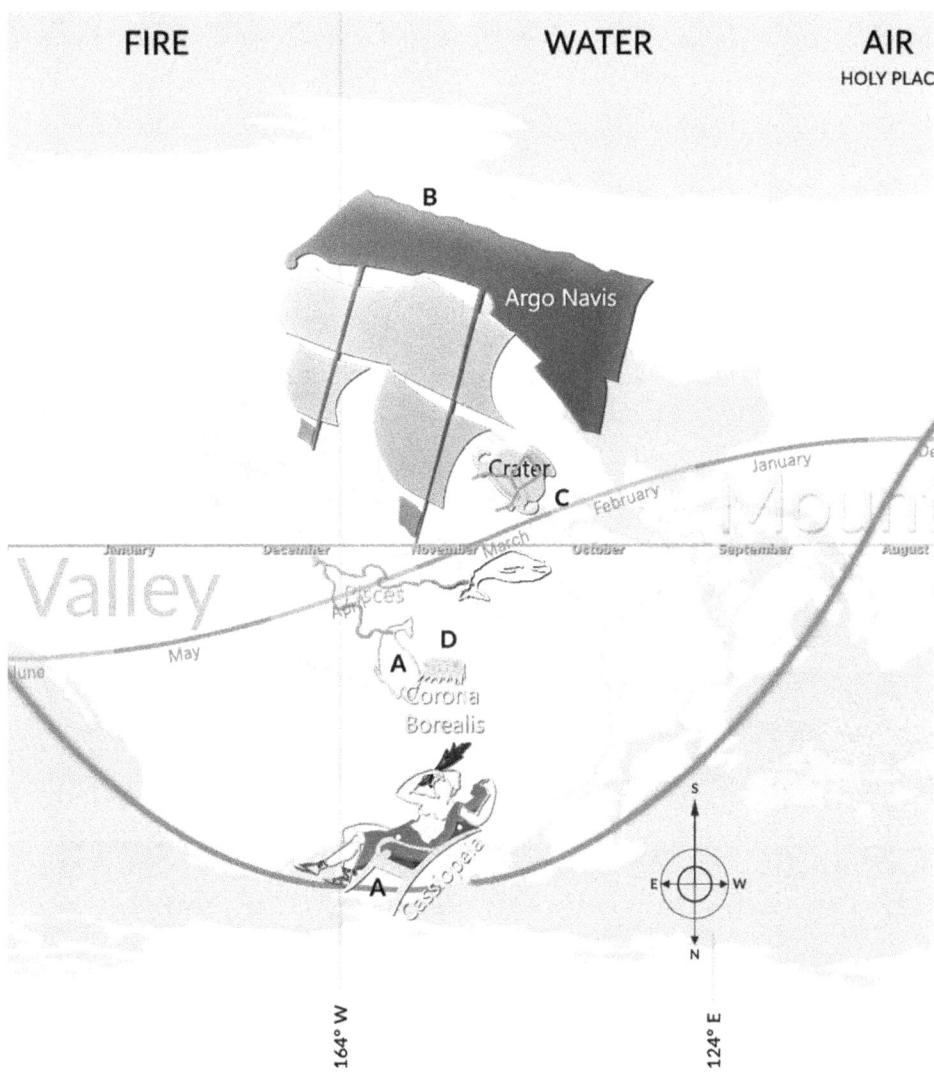

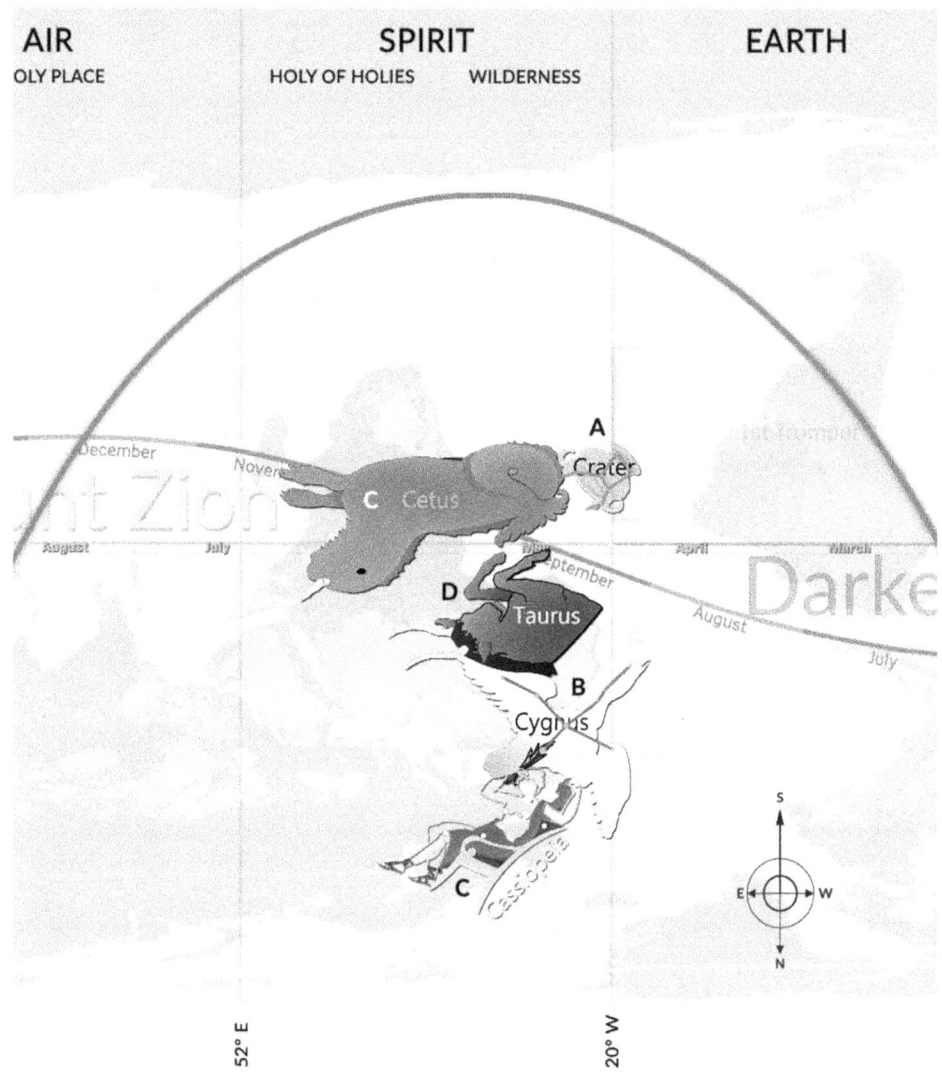

beast with seven heads and ten horns. In the initial account, John is informed of the great harlot being seated on many waters. However, upon observing the woman, clothed in purple and scarlet, John finds that she is depicted as seated on the scarlet beast. As illustrated, the constellation Cassiopeia is aligned with the constellation Taurus, which is positioned adjacent to the constellation Cetus. According to this depiction, the scarlet beast is distinct from the ten horns, and the harlot sits on both.

Additionally, John portrays the harlot as being drunk with the blood of the saints and martyrs of Jesus, as referenced in Revelation 17:6. The cup from which the great harlot drinks from is represented by the constellation Crater, which is filled with the blood of the saints, as symbolized by the Northern Cross asterism. A notable distinction emerges in the manner of intoxication between the harlot and the inhabitants of the earth, whereby the inhabitants of the earth are made drunk by the wine of her fornication. This contrast suggests that the inhabitants are made drunk, signifying a strategic subjugation of the kingdoms of the world by the harlot through the instrument of corruption. This dynamic enables the harlot to perpetuate her dominion by excluding those who voice opposition to her actions.

The Seventieth Week to the Covenant

In Daniel, chapter nine, an account is provided of seventy weeks that have been decreed for the city of Jerusalem to finish the transgression and to bring in everlasting righteousness. In this prophetic text, the reference to the week is employed to denote a seven-year interval. Although the week is illustrated by a single year, the day for its midpoint is approximately equivalent to the midpoint of a seven-year period, provided that the time frame is initiated on the same day. Consequently, the total duration of the prophetic period is equivalent to four hundred and ninety years.

The prophecy is comprised of three sections: seven weeks, sixty-two weeks, and the seventieth week. According to the prophecy, the restoration of the open square and the city walls of Jerusalem is to be completed before the start of the seventieth week. Following the period of sixty-two weeks, the Messiah will be cut off. Therefore, the ascent of the male child to God and His throne is associated with the beginning of the seventieth week.

The advent of the seventieth week is not contingent on a covenant established by the beast with many for one week, which is referenced

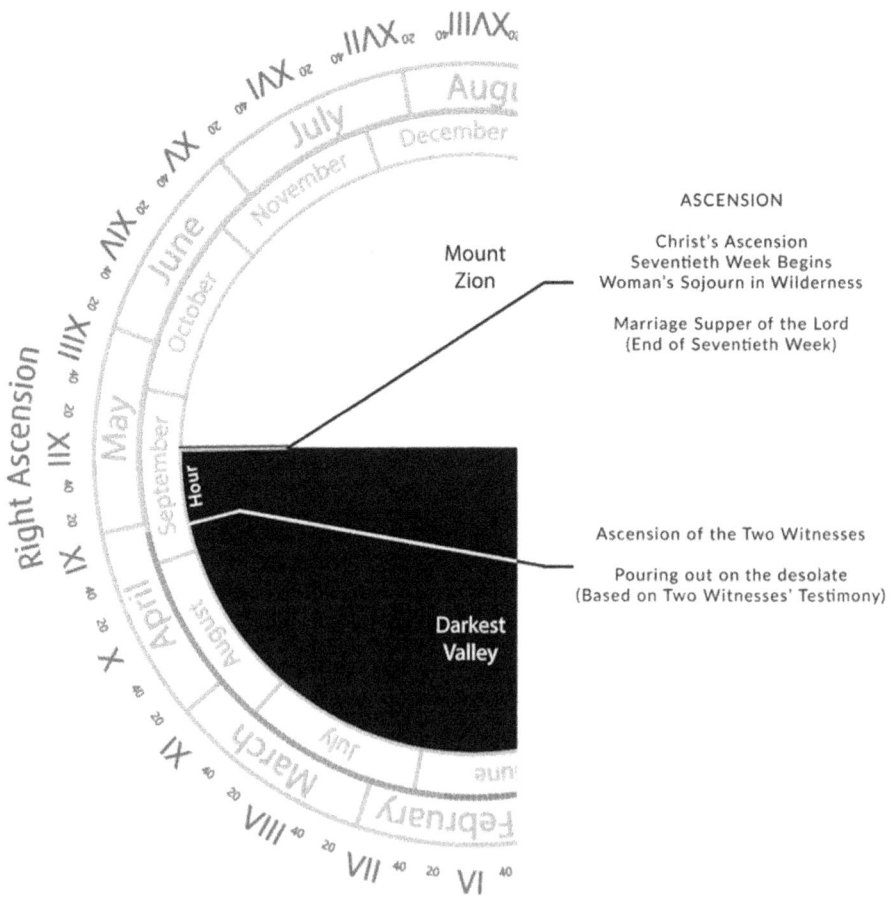

in Daniel 9:27. The preceding verse indicates that the prince of the people, who is to come, will first destroy the city and its sanctuary. Afterwards, a covenant is confirmed; nevertheless, it will be broken halfway through, corresponding to the closing of the second half of the seventieth week. Therefore, a period of half a week transpires between the ascension of the male child and the confirmation of the covenant.

The seventieth week is initiated by the correlation between the ascension of the male child, the initial departure of the woman into the wilderness, and the conflict between the Devil and the Archangel

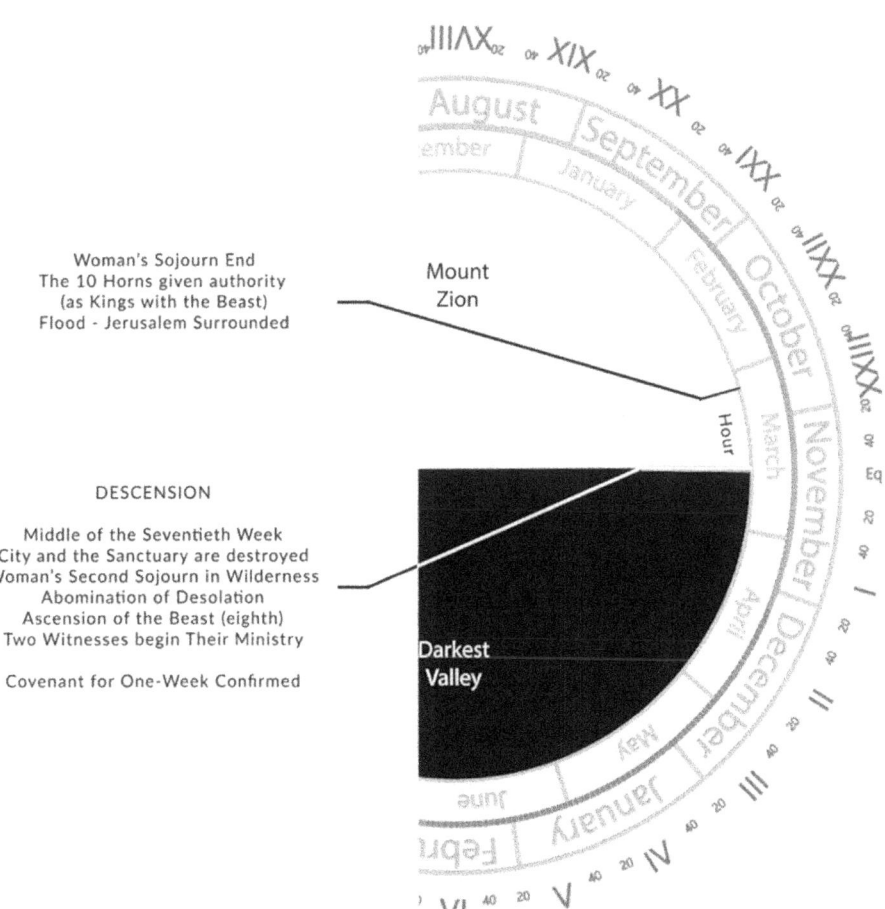

Michael in the heavens. At this point, the beast has not yet emerged from the sea to receive power from the dragon. The absence of this event suggests that the great apostasy, the trampling of the earth, and the removal of the one who restrains have not yet occurred. Therefore, it can thus be deduced that a period of time must occur between the ascension of the male child and the actual destruction of the great city.

The impending destruction of the great city is predicted to occur within a span of one hour. The kings of the earth will proclaim that judgment has come in one hour. Merchants of the earth will also attest to the loss of great riches within the same amount of time. Those who had ships on the sea will claim that the city has been made desolate in one hour. Thus, the judgment of God against the great city is fulfilled in one hour, profoundly impacting many global economies.

In the aftermath of the complete fall of Babylon at the hands of the people of the prince who is yet to come, a one-week covenant is established between the beast and many. As a result of this agreement, it appears that the beast will proceed to persecute the saints of the Most High and prevail over them. The beast will have gained authority over every tribe, tongue, and nation, and will be worshipped by those whose names have not been inscribed in the Book of Life. Therefore, following the destruction of the great city, the beast will emerge from the sea as a symbol of the collective power, wielding authority over all the preceding kingdoms of the earth.

The downfall of Babylon corresponds with the removal of the one who restrains, as stated by the Apostle Paul in 2 Thessalonians, chapter two. This great city is identified as the place where Jesus was crucified, as set forth in Revelation 11:8, and thus can be interpreted as implying Jerusalem. Despite the devastation, the great city will maintain its spiritual identity as Sodom and Egypt, thereby expressing hostility toward the true God. Therefore, the great apostasy, facilitated by Babylon, will persist under the reign of the beast.

Time, Times, and Half a Time

According to Luke 21:20, Jerusalem will be encircled by armies, identified as the people of the prince who is to come, in conjunction with the prophecy given in Daniel chapter nine. It is incumbent upon the inhabitants of the city to recognize that the abomination that makes desolate is imminent. In the event of the abomination, those residing in Judea are to seek refuge in the mountains, as outlined in Matthew 24:15-16. Moreover, those residing in the midst of the city should evacuate and prevent those in the country from entering Jerusalem. In essence, individuals who discern the impending divine judgment upon the city will avoid experiencing it directly.

The devil, having been expelled from heaven as a result of his war with God in heaven, will persecute the woman who gave birth to the male child. In the illustration, the woman is represented by the constellation Virgo, and in this instance, she is situated in the presence of the serpent, the constellation Hydra. The woman is then given wings like that of a great eagle, which can be symbolized by those of Pegasus, a constellation depicted as rising up out of the water. This dynamic gives the woman the necessary means to escape the presence of the serpent and reach her place where she will be nourished, as described in Revelation 12:14. Therefore, the woman will experience a liberation in the wilderness similar to that of those in heaven following the expulsion of the devil.

The hour-long judgment against the great city, as indicated in Daniel 9:26, concludes with a flood, which is represented by the water flowing from the jug held by the figure in the constellation Aquarius. This event corresponds to the serpent, which will spew forth from its mouth something like a flood in pursuit of the woman, with the intention of carrying her away. This water signifies a military pursuit by the people of the prince to come; however, the earth assists the woman

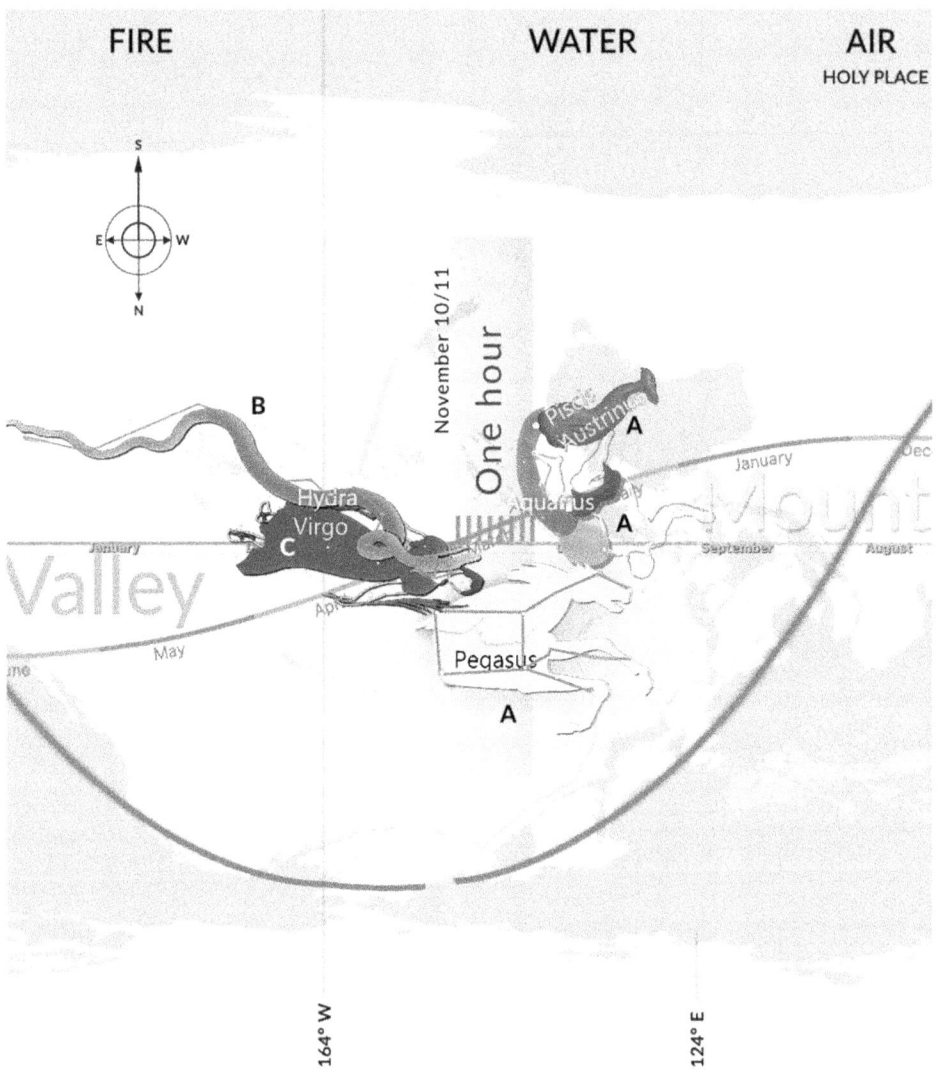

by opening up and swallowing the flood, akin to how the constellation Piscis Austrinus drinks the water from the jug of the constellation Aquarius. This suggests that the woman and the earth share common ground, a notion that the dragon will address when establishing the beast from the sea, thereby disrupting sympathy towards the woman.

The period referred to as "time, times, and half a time" starts with the abomination that causes desolation and concludes with the power of the holy people being completely shattered. The abomination prompts the woman to flee the presence of the serpent, which then prompts the dragon to engage in warfare with the rest of her offspring, as outlined in Daniel 7:25. The death of the two witnesses is likely a reference to the power of the holy people being completely shattered, as foretold in Daniel 12:7, marking the end of this period. Therefore, the period begins with the final composition of the kingdoms as the eighth, and of the seven, until the times of the Gentiles are fulfilled, and the nations are judged by God.

Armistice Day

The ten horns will become kings for one hour and destroy the great city. Following the destruction of the great city, the ten kings who are of one mind will give their authority to the beast, which is to become the eighth, and is of the seven. The conclusion of these events corresponds with the passage in Daniel 8:12, which describes the little horn being given an army to oppose the daily. At that juncture, the kingdom of the beast from the sea is established.

People will proclaim peace and security, suggesting a kind of Armistice Day observed on November 11. This declaration is illustrated to take place on that date on the celestial calendar. Those who dwell on the earth will proclaim, "Who is like the beast? Who is able to make war with him?" Thus, they will give honor to the beast.

However, the populace will not experience peace, as the dragon is enraged by the flight of the woman who gave birth to the male child. As described in the thirteenth chapter of Revelation, the dragon, in conjunction with the antichrist and the false prophet, will engage in warfare against the rest of her offspring. The inability of the dragon to maintain a presence in heaven serves as a motivating factor in his quest to eliminate all those who have a personal relationship with God on Earth. In a manner paralleling his expulsion from heaven, the dragon seeks to remove from the earth every work of the kingdom of God. Therefore, his wrath will persist until such a time as he is able to claim irrefutable victory over God by continuing his deception over the kingdoms on the earth.

Restoration, Abomination, then Restoration

The time of the abomination that causes desolation is set in opposition to two key events: the ascension of the ultimate atonement of God to heaven and to the throne of God, and the establishment of the kingdom of God at the conclusion of the seventieth week. The abomination is described as the image of the beast from the sea that is standing within the holy place, as outlined in Mark 13:14. The image will have been created by the people of the earth, and the beast from the earth gives it its breath. In this way, the establishment of the beast represents a contrast to the moment when the kingdoms of the world become the kingdoms of our Lord and of His Christ.

An oppositional narrative structure is evident in the anticipated restoration of the Earth, which will coincide with the millennial reign of peace. This restoration contrasts with the desolation and establishment of the beast, which did not accomplish peace but rather brought war. The restoration of the earth at the conclusion of the seventy weeks correlates with the rebuilding of Jerusalem by the end of the sixty-ninth week, which stands in stark contrast to its destruction. In summary, the seventieth week appears to exhibit a pattern of alternating between periods of peace and war, restoration and destruction, ultimately concluding with peace and restoration.

It should be noted that additional instances of such oppositional dynamics exist. One such example is the ascent of the male child to heaven and to the throne of God, which is in contrast to the revelation of the man of sin, who enters the temple of God to proclaim that he is God. In the midst of the final week, an army is given to the beast to oppose the daily, which is a counterpoint to the reestablishment of the sacrifice and offerings at the end of the seventieth week. Moreover, the

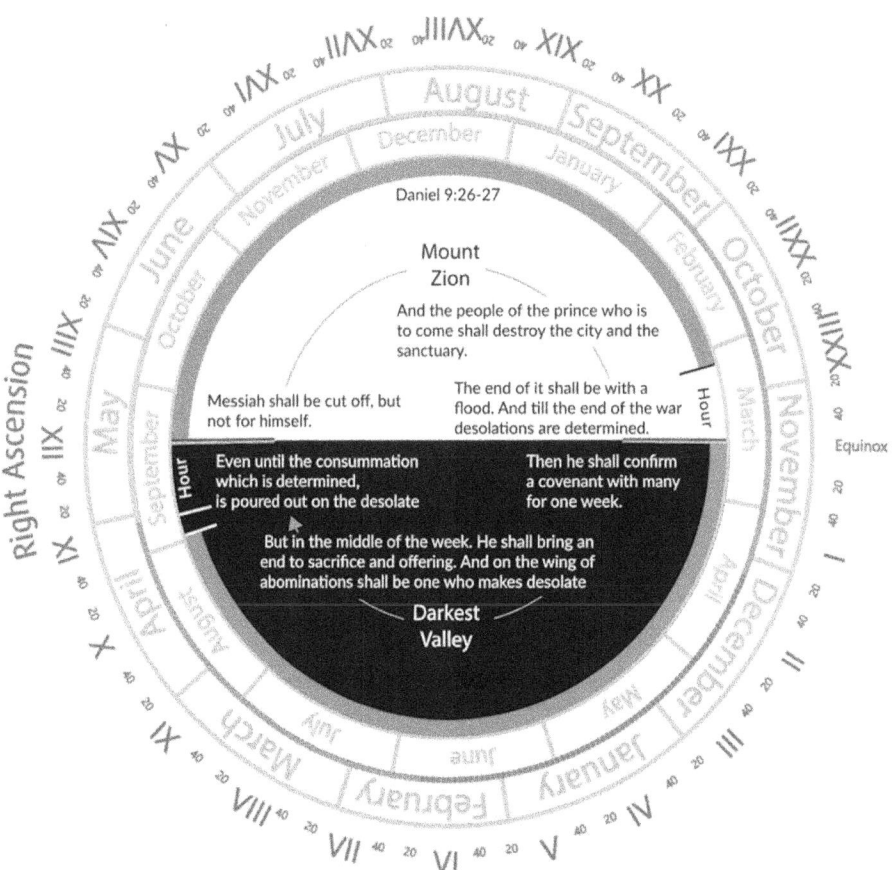

covenantal union between the people of God and the Lamb of God functions as a counterpoint to the week-long covenant confirmed with the beast and many. The imagery associated with the marriage feast of the Lamb functions as a counterpoint to the narrative surrounding the acceptance of the mark of the beast.

As indicated in Daniel 9:24, the seventieth week will reach its conclusion with the anointing of the Most Holy, thereby reestablishing sacrifice and offerings. According to Ezekiel chapters forty through forty-eight, in a vision of a new temple, millennial sacrifices are to be made, including grain, peace, sin, guilt, and drink offerings. This study suggests that the interpretation of Daniel 9:27 indicates that the beast will enter into an agreement with many at the time of the abomination of desolation. The passage continues with the phrase "But in the middle of the week," which is taken to refer to the seventieth week rather than the week-long agreement. Therefore, in terms of the calendar, the confirmation of the covenant that signifies the cessation of sacrifices and offerings occurs opposite the commencement of the millennial sacrifices and offerings.

11
Angelic Proclamations

In Revelation chapter fourteen, John describes a scene in which one hundred and forty-four thousand sealed servants of God stand with the Lamb of God on Mount Zion. Twelve of the fourteen tribes of Israel are represented by twelve thousand individuals, with the exception of the tribes of Ephraim and Dan. These servants of God will be redeemed from the earth and are characterized by spiritual purity, which is a result of their unwavering allegiance to the Lamb of God. Moreover, this loyalty is accompanied by a very deep sense of frustration regarding the abominations of the harlot, the great city, as well as the beast from the sea. Consequently, the one hundred and forty-four thousand servants exhibit an unwavering devotion to God, against a backdrop of widespread apostasy.

The following illustration can be described as follows: the Lamb is symbolized by the constellation Aries, and the sealed servants are represented by the constellation Andromeda, whose feet are aligned near the summit of Mount Zion. The star Alpheratz, which is located on the forehead, represents the seal of the living God in this context. Before the throne of God, which is represented by the constellation

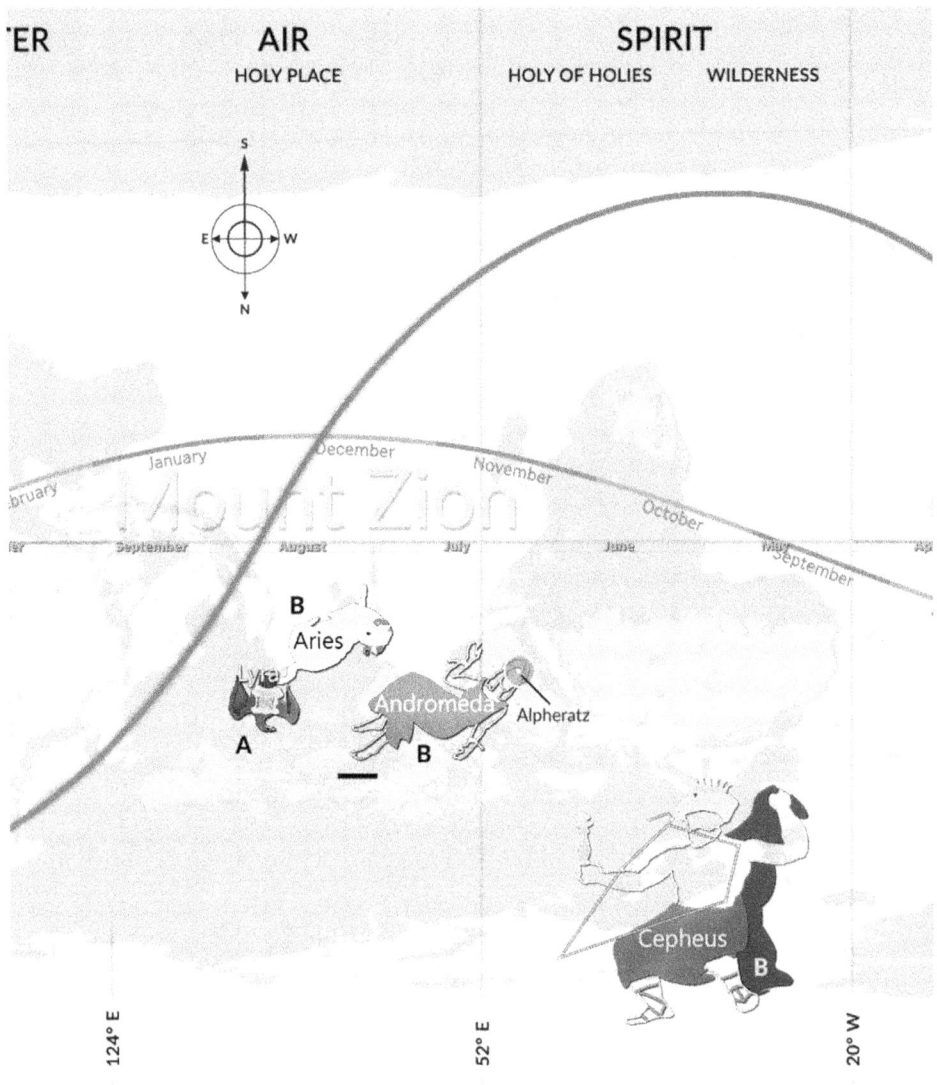

Cepheus, the servants will sing a new song in remembrance of their experiences. The harpists will play on stringed instruments, which are symbolized by the constellation Lyra.

Following the depiction of the sealed servants of God, John mentions three angels who will issue proclamations. The proclamation made by the first angel occurs prior to the judgment and destruction of the great city and corresponds to the gospel being preached in all the world before the people of the prince surround the great city. The second angelic proclamation pertains to the destruction of the great city. The third angelic proclamation concerns the establishment of the beast and the consequences of aligning with this kingdom. Therefore, the three proclamations signify a transition from the time of the great city to the beast, which is the eighth, and of the seven.

The first angel, flying in the midst of heaven, will have proclaimed the everlasting gospel to all the inhabitants of the earth. In Matthew 24:14, Jesus states that the gospel of the kingdom will have been preached to all the inhabitants of the earth as a witness to the nations before the end. According to Romans 1:20, those who observe creation yet deny the eternal power and divine nature of the Creator, the invisible God, have no excuse. The nature of God and His actions, as revealed in the gospel, therefore calls for a response from everyone.

The angelic proclamation aligns with the message conveyed to the nations, tribes, tongues, and peoples, which urges the people to depart from the great city. The scarlet beast, which serves as a throne for the great harlot, is filled with blasphemous names. For this dynamic to exist, the great city must justify sin, thereby distancing itself from God. Therefore, a distinction is made between individuals who maintain their faith and those who have renounced it.

The proclamation by the second angel concerns the fall of the great city, which has been judged by God. As stated in Luke 21:22, these days will be the days of vengeance, when all things that are written will be fulfilled. The downfall of the great city can be compared to the reference in the second trumpet judgment, which describes something akin to a burning mountain being cast into the sea. The fulfillment of all things written is related to the curses outlined in the Mosaic covenant and to the prophecy of seventy weeks. Given these considerations, the proclamation corresponds to the trampling of Jerusalem by the Gentiles, which will continue until the times of the Gentiles are complete.

The angel asserts that all nations have drunk the wine of the wrath of her fornication. As indicated in Revelation 17:6 and 18:24, the blood of the prophets, saints, and all those who were slain on the earth is found in her. It can be inferred that the blood of those who have been slain, having cried out for justice and vengeance, will have their supplications answered by God. Therefore, the harlot engaged in these actions with the kings and merchants of the earth in addition to the mariners, all of whom will mourn the destruction of Babylon.

Three States of the Beast

In the seventeenth chapter of Revelation, the beast that carries the harlot is described in three distinct phrases, each beginning with the phrase "the beast that was, and is not." The first phrase concludes with the assertion that the beast will ascend from the bottomless pit and ultimately be subject to perdition, thereby depicting the current scene of the harlot sitting on the beast. The second phrase, "and yet is," alludes to the destruction of the great city, while the third phrase concludes with the assertion that the beast is "also the eighth, and is of the seven, and is going to perdition," signifying the establishment of the beast following the fall of Babylon. These phrases delineate a progression, beginning with the harlot sitting on the beast, then to the beast in its association with the ten kings, and finally leading to the eventual consolidation of power under the reign of the beast.

The second phrase is found in verse eight, where it concludes with "and yet is." The beast is regarded as a potential threat to the great city and functions as a means of divine punishment due to her continued disobedience towards God. The beast is comprised of individuals whose names have not been written in the Book of Life and is distinct from the apostasy of the harlot, as iron does not mix with clay. Therefore, when the harlot is judged, the divine purpose of God will be fulfilled by the beast, which maintains its own identity.

In verse eleven, the third phrase concludes with a reference to the beast, following the downfall of Babylon. The beast is regarded as the eighth and of the seven, and is destined for perdition. The eighth king, the little horn, is granted authority by the dragon over all of the kingdoms that had emerged from the great sea, as referenced in Daniel chapter seven. This reference to the little horn corresponds with Revelation 13:4-7, which states that the beast is given a mouth to speak great things and for a period of time, able to make war against the saints. Therefore, the little horn ascends as leader over the beast and the kings of the earth, having been given this authority by the dragon.

Resurrection of the Beast

The authority acquired by the little horn over the other kingdoms gives rise to the description of the beast from the sea in Revelation, chapter thirteen, which differs from the beast on which the harlot sat. In Daniel 7:24, the passage states that a future king will emerge following the ten horns and subdue three kings. The three kings are associated with the first three beasts, which are represented by the lion, the bear, and the leopard. It is noteworthy that Revelation 17:13 states that the ten kings would give their authority to the beast. Therefore, the description of the beast from the sea can be interpreted as a combination of all the beasts that emerged from the sea, thereby signifying that he has subdued the entire earth.

Those whose names are not inscribed in the Lamb's Book of Life

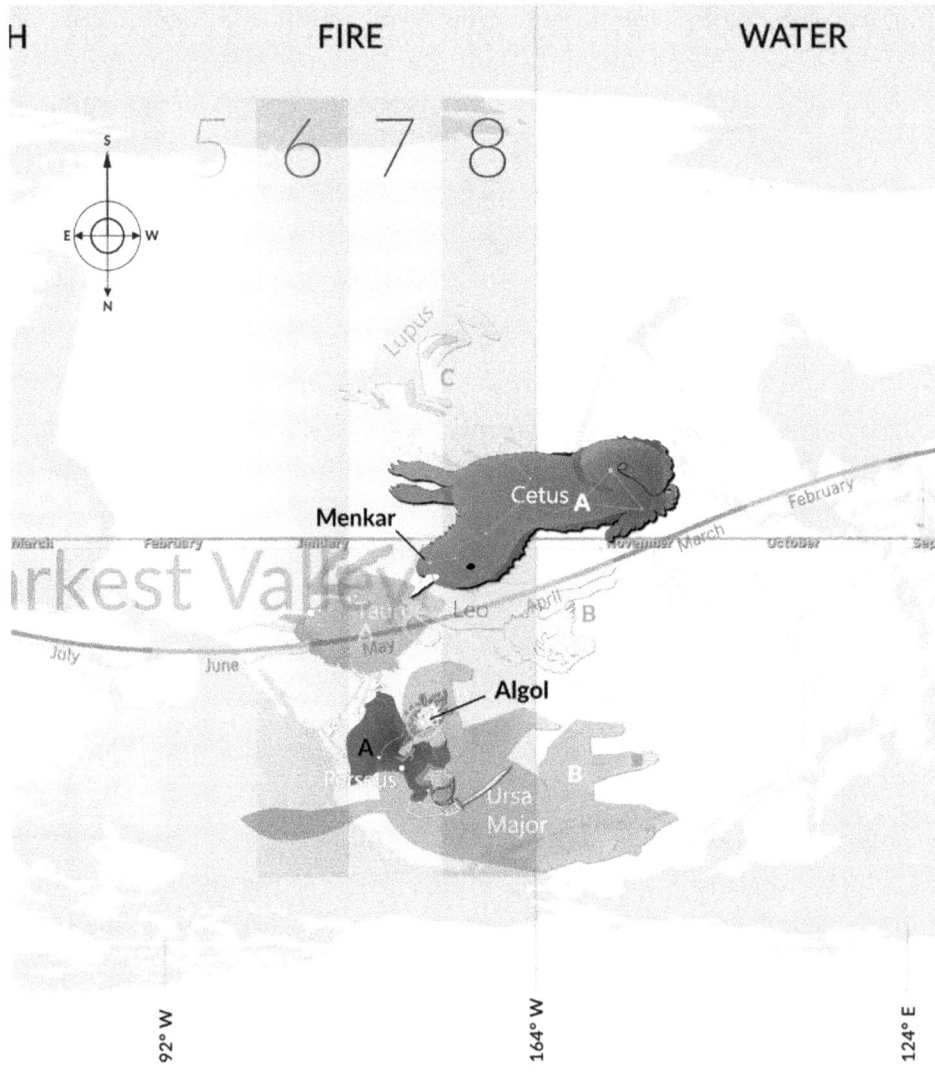

will be amazed at the recovery of the beast from its mortal wound, as described in Revelation 13:8 and 17:8. On three occasions in Revelation chapter thirteen, specifically verses three, twelve, and fourteen, states that the beast recovered from a mortal wound that one of its heads received from a sword. It is noteworthy that the Greek word for slain is identical to that used for the Lamb in Revelation 5:6, where the wounds of the Lamb remain clearly discernible. This observation suggests that both the Lamb and the beast have physical evidence of their respective deaths.

In the illustration, the constellation Perseus is depicted holding the decapitated head of Medusa, a Gorgon in the context of Greek mythology. This imagery features her snake-haired appearance, and in her head is the location of the star Algol. The name of the star translates to demon's head in Arabic. This star is nearly aligned longitudinally with Menkar, a star in the constellation Cetus that symbolizes the jaw of the seventh beast. In light of these considerations, the celestial reference to the severed head of Medusa may symbolize the action that has been taken against the beast.

Beast from the Earth

In Revelation 12:12, a voice in heaven issues a warning to those who dwell on the earth and the sea. This warning is associated with the appearance of two beasts, one emerging from the sea and the other from the earth. The first beast is depicted as emerging from the water element, and the second beast emerges from the earth, which is illustrated by the earth element. Therefore, following the expulsion of Satan from heaven, the beast from the sea and the beast from the earth are established by the dragon to perpetuate his war against the saints of the Most High.

The second beast is only described physically by its horns, which resemble those of a lamb, while its speech is like that of a dragon. This

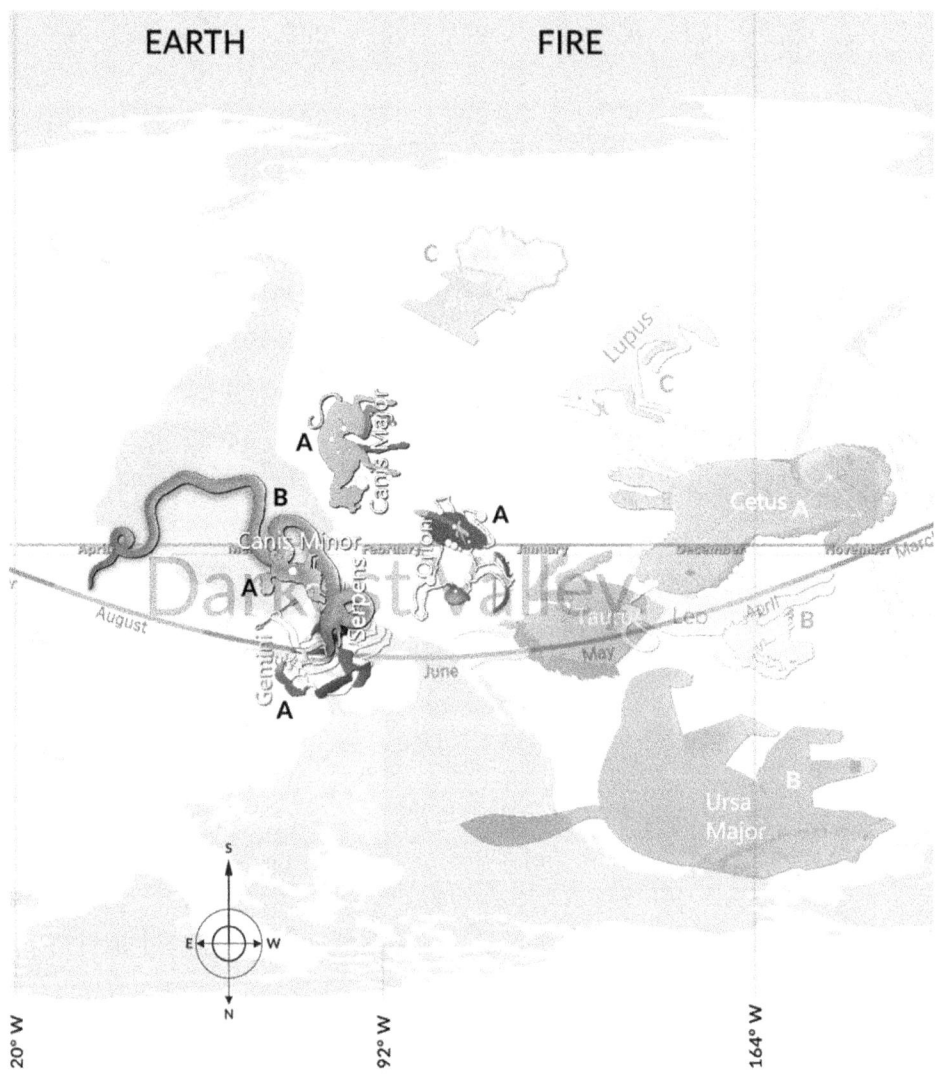

results in a figure that appears benevolent on the surface but is in fact malevolent in its intentions. The duality of the second beast can thus be likened to that of wolves in sheep's clothing.

The words of the second beast, also known as the false prophet, are derived from the devil himself. In the illustration, the rhetoric of this beast is symbolized by the mouth in the constellation Serpens. The true nature of the beast is symbolized by two wolves in the earth element, represented by the constellations Canis Major and Canis Minor. The horns of the beast evoke a sheep-like appearance and align with the two figures in the constellation Gemini, thereby concealing the true nature of the beast. In this manner, the false prophet will deceive those who dwell on the earth.

The constellations of Canis Major and Canis Minor are interpreted as encircling the constellation Orion while they are in a state of extreme hunger. This behavior is observed from the beginning of Orion's spiritual journey, which begins in the darkest valley between the beast from the sea and the beast from the earth. The position of the false prophet may be indicative of its message, which is to turn one away from God and the message of the cross symbolized by the brazen altar, and become dependent on the beast from the sea. Based on these considerations, the beast from the earth, akin to ferocious wolves in sheep's clothing, manifests a spiritually deceptive nature.

The false prophet exercises all the authority of the beast from the sea in its presence, as stated in Revelation 13:12. The inhabitants of the earth are deceived by the false prophet to construct an image of the first beast, which is from the sea, and whose fatal wound was healed. The false prophet gives breath to the image, thereby enabling it to speak and cause any individual who refuses to worship it to be killed. The objective of the false prophet is therefore to solidify the dominion of the first beast through the words of the dragon.

Mark of the Beast

The third angelic proclamation concerns the condemnation by God of those who worship the beast and his image and who receive the mark of the beast. In Revelation 14:10-11, the angel issues a clear pronouncement regarding those who engage in these actions, stating that they will be subject to torment by fire and brimstone, with the smoke of their torment rising forever and ever. This torment will be unending, as these individuals will experience a state of constant unrest, both during the day and night. Those who engage in the worship of the beast and his image and receive his mark must understand that they are opposing God and will be subject to His judgment, which will be severe and catastrophic.

The mark of the beast serves as a means of intimidation and identification, in part to facilitate the establishment of the kingdom of the beast. In this way, the image of the beast forms alliances to ascertain one's position in a time of war. Upon receiving the mark, the individual thereby indicates their opposition to the Creator. Conversely, those who oppose the worship of the image of the beast will be killed by the beast. The mark, thus, serves as a means of implementing the agenda of the devil for the world, which involves the weakening of nations.

Those who receive the mark of the beast are effectively separated from the kingdom of God and aligned with the devil. This mark is of significant concern to those engaged in commercial activities, as well as to their potential customers. The mark of the beast can be regarded as the counterpart of the seal of the living God, which was given to the one hundred and forty-four thousand servants of the twelve tribes of Israel mentioned prior to the opening of the seventh seal. In a manner similar to the unwavering devotion of the sealed servants of God to the Creator, those who receive the mark of the beast are unwavering in their devotion to the beast and the worship of Satan. Therefore, the acceptance of the mark of the beast signifies their endorsement of the business practices within the kingdom of the beast.

Patience of the Saints

Following the three angelic proclamations, John hears a voice from heaven that says, "Blessed are the dead who die in the Lord from now on," according to Revelation 14:13. The blessed are the saints who adhere to the commandments of God and the faith of Jesus. The proclamation concludes with the assertion "that they may rest from their labors, and their works follow them." The statement indicates that those who die in the Lord will attain rest, in contrast to those who receive the mark of the beast. Thus, the decision to pursue or reject a relationship with the Creator carries profound and eternal implications.

As previously illustrated, the predicament confronting the saints, who are symbolized by the constellation Orion at the brazen altar, is that they are surrounded by the two beasts. The beast from the earth, emerging from the earth element on the one side of the constellation Orion, deceives people by performing great signs and wonders. These actions may, if possible, even influence the elect during this period of great tribulation, as referenced in Matthew 24:24. Those who receive the mark of the beast effectively turn away from the brazen altar, which represents a place for reconciliation with God, and align themselves with the false prophet. Therefore, the beast from the earth seeks to prevent the establishment of a correct relationship with God by disrupting the spiritual journey of those who might seek it.

Those who adhere to the principles set forth by God will be engaged in conflict with the beast from the sea by continuing their spiritual journey. This conflict is illustrated by a confrontation between the constellation Orion and the beast that emerged from the water element. The scriptures indicate that the beast will engage in war with the saints and will overcome them. Nevertheless, the patience and the faith of the saints is to know that he who leads into captivity shall go into captivity; he who kills with the sword must be killed with the sword. Therefore, the saints are to remain faithful, whether they are captured or killed, with the understanding that the power of the beast will be completely shattered in the end.

12
Seventh Trumpet

Following the ascension of the two witnesses and a great earthquake, John writes that the second woe has passed and the third woe will come quickly. The third woe is closely associated with the sounding of the seventh trumpet and the subsequent pouring out of the seven plagues. These events transpire between the conclusion of the times of the Gentiles and the advent of the millennial reign of Christ. The kingdom of God is not established by these judgments; rather, it is established at the return of the Son of Man, at which point the angels separate the wicked from the righteous. The third woe, therefore, signifies a transitional period that has been determined, commencing at the conclusion of the times of the Gentiles.

In heaven a proclamation is made in response to the sounding of the seventh trumpet that "The kingdoms of this world have become the kingdoms of our Lord and of His Christ." While the voices in heaven rejoice, they perceive that the victory has already been secured, prior to the occurrence of any other event. Moreover, Revelation 10:7 states that the mystery of God will be brought to completion during the days of the sounding of the seventh angel. The seventh trumpet is

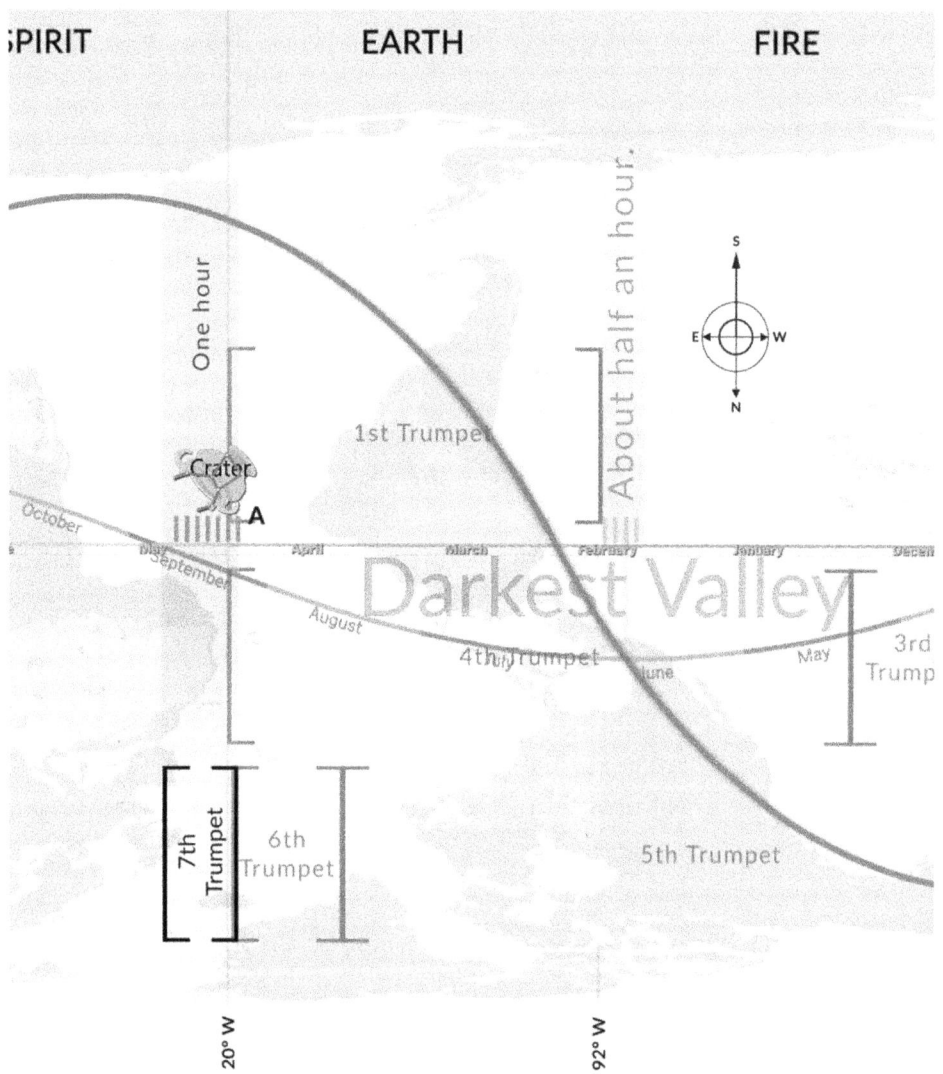

thus understood to signify both the imminent arrival of the Day of the Lord and the full revelation of God.

In response to the sounding of the seventh trumpet, the twenty-four elders, seated on their thrones before God, prostrate themselves in worship of God. Thereafter, they proceed to delineate events that are to occur as a direct result of the seventh trumpet. These actions encompass the wrath of God against the nations, the judgment of the dead, and the vindication of the righteous, including the servants, prophets, saints, and those who fear God. Moreover, those who engage in the destruction of the earth will be destroyed. In summary, the events stated by the elders will be accomplished by God as His kingdom is established on earth.

At this juncture in the narrative, seven angels, each having a distinct plague, will emerge from the temple. At that moment, each of the seven angels will be provided with a bowl full of the wrath of God by one of the four living creatures. Thereafter, the temple of God is filled with smoke from the glory of God. From this point forward until the judgments brought about by the seven angels have been completed, no individual is permitted to approach the dwelling place of God.

Celestial Calendar			Observances
April	27	10:04 P. M.	Ascension of the Two Witnesses
			One Hour according to Right Ascension (~15.2 Days), Days of the Seventh Trumpet
May	13	Day 40	Ascension of Jesus
May	14		Feast of Tabernacles (solar calendar)

The table delineates a correlation between the ascension of the two witnesses and the day corresponding to the ascension of Jesus. This interval corresponds to the constellation Crater, which is located in both the darkest valley and spirit element, representing the bowl judgments. This period, spanning approximately fifteen to sixteen days, concludes at the equinox with the destruction of the beast, a reference that is opposite to the one-hour period during which the great city was destroyed on the calendar wheel. It is noteworthy that the duration of the third woe, the bowl judgments, and the seventh trumpet is not explicitly stated in Scripture. In consideration of these factors, this correlation can serve as a framework for understanding this period.

Bowl Alignments to the Exodus

The final years of the Exodus, extending up to the collapse of the walls of Jericho, align chronologically with the sounding of the seventh trumpet and the seven angels pouring out bowls of the wrath of God. The eighth chapter of this study demonstrates that the first five trumpets correlate with the sequence of events pertaining to the Exodus up until the death sentence is handed down by God, which corresponds to the sound of the sixth trumpet. According to Deuteronomy 2:14, the death sentence was completed after a period of thirty-eight years, at which point the Israelites were instructed to journey a second time to the land of promise. Therefore, the period between the fulfillment of the death sentence and the destruction of the walls of Jericho corresponds to the bowl judgments, which are succeeded by the establishment of the kingdom of God on Earth following the tribulation.

First Bowl

In the twenty-first chapter of Numbers, the Israelites expressed their displeasure with God and Moses. In response to this discontent, God sent fiery serpents to bite the people as punishment, leading to a significant number of deaths. In order to remedy this situation, Moses created an image of a fiery serpent and erected it on a pole, as instructed by God, as a symbol of redemption. It was only through repentance and faith that those who had been bitten by the serpents, were healed upon looking at the image of the fiery serpent.

This plague can be regarded as a type of divine retribution, akin to the first bowl of the wrath of God that is to be poured out upon the earth. Instead of demonstrating reverence for God and giving Him glory, the people chose to accept the mark of the beast and to worship the image of the beast. Due to their defiance of God, a foul and loathsome sore came upon them. The plague of the first bowl appears to function as a means to distinguish those who are destined for destruction, in a manner similar to those who had sustained bites from the fiery serpents during the Exodus.

Second Bowl

The Israelites would engage in two pivotal battles before they could once more reach the land of promise. As the Israelites advanced toward the land of promise, they engaged in combat with the Amorite king, Sihon. The Israelites emerged victorious and proceeded to occupy all of the Ammonite cities and settlements. Thereafter, King Og of Bashan, along with his entire army, engaged in combat with the Israelites, leading to their complete annihilation, with no survivors. Following these events, the Israelites assumed control over the territories that had previously been held by King Og.

These battles and their effects are likened to the second bowl that is poured out on the sea. The result of this plague is that the sea becomes blood as of a dead man and is transformed into an environment devoid of life. Thus, the second bowl signifies major military operations that result in widespread and complete destruction and death.

Third Bowl

The Israelites would later engage in harlotry and idolatrous practices with the women of Moab. As a result of their actions, the Lord became angry and informed Moses that all who had offended Him by joining themselves with their false gods were to be executed by hanging. Moreover, Psalm 106:28-30 makes reference to the plague that broke out among them, which was stopped when Phinehas, the son of Eleazar, intervened. By that time, a total of twenty-four thousand individuals had perished as a result of the plague. These events were a successful result and a direct consequence of the seductive schemes of the Midianites.

The third bowl correlates with the period during which the Israelites initiated a holy war, undertaken in the name of the Lord, against the Midianites. They proceeded to kill all the males, including the kings. Additionally, they would kill all male children and every woman who had been sexually intimate with a man. In light of these considerations, the third bowl represents divine retribution against those who conspire against God and make war with the saints.

The pouring out of the third bowl results in the transformation of the rivers and springs of water into blood. The angel of the waters declares that God, in His judgment of these matters, is righteous, a claim that is reiterated by the altar. The unrighteous, apathetic to the messages of the saints and the prophets, have shed the blood of the saints and the prophets. Thus, due to their conspiracies against the righteous, the unrighteous face divine retribution.

Fourth Bowl

In the thirty-third chapter of Deuteronomy, Moses gives his final blessing to the children of Israel before his death. In this blessing, Moses states that the Lord came with innumerable company of angels and from His right hand went rays of fire like arrows shot forth, a law. Those who adhere to the teachings of God are blessed, while those who stray from His word are cursed, as a sign of His holiness. The metaphor of fire is employed to illustrate the intense and purifying nature of the word of God, which is used to search, purge, and examine the hearts of the people. In light of these observations, it is evident that the covenant relationship between God and His people establishes blessings and curses as the consequences of obedience and disobedience, respectively.

The pouring out of the fourth bowl on the sun corresponds to the Exodus, when the covenant between the people of Israel and God was renewed in Moab. As a result of the fourth bowl, the sun is given power to scorch men with fire, thereby serving as a stark reminder that they have forsaken the covenant of the Lord, the God of their fathers, which He established with them when He led them out of the land of Egypt. Despite the severity of this affliction, the unrighteous do not perceive, their eyes do not see, and their ears do not hear; instead, they blaspheme His name. Therefore, the fourth bowl underscores the awareness of the covenant and the pivotal choice between life and death, blessing and cursing.

Fifth Bowl

Prior to the entry of the Israelites into the land of promise, two spies were dispatched to the city of Jericho. In the city, the spies encountered Rahab, who informed them that the victories of the Israelites over Sihon and Og had eroded the resolve of the inhabitants of the city. In addition, the inhabitants were aware that they were situated along the route of the Israelites and that spies were present within their city walls. This context suggests that the prevailing atmosphere in Jericho would be characterized by a state of pervasive darkness, fear and uncertainty.

The fifth bowl is associated with the city of Jericho during a period of uncertainty, a fog of war. During the last days, the fifth angel proceeds to pour out his bowl of the wrath of God upon the throne of the beast, thereby enveloping the kingdom of the beast in darkness. The beast and his followers gnaw their tongues in agony due to the pain, and are unwilling to acknowledge the holiness of God. The kingdom of the beast is aware of the imminent Day of the Lord, a scenario that likely transpired behind the walls of Jericho in anticipation of the siege by the Israelites. Despite this, they continue in their defiance of God, relying on their conviction that they can overcome their predicament.

Sixth Bowl

The priests bearing the ark of the Lord approached the river Jordan and stepped at the edge of the water. The waters upstream stood still, rising a considerable distance away, thereby enabling the Israelites to cross the river Jordan as if on dry land, as described in Joshua 3:15-17. This crossing is similar to the crossing of the sea of reeds, where the waters remained parted until all the Israelites had passed. In commemoration of this event, twelve stones were taken from the Jordan and set up in Gilgal. Therefore, the stones would serve as a reminder for the children of Israel, and all peoples of the earth would attribute the crossing to the Lord and fear Him.

Prior to the conquest of Jericho, the Lord directed Joshua to instruct the sons of Israel to undergo circumcision. It is noteworthy that this procedure had not been performed on the people born in the wilderness. The place of this event was named by God as Gilgal, which was situated on the eastern border of Jericho, as recorded in Joshua 4:19. After they had been circumcised, God says that He had rolled away the reproach of Egypt. The Israelites remained encamped until they were healed.

The crossing of the Jordan River by the Israelites in their approach to Jericho from the east corresponds to the description of the sixth bowl, which is described as being poured out on the river Euphrates. The outcome of the sixth bowl is the drying up of the water, thus enabling the approach of kings from the east. The advance of the kings from the east, from the direction of the rising of the sun, may be indicative of an impending battle with the beast. This event bears resemblance to the history of the Amorites and the Canaanites, who, upon hearing of the drying up of the waters of the Jordan by the Lord, became greatly afraid. In a similar manner, the inhabitants of the land and the people of the earth are troubled by the drying up of the river Euphrates, which is perceived as divine intervention for the kings of the east.

In the period before the Day of the Lord, unclean spirits will emerge from the mouths of the dragon, the beast, and the false prophet. These spirits of demons are described as frogs that will perform signs directed towards the kings of the entire world, with the intention of recruiting armed forces to battle on that great day of God Almighty, as stated in Revelation 16:14. This gathering of the armies is to take place at Mount Megiddo, also referred to as Armageddon. In consideration of the factors, it can be proposed that the troubling news from the east functions as the catalyst for the beast, the dragon, and the false prophet to amass a formidable military force.

Preparation of Armageddon

Prior to the battle of Jericho, Joshua encountered a man with a sword drawn and inquired as to his allegiance. The man identified himself as the Commander of the army of the Lord and informed Joshua that he was not aligned with either side in the impending conflict. Nevertheless, he had arrived at this time to lead the Israelites. Upon hearing this, Joshua immediately prostrated himself in deep reverence and proclaimed his devotion to the Lord.

A military assembly at Megiddo, comprised of the armies of the kings of the whole world, will have been amassed by the spirits of demons. Those who gather there listen to the false prophets and false christs, which is in direct opposition to the teachings of Jesus in Matthew 24:24-28. This military operation appears to be directed against the kings of the east, who have crossed the river Euphrates as though on dry land. According to Daniel 12:1, at this pivotal moment, Michael, the great prince, will stand up, which corresponds to the appearance of the Commander of the army of the Lord before the Israelites advanced on the city of Jericho. In light of these considerations, it can be concluded that the conflict is imminent and the great tribulation is about to come to a close.

In Revelation 6:15, the Lord states that those who watch and keep their garments will be blessed, as the Lord is coming as a thief. The outcome of this battle will not be determined by which side people believe God is on, but rather, the elect will be those who seek to align themselves with God. Moreover, such individuals will not be deceived by the false christs and false prophets. Therefore, the elect must remain vigilant, discerning the characteristics and scriptural warnings pertaining to the spirits of demons.

Seventh Bowl

In the siege of Jericho, the city was effectively shut up, preventing anyone from entering or leaving. The priests, bearing the ark of the covenant, together with seven other priests, each with a ram's horn, and men of war, proceeded to circled the walled city once a day for six consecutive days in silence. On the seventh day, the procession circled the city seven times in silence, after which a prolonged blast of the trumpets commenced. In tandem with the blast, the people let out a shout, for the Lord had given them victory over the city. As a result of this action, the walls of Jericho collapsed completely.

The events surrounding the siege of Jericho and the collapse of its city walls can be correlated with the seventh bowl. When the seventh bowl is poured out into the atmosphere, a loud voice comes from the temple, from the throne, proclaiming, "It is done!" The voice is understood to be that of God Himself, speaking as the seventh bowl is being poured out, reminiscent of the prolonged blast of trumpets that sounded during the siege of Jericho, accompanied by the shouts of the people. In the aftermath of the bowl, a great earthquake splits the great city into three parts, all of the islands and mountains disappear, and great hail falls from heaven. These events result in the complete collapse of the nations.

The seventh bowl is regarded as the final judgment in the great tribulation against those who refuse to worship the Creator and acknowledge His glory. Despite the evident devastation caused by the earthquake, the men will persist in their blaspheming of God due to the severity of the hail plague that follows. This plague can be likened to the stones from the city walls of Jericho falling down on the people within the city. Nevertheless, throughout this period, the men persist in their failure to recognize the holiness and majesty of God.

13
Following the Tribulation

The temple in heaven is set to reopen following the pouring out of the seven bowls of wrath. When the temple opens, the Son of Man will appear in the heavens, and with the great sound of a trumpet, he will dispatch his angels to gather the elect from the four winds, as described in Matthew 24:31. In this context, the elect refers to the servants of God who are dispersed across the world and who are to be gathered to meet with the Lord as He approaches in preparation for the establishment of the kingdom of God on Earth. At this juncture, the kingdoms of the world have become the kingdoms of our Lord and of His Christ.

In the parable of the wheat and the tares, Jesus states that the field represents the entire world, which will be harvested at the end of the age prior to the wedding feast of the Lamb. Although the tares may appear similar to the wheat in the early stages of growth, they become distinguishable as they ripen. It is noteworthy that God's intention is for the wheat and the tares to coexist until the harvest. The tares, which symbolize evil or false believers, are separated from the wheat by angels and thrown into a furnace to be burned.

In the fourteenth chapter of Revelation, the references to the harvest of the earth and the harvest of the vine of the earth are utilized to describe the gathering of those who have already died and those who are still living, respectively. In the context of the first resurrection, those who are reaped from the dead are those who were beheaded for their testimony of Jesus, as indicated by Revelation 20:4-5. In contrast, the reaping of the living can be interpreted as a symbol of the separation of the tares from the wheat, which begins following the cry from an angel at the brazen altar. It is through these harvests that the kingdom of God establishes an era of peace on Earth.

Those who are resurrected and transformed will be considered blessed and will participate in the marriage supper of the Lamb. This sequence of events is consistent with the account presented in 1 Corinthians 15:52. The passage states that those who have died in Christ will be raised imperishable. Afterwards, those who are alive and who have kept the commandments of God will undergo a transformation, assuming festive garments for the wedding feast as described in Matthew 13:43. In this manner, they will inherit the kingdom that was prepared from the foundation of the world.

Harvest of the Earth

The harvest of the earth comprises those who have been beheaded for their witness to Jesus and for the word of God. In the narrative of the fifth seal, John observes that those who have been killed for their faith in the word of God and for their testimony are given white robes. They are instructed to rest until the number of their fellow servants and their brethren killed as they were is complete. This period of rest would therefore end with the conclusion of the tribulation period, when the temple in heaven is reopened.

Once the harvest of the earth is ripe, an unidentified angel will emerge from the temple and call out to the one who is like the Son

of Man. In the illustration, the figure representing the one who is like the Son of Man is the constellation Cepheus, which in this instance is associated with the earth element and the return of the Lord. In Revelation 14:14, the figure is described as wearing a golden crown and holding a sickle, which is represented by the sickle asterism in the constellation Leo. This figure will proceed to reap the earth of those who are part of the first resurrection and thus belong to the Lord.

Reaping the Grapes of Wrath

In Revelation 14:17-18, John sees a vision of two angels: one emerging from the temple in heaven and the other from the altar. The following illustration portrays the angel that appears from the brazen altar as the constellation Auriga. This angel, coming from the same altar where the martyrs once cried out to the Lord to avenge them, proclaims with a loud voice to the angel at the temple to commence the harvesting of the vine of the earth. Thus, the act of harvesting the grapes signifies the moment when those who oppose God will be unable to approach the brazen altar and seek mercy.

The angel who emerges from the temple to reap this harvest is not described in detail. Nevertheless, the following illustration employs the constellation Cepheus to symbolize this figure. John states that the angel holds a sharp sickle, which corresponds to the sickle asterism in the constellation Leo. Those who are wicked will not find refuge from this harvest, as indicated by Matthew 13:40-42, which states that the angels will first gather out of the kingdom all things that offend. Those who choose to disregard the invitation to the wedding feast, become preoccupied with matters of lesser importance, or who even kill the messengers of God will be destroyed.

The vineyard symbolizes the whole earth, given that the gospel message would have been preached in all the world. In the fourteenth chapter of Revelation, the proclamations of the three angels serve as a warning, foreshadowing the consequences of disobedience. Their proclamations affirm that those who dwell on earth are expected to produce good fruit in accordance with the divine principles of righteousness. God deems the harvest of the vine of the earth, those who do not comply to His mandates, to be akin to wild grapes, or bad fruit. Therefore, the judgment pronounced by God is indicative of the failure of the people to produce spiritual fruit, which speaks to their failure to fellowship with Him.

Once the clusters of grapes have been gathered, they will be thrown into the great winepress of the wrath of God and crushed, as described in Revelation 14:19-20. The following illustration depicts the altar outside the city as the location of the winepress, which is symbolized by the foot of the constellation Ophiuchus. The grapes of wrath will be trodden there, as illustrated near the shaft to the bottomless pit, where Satan will be bound for a thousand years. Therefore, the winepress located outside the camp symbolizes where the wrath and judgment of God will take place.

According to Revelation 14:20, from the great winepress, blood will flow for a distance of approximately two hundred miles at a height corresponding to the bridles of the horses. The horses are represented by the constellations of Sagittarius and Centaurus, with a line delineating the height of the blood relative to the foot of the constellation Ophiuchus. This event can correspond to the third verse of chapter ninety-eight of Enoch, which states that the horse will traverse the blood of sinners up to its chest. In summary, the overall portrayal of the harvest represents the removal of those deemed to be wicked.

Go'el

The Lord is both the avenger who exacts vengeance in the winepress of His wrath and the redeemer who offers salvation. At the time of the fullness of the Gentiles, the nation of Israel will be delivered, as

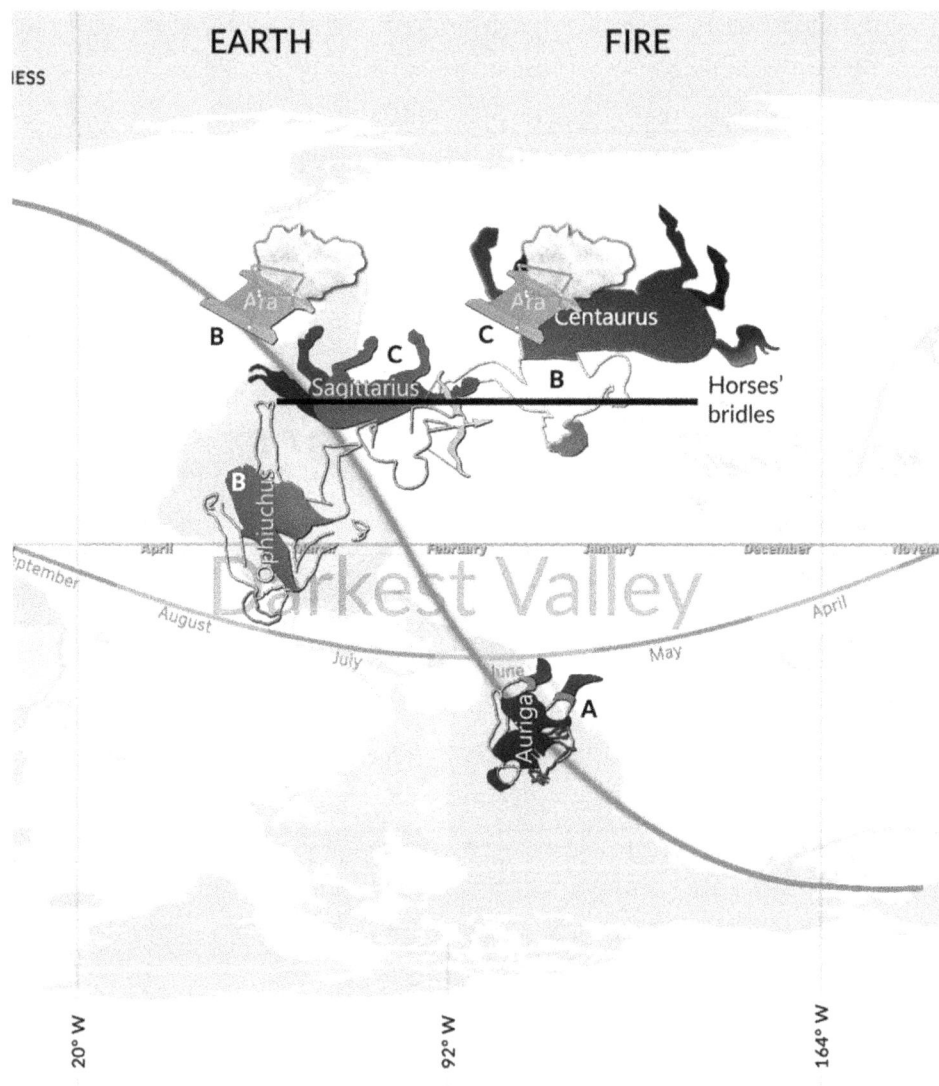

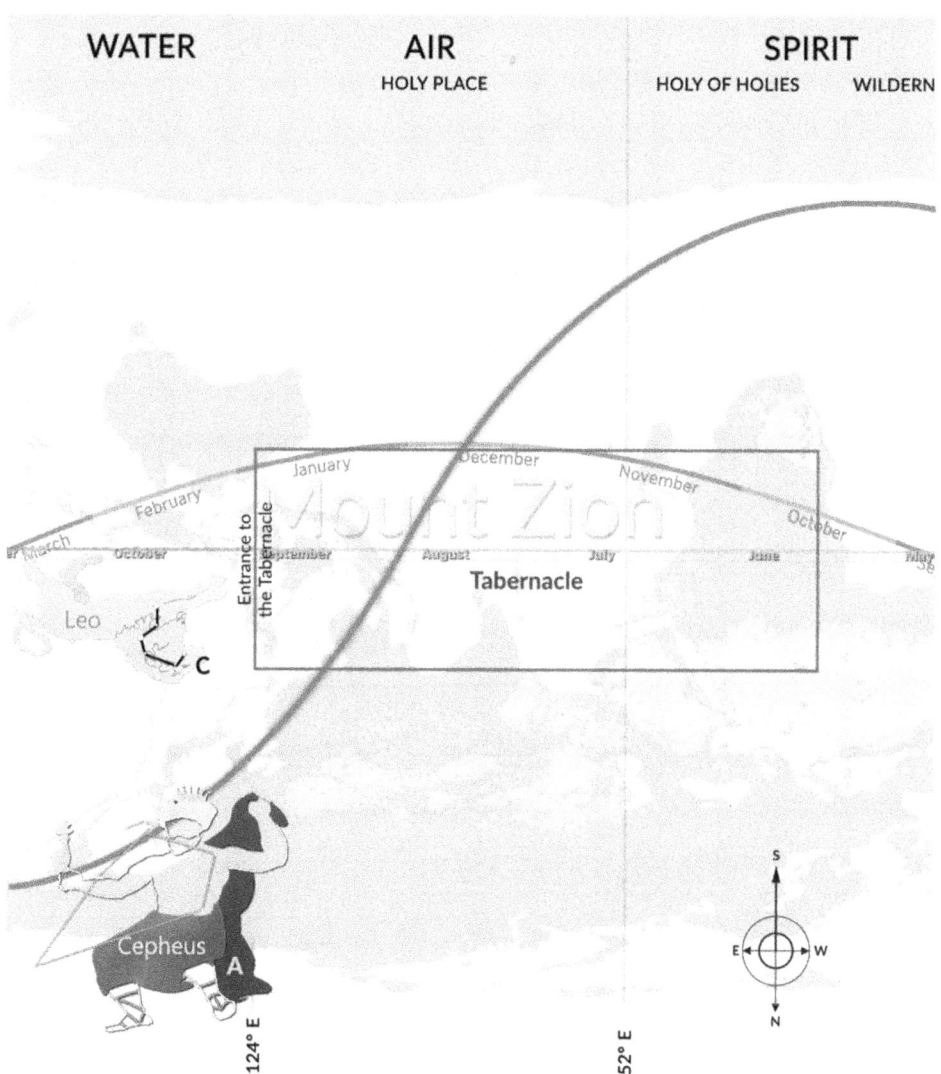

stated in Romans 11:26. The Deliverer will come out of Zion and turn away ungodliness from Jacob. It is worth noting that these concepts are encapsulated in a single Hebrew word, go'el. Therefore, the return of the Lord is understood to signify both redemption and the avenging of the blood of the righteous.

At the advent of the Messianic era, the Messiah will reunite the remnant of Israel by returning them to the land, as described in Jeremiah 31:1-4. In Psalm chapter fourteen, the author expresses a desire for a future in which the judgment of God will remove the wicked from the earth, thus paving the way for the restoration of the people of God. Furthermore, the psalmist makes an assertion that the salvation of Israel will come from Zion. These passages are consistent with Revelation 14:4 and the one hundred and forty-four thousand servants of God standing with the Lamb. As the first fruits to God and the Lamb, these servants are gathered on Mount Zion in the establishment of the kingdom of God.

Transition Illustrated

In the illustration, the pouring out of the seven bowls is represented by the constellation Crater, which is a period that ends before the alignment of two stars, Al Chiba and Alpheratz. The star Al Chiba is regarded as the beak of the constellation Corvus, which is depicted as pecking at the flesh of the Hydra constellation. This event corresponds with the great supper that God will hold, as described in Revelation 19:17-21. The star Alpheratz, which is part of the constellation Andromeda, represents the everlasting joy experienced by the ransomed of the Lord who have returned to Zion, as indicated in Isaiah 35:10. Therefore, the great supper of God and the return to Zion can be illustrated as occurring after the conclusion of the bowl judgments with the transition to Mount Zion.

Alpheratz is aligned with the first day of the Feast of Tabernacles,

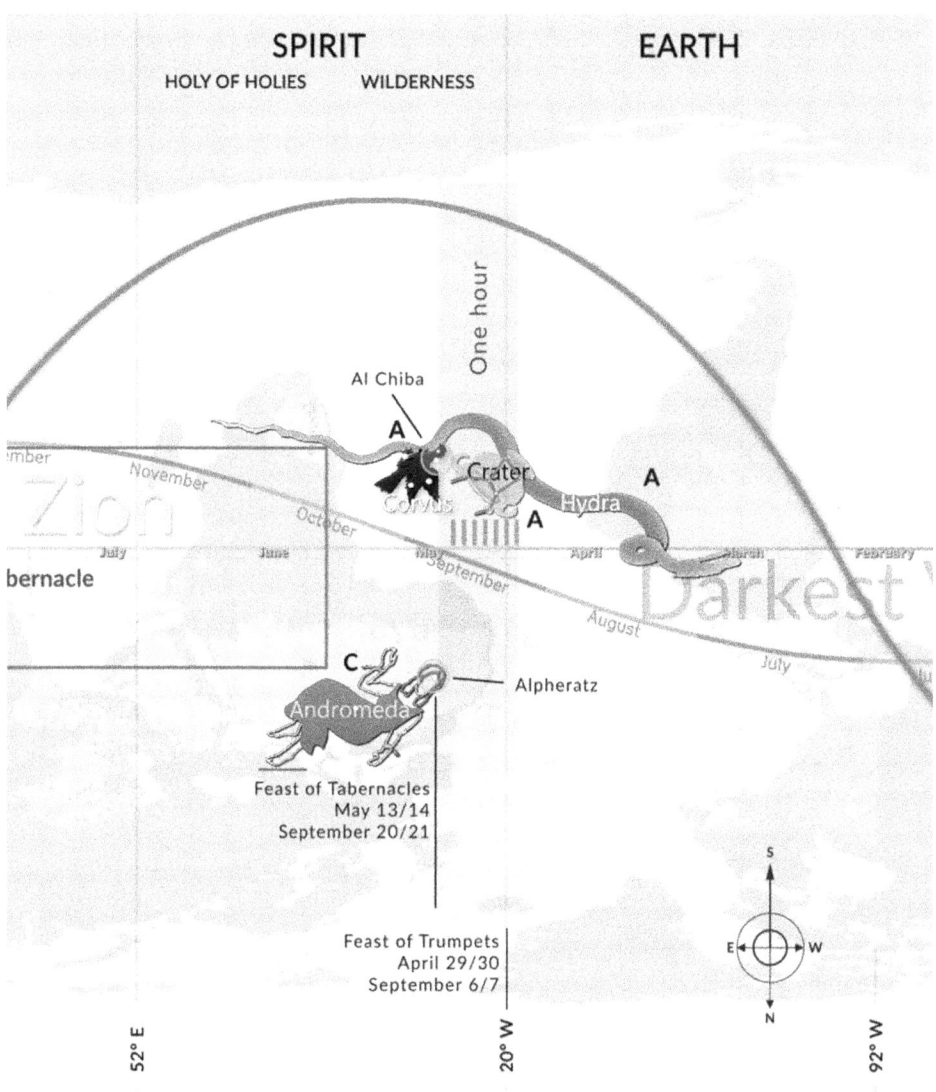

also known as the Feast of Ingathering. In accordance with Leviticus 23:42-43, the Israelites were instructed to dwell in booths they had constructed for the occasion for the entire seven-day celebration. In this manner, the people would be reminded of the grace, compassion, and protection that those who departed Egypt had received from God during their journey in the wilderness. Furthermore, this observance is a celebration and acknowledgment of the faithfulness of God with respect to the harvest and the conclusion of the agricultural year, as indicated in Deuteronomy 16:13. Thus, the observance can be regarded as being associated with the harvest, the ingathering, and redemption.

The Israelites were expected to acknowledge the provision of God from both the threshing floor and the winepress, which may be interpreted as a symbol of the redemption of the people of God from their enemies. During the millennial reign of Christ, the Feast of Tabernacles will be observed as a memorial for all that Christ has done. It is to be expected that all nations that had previously attacked Jerusalem will be required to participate in this annual festival in Jerusalem, thereby expressing gratitude to God for the blessings they have received. Therefore, this observance speaks of a period when Israel will be redeemed and represents the hope for the establishment of the Kingdom of God.

These events are indicative of the establishment of everlasting righteousness and the anointing of the Holy of Holies. Individuals who have faith in God will be permitted to attend the wedding celebration and will be clothed in the appropriate wedding attire. Individuals who are either in apostasy, characterized by a lack of faith, or engaged in wicked behavior will be cast into outer darkness. The establishment of this period of peace is marked by the return of the Messiah, the anointed king, who will restore the offerings and sacrifices. Therefore, the harvest at the end of the age involves the gathering of the elect and the destruction of the wicked.

Consuming the Nations

In Proverbs chapter sixteen, the author claims that the Lord weighs the spirit. The same idea is found in Proverbs chapter twenty-one, where the author states that the Lord weighs the heart. In this way, the everlasting and evaluative nature of God provides encouragement that He is a fair and impartial judge. It can therefore be concluded that God is aware of the actions and motivations of all individuals and will judge all nations and peoples fairly.

In the seventh chapter of the book of Daniel, the figure of the Ancient of Days is described as seated on a throne, with the books being opened. In the illustration, the constellation Cepheus, which in this instance aligns with the Holy of Holies, represents the figure of the Ancient of Days. A comparison of Daniel 7:10 and Revelation 7:14-15, reveals that the multitude of a "thousand thousands" can be interpreted as individuals from the great tribulation who are described as having washed their robes in the blood of the Lamb and who are seen serving the Ancient of Days. During this judgment of the beast, "Ten thousand times ten thousand," representing the elders, angels, and innumerable servants, will be in attendance. Thus, this judgment is set to occur following the great tribulation, when the beast is captured, coinciding with the great supper of God.

During the course of the court proceedings, the beast will speak blasphemies until the judgment is rendered. The beast is slain, its body destroyed and consumed by a burning flame, as described in Daniel 7:11 and 7:26. According to Revelation 19:20, both the beast and the false prophet are cast into the lake of fire, which is described as burning with brimstone. This judgment signifies the destruction of the dominion of the beast, which is then followed by God establishing a kingdom for the saints of the Most High, which will consume the other nations, as described in Daniel 2:44 and 7:27. Accordingly, the

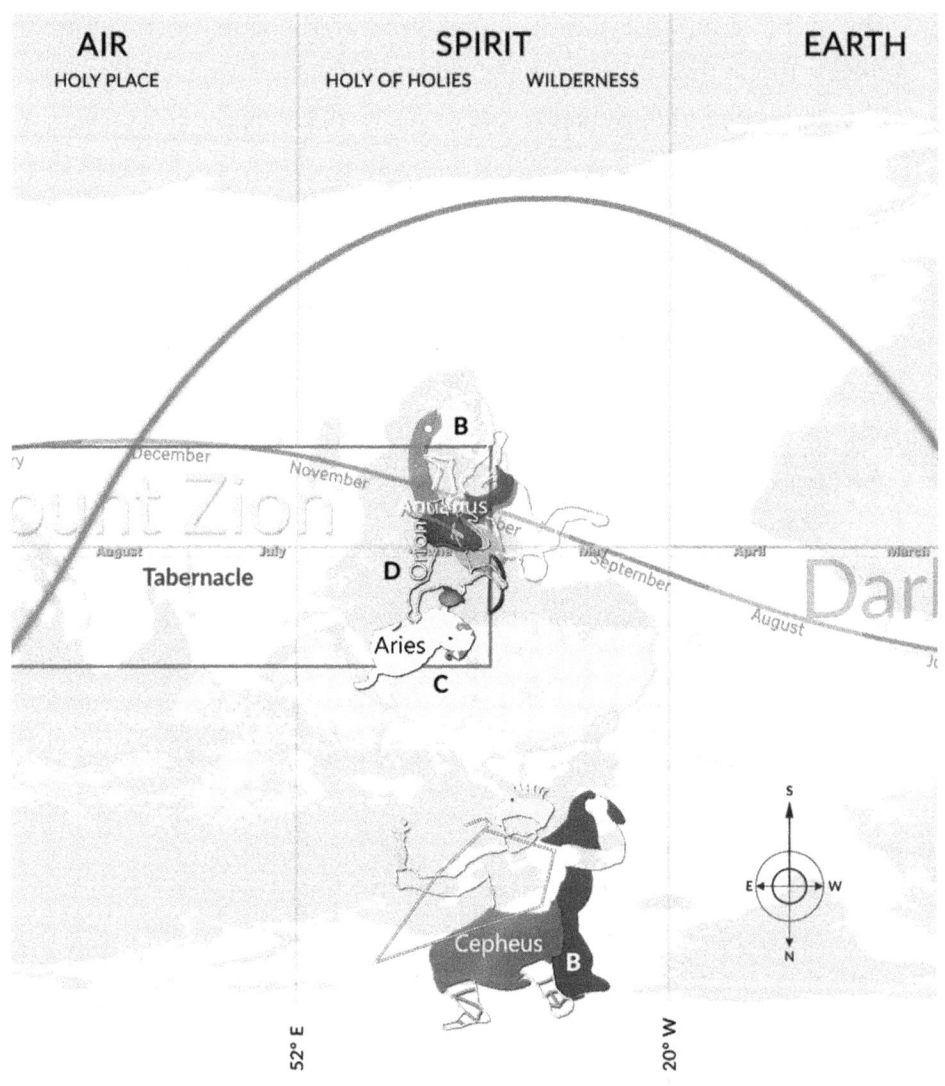

earth will have been purified by fire, which is a symbolic representation of the advent in the reign of the saints of the Most High.

In a night vision, Daniel sees a figure representing one like the Son of Man, arriving with the clouds of heaven and presenting himself before the Ancient of Days. This figure, depicted in human form, is represented through the constellation Orion and symbolizes the saints who will receive a kingdom that will never pass away, as described in Daniel 7:18, 7:22, and 7:27. The saints are defined as individuals who have led virtuous lives and have believed in and walked in the light of the word of God. Therefore, this event can be attributed to the angels having gathered the elect belonging to the Lord from the four winds, from one end of heaven to the other, for the Messianic kingdom.

Those who have made their robes white in the blood of the Lamb will be guided by the Lamb of God in heaven. Despite the absence of physical thirst in heaven, the Lamb will lead them to the fountains of the waters of life. The Lamb is symbolized by the constellation Aries, positioned at the throne, while the fountain of the waters of life, which flows out from the throne, is represented by the water from the jug of the constellation Aquarius. The premise under consideration is that the waters of life are associated with spiritual renewal, cleansing, and eternal life for the soul. Thus, the shepherding concept proposes that thirst signifies self-awareness and a spiritual longing for God.

Following the Millennial Reign

Following the millennial reign of the saints of the Most High, the final scene of judgment will take place before the great white throne of God. Individuals who are not found in the Book of Life are subject to the second death, which results in being cast into the lake of fire. The devil, death, and hades will also be cast into the lake of fire. Therefore, the definitive separation of those deemed unworthy from those in the Book of Life is complete.

Following the great throne judgment, God creates a new heaven and a new earth without a sun, which can be likened to the experience of a priest who, while within the tabernacle, is no longer able to perceive the sun. In the first creation, God divided light from darkness. In the new heaven and the new earth, darkness is no longer a factor, as its elements have been cast into the lake of fire. In this manner, the radiance of the Creator's light serves to illuminate the relationship between Him and His people. Thus, the people will walk in the light of His word for all eternity.

According to Revelation 21:1, the new heavens and the new earth will be without a sea, which is indicative of the absence of nations. The Lamb's bride, New Jerusalem, will descend from heaven, and it will have no temple. The Lord God and the Lamb of God will serve as its temple and dwell among the people. In this manner, the kingdom of God will reign over the people forever and ever.

14
Conjunction of the Ages

T he position of the Earth relative to the Sun over the course
of a year is a fundamental factor in the illustration of the
pattern; however, it can also delineate the concept of the
precessional ages over many millennia. From our vantage point, the
Sun appears to move from east to west across the sky on a daily basis
due to the Earth's rotation on its axis. When evaluated in relation to
the previous day's position, the Sun appears to have a slight eastward
shift along the ecliptic plane. An investigation into the position of the
Sun in relation to the stars would indicate a position slightly west of
its position from one year prior. This latter observation gives rise to
the phenomenon of the precession of the equinoxes, along with the
concept of the astronomical ages.

The ages of precession under consideration in this study are
represented by the constellations of Gemini, Taurus, Aries, Pisces, and
Aquarius. These ages, as indicated by the position of the Sun along
the ecliptic during the March equinox of the given year, provide
further insights into the biblical narrative surrounding the themes of
sin, atonement, and resurrection. In addition, these five astronomical

ages are associated with key historical periods and religious traditions, including the Garden of Eden, the patriarchal age, the Levitical priesthood, the body of Christ, and the anticipated Kingdom of God on Earth. Consequently, the distinctive characteristics of each age can be correlated with the respective celestial representations.

It should be noted that the five precessional ages are considered in part based on the length of time derived from the Maya calendar. The full cycle of precession is thus estimated to be a period of approximately twenty-five thousand, six hundred and twenty-seven years. Moreover, the objective of this exercise is not to ascertain a specific time for any event; rather, it is to illustrate that the events described in the scriptures can be observed in the sky in relation to astronomical ages, as well as the transitions into these ages.

Transitional Events of the Ages

The table demonstrates the transitions between the five ages under consideration and their correlation with pivotal events in biblical history. These pivotal events include the sin of Adam and the woman in the Garden of Eden, the inaugural Passover observance by the Hebrews in Egypt, the wine and bread given to the apostles during the Last Supper, and the defeat of the armies of the beast by the Lamb of God.

Sign	Start of the Age	End of the Age
Gemini		Sin in the Garden
Taurus	Promise of the Redeemer	Slaves to the Egyptians
Aries	Delivered from Egypt	Lamb of God Dies
Pisces	Ascension of Christ	Day of the Lord
Aquarius	Kingdom of God on Earth	White Throne Judgment

In each of these ages, a new standard is established based on a new revelation. In essence, the fundamental principles of the preceding ages remain intact with the advent of each subsequent age. In John 13:34-35, Jesus states that his true disciples will love one another as he loved them, thereby expanding on the Mosaic commandment to "love your neighbor as yourself." In this way, the love of God, as demonstrated by Jesus, serves as a model to be emulated by all individuals throughout all periods of time going forward. It can thus be proposed that the primary objective of each astronomical age, in conjunction with our relationship with God, is based on new developments that marked the conclusion of the preceding age.

There are additional instances that illustrate this concept. For example, the patriarchal age is established when the woman is informed by God that her husband will have authority over her as a consequence of her having been deceived and having given the forbidden fruit to Adam. Furthermore, as stated in Exodus chapter twelve, the Passover is to be observed annually by all subsequent generations as a distinctive festival in honor of the Lord, to commemorate how God delivered their families from Egypt. In the Last Supper, Jesus institutes the Eucharist and also issues a command to his followers to celebrate it in remembrance of him and his sacrifice. Therefore, the primary theme that emerges at the outset of each age serves as a blessing based on the recollection of a past act.

With respect to the fifth period under consideration, once the Kingdom of God is established on earth, all those remaining of the nations that attacked Jerusalem will ascend there annually to worship the King, the Lord of hosts, and to observe the Feast of Tabernacles, as stated in Zechariah 14:16. Furthermore, it is stated that those families residing on the earth who do not come to Jerusalem during that time will experience no rain. Thus, the condition is established at the outset of the age, and those who do not adhere to the words of the Lord will face consequences as a result.

These pivotal moments represent transitions in the astronomical ages

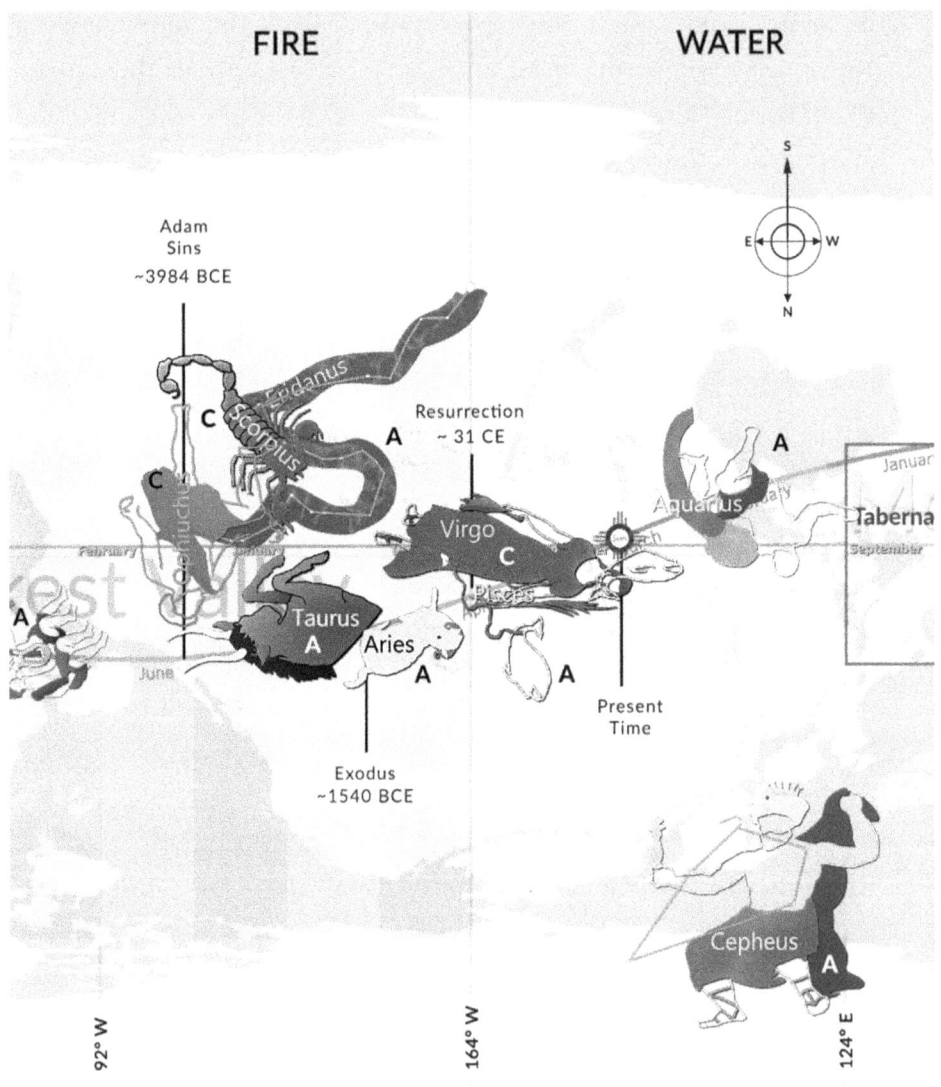

and are illustrated in relation to the estimated position of the Sun along the ecliptic on the vernal equinox. The first transgression committed by Adam is estimated to have occurred in 3984 BCE (three and a half years after his creation, thereby drawing a contrast between the start of his spiritual life and the onset of his transgression). The exodus of the Israelites from Egypt is estimated to have occurred in 1540 BCE, and the death and resurrection of Jesus is depicted as occurring in 31 CE. At the present moment, on the first day of spring, the Sun is positioned beneath the western fish in the constellation Pisces and is moving toward the constellation Aquarius. As illustrated, precession is only an approximation, as these and future events may transpire on any day of the year.

The constellation Aquarius, as well as the constellation Cepheus, will give way to the entrance of the tabernacle with respect to precession. According to Revelation 21:3-4, a great voice will proclaim that the tabernacle of God is with men, and those who are spiritually thirsty for righteousness will have the capacity to enter the tabernacle. As the table shows, the great white throne judgment signifies the conclusion of the astronomical age of Aquarius, which will be followed by the establishment of a new heaven and new earth. It can thus be concluded that passing through the door of the tabernacle corresponds to the individual who leaves behind the experience of the old heaven and earth. Therefore, the transition from the age of Aquarius to the representation of the tabernacle underscores the presence of God among humanity.

Week of Unleavened Bread Precession

The sequence of astronomical ages symbolizes the individual's progression from the brazen altar to the door of the tabernacle, where one will begin their new life in Christ. This approach corresponds with the day of preparation and the Week of Unleavened Bread, as the spiritual journey commences at the brazen altar with the deliberate

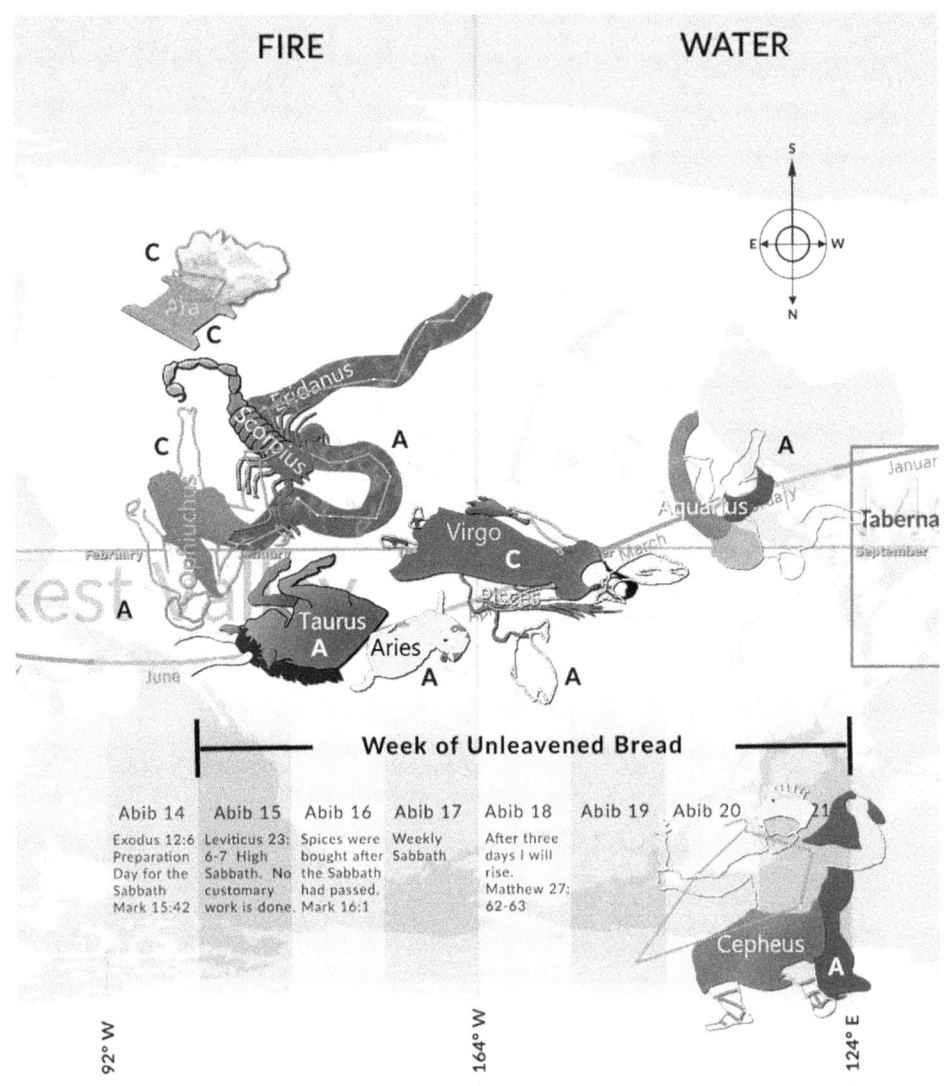

FIRE

WATER

C
C

Eridanus

Scorpius

C   A   A

Ophiuchus   Virgo C   Aquarius
                                        Taberna
February   March   September

Darkest valley

A   Pisces

Taurus
A   Aries
               A   A

Week of Unleavened Bread

Abib 14	Abib 15	Abib 16	Abib 17	Abib 18	Abib 19	Abib 20	21
Exodus 12:6 Preparation Day for the Sabbath Mark 15:42	Leviticus 23: 6-7 High Sabbath. No customary work is done.	Spices were bought after the Sabbath had passed. Mark 16:1	Weekly Sabbath	After three days I will rise. Matthew 27: 62-63			

Cepheus
A

92° W   164° W   124° E

decision to remove sin from one's life, becoming a representative of the new creation upon entry into the tabernacle. The spiritual journey, therefore, can be understood through the interweaving of these concepts, thereby signifying the death of the old self at the brazen altar and the subsequent new creation that can enter the tabernacle.

The day of preparation and the days in the Week of Unleavened Bread correspond to particular segments of the courtyard, similar to the eight kingdoms having been identified in the courtyard. Within the framework of precession, these segments delineate the progression from the brazen altar with the day of preparation and conclude the Week of Unleavened Bread with the entrance into the tabernacle. Consequently, the astronomical ages are subdivided to symbolize this spiritual journey, its beginning with Adam and his transgression, which corresponds to a decision each individual must make regarding sin in their lifetime. Therefore, the observance of the Week of Unleavened Bread is contingent upon the reconciliation of sin.

The ultimate atonement of God provides a means for believers to *passover* from a state of sinfulness to one of righteousness. The day of preparation as delineated in the initial segment of the fire element represents an eastward approach to the brazen altar and the message of the cross. The significance of the day is the ability to discern between that which is regarded as profane and that which is considered holy, which can be seen through the actions and behaviors exhibited by individuals and communities. From that point, there are seven segments to the door of the tabernacle, corresponding to the Week of Unleavened Bread. Therefore, it can be proposed that an individual's disposition during the day of preparation is equivalent to their position toward sin and the brazen altar.

It is evident that the significance of abstaining from sin in order to sustain a proper relationship with God is illustrated, as an individual cannot stay in the tabernacle and on the path to enlightenment otherwise. During the Week of Unleavened Bread, the consumption of leavened bread is prohibited, as leaven must be removed from the home before the week begins. Individuals who approach the tabernacle are expected to maintain a state of spiritual purity by refraining from leaven; those who consume leavened bread during this period will be excommunicated from the community of the people of God. Therefore, from a spiritual perspective, the Week of Unleavened Bread signifies a period during which individuals may undergo personal transformation through faith in God.

Ultimate Atonement

In Romans 5:12-17, Paul asserts that spiritual death has spread to all of humanity as a direct consequence of the transgression committed by the first man, Adam. The illustration delineates the moment when Adam ate the fruit of the Tree of the Knowledge of Good and Evil by the star Ophiuchus Theta in relation to the astronomical ages. The star is located in the foot of the constellation and is impacted by the stinger in the constellation Scorpio. The integration of the day of preparation with the brazen altar, serves to underscore the application in the propitiation of the ultimate atonement of God. An individual who arrives at the brazen altar in search of forgiveness and a relationship with God will be redeemed from spiritual death.

The ultimate atonement is provided by the grace of God to serve as propitiation for the sin of humanity, as individuals are unable to establish a relationship with God on their own terms. In John 10:11, Jesus states that he is the Good Shepherd who lays down his life for the benefit of the sheep. It is noteworthy that the constellation Auriga is associated with the figure of the good shepherd and is shown to align with the constellation Ophiuchus and the brazen altar. It is therefore through grace that an individual may receive the gift of eternal fellowship with God.

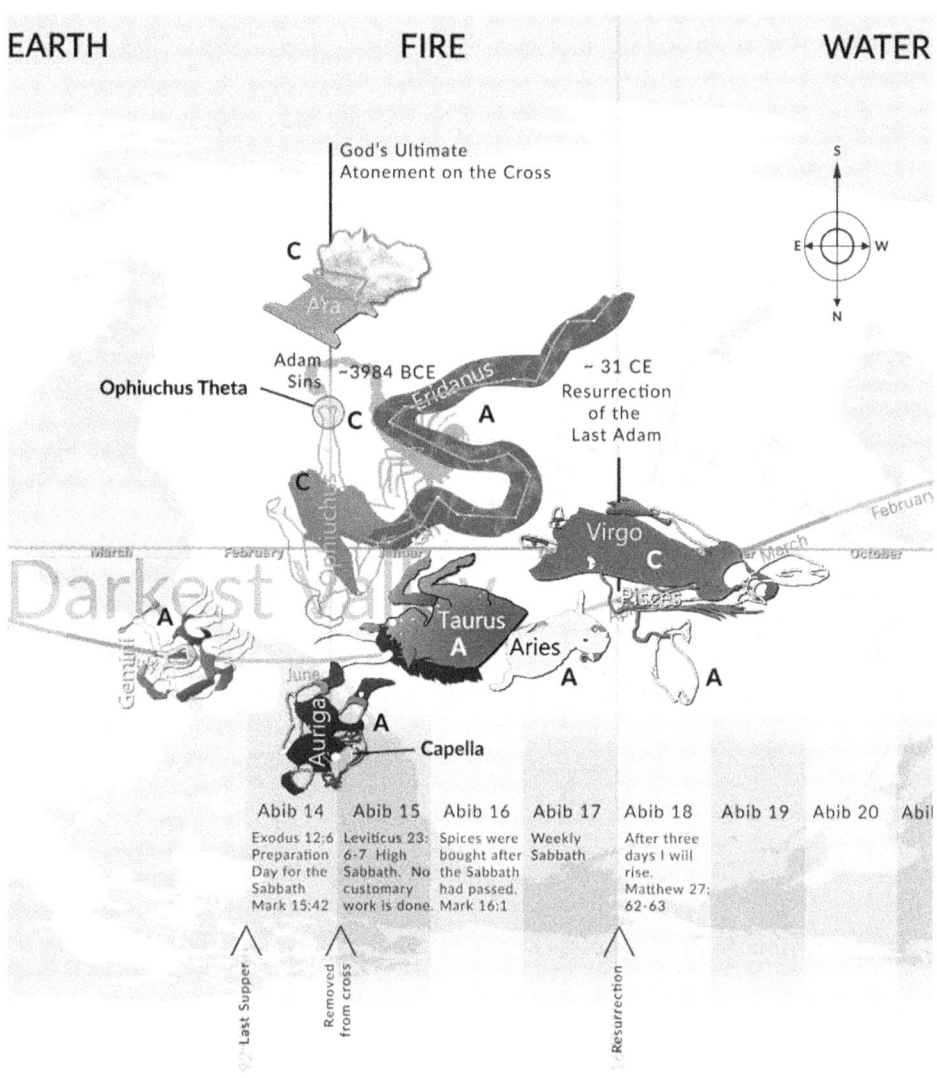

EARTH   FIRE   WATER

God's Ultimate
Atonement on the Cross

S
E — W
N

Adam
Sins   ~3984 BCE   ~ 31 CE
Ophiuchus Theta   Resurrection
                                         of the
                                         Last Adam

Darkest Valley

Virgo

Taurus

Aries

Auriga

Capella

Abib 14   Abib 15   Abib 16   Abib 17   Abib 18   Abib 19   Abib 20   Abi

Exodus 12:6 Leviticus 23: Spices were Weekly   After three
Preparation 6-7 High   bought after Sabbath   days I will
Day for the Sabbath. No the Sabbath   rise.
Sabbath   customary   had passed.   Matthew 27:
Mark 15:42   work is done. Mark 16:1   62-63

Last Supper   Removed from cross   Resurrection

The sacrifice of Christ annulled the sin of the world once and for all at the conjunction of the ages, as stated in Hebrews 9:26b, thereby providing eternal redemption and justification. While the definitive act of the ultimate atonement of God did not occur until approximately 31 CE, the blood of the Lamb has atoned for sin since the foundation of the world. The period, spanning from the first transgression in the Garden of Eden to the Good Shepherd laying down his life, is represented by the constellation Eridanus, which is emblematic of the scarlet thread of redemption, salvation, and forgiveness. In this imagery, the source of the scarlet thread is the sacrifice of the Good Shepherd in relation to the precessional day of preparation, which extends to the actual death of the Lamb of God in relation to the precession.

The following table presents the precessional segment designated as the day of preparation in relation to a twenty-four hour day, which begins at 6 p.m. This assignment enables the position of the star Ophiuchus Theta to correlate with the approximate time of the death of Jesus on the cross. The Gospels of Matthew, Mark, and Luke provide accounts of the crucifixion of Jesus, placing the time of his death at approximately three in the afternoon, which corresponds to the ninth hour of the day. This moment also corresponds with the lamb offerings at the temple, which would commence at that time for the Passover meal in the evening. Therefore, the proposed time for his death on the cross can coincide with the outline of the precessional segment designated as the fourteenth of Abib.

Segment	Abib 14	Star	24-hour Day
Begins at	Feb. 15, 6 p.m.		6 p.m.
	Jan. 30, 9:47 p.m.	Ophiuchus Theta	~ 2:50 p.m.
Ends at	Jan. 28, 12 p.m.		6 p.m.

Courtyard Associations

The period during which Jesus was in the tomb prior to his resurrection is illustrated as three full days. Some scriptural passages, such as Luke 24:46, indicate that Jesus would rise on the third day, while others, such as Mark 8:31, state that he would rise after three days. In Matthew 12:40, Jesus states that the Son of Man will be in the heart of the earth for three days and three nights, which is the same amount of time the prophet Jonah spent in the belly of the great fish. In their discussion with Pontius Pilate, the chief priest and the Pharisees corroborate the assertion of Jesus that he would remain in the tomb for three days and request that guards be stationed at the tomb until the third day, as recorded in Matthew 27:62-64. Based on these passages, it is reasonable to infer that Jesus was in the earth for the entirety of the three days and three nights.

In addition to the statements made by Jesus and the other accounts concerning the time that the Son of Man is in the earth, there is also the sequence of events pertaining to Mary Magdalene, Mary, and Salome that corroborates the same amount of time. According to Leviticus 23:6-7, no customary work is performed on the fifteenth day of Abib, as it is a high Sabbath. Following the observance of the high Sabbath,

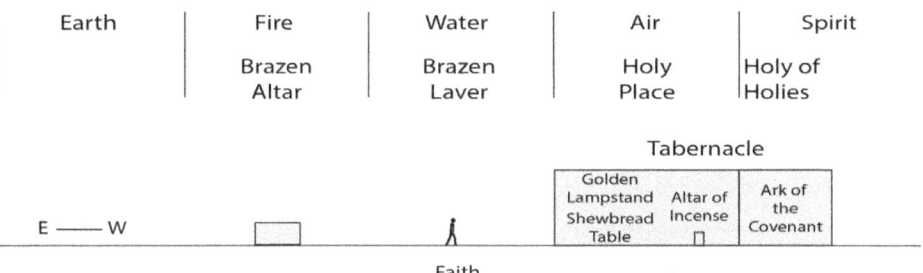

the three women purchase spices, as documented in Mark 16:1. The women then prepared the spices and the fragrant oils, and as stated in Luke 23:56, they observed the weekly Sabbath. Accordingly, following a period of two Sabbaths and one day of shopping, they proceeded to the tomb in the early morning hours of the first day of the week.

The sequence of events described and the time indicated by Jesus substantiates the assertion that the Son of Man remained in the earth, in the tomb, for a period of three days and nights. The presented timeline lends support to the precessional framework of the Week of Unleavened Bread, with the concept of the scarlet thread of redemption aligning with the last three segments of the fire element. The resurrection of the ultimate atonement eliminates the necessity for further atonement for sin, thereby bringing humanity to the threshold of faith, symbolized by the water element. Thus, the framework of the Week of Unleavened Bread establishes two fundamental concepts for individuals to have fellowship with God: the atoning work of Christ on the cross and faith in the Creator.

The tabernacle is a symbol of the desire of God to dwell with and relate to His people. The entry of the believer into the tabernacle is attributed to the Creator providing the ultimate atonement, as well as His spirit uniting them with Christ. In John 2:19, Jesus employs the metaphor of his body as a temple, thereby symbolizing the presence of God and fulfilling the purpose of the tabernacle. The application for the believer involves the establishment of an ongoing relationship with God as well as the encouragement and edification of fellow believers. Thus, those who believe in the Creator are considered part of the tabernacle, thereby embodying the concept of being in Christ.

15
Chronological Adjustments

A well-defined chronology extending from the time of Adam to the fall of Jerusalem can be derived from an analysis of Scripture and the study of past civilizations. The study commences with the generally accepted date of the fall of Jerusalem in 586 BCE and proceeds in reverse chronological order, concluding in the year 3988 BCE. In the period spanning from Adam until the Exodus, the age of the father at the time of the child's birth is used. In the period following this, and extending until the fall of Jerusalem, the non-accession year method is applied. Therefore, two distinct methodologies are employed in order to measure the passage of time from Adam to the fall of Jerusalem.

Pre-Exodus Time Keeping

The chronology presented in this study calculates the time from the creation of Adam to the Exodus to be two thousand four hundred and forty-eight years. This period corresponds to the year 2448 in the Hebrew calendar, which corresponds to the year of the Exodus from Egypt. During this period, the Bible does not provide years for how long Levi and Kobath were in Egypt. However, this study utilizes the period of four hundred and thirty years, as referenced in Exodus 12:40, for this determination. While the birth dates of Levi and Kobath can be shown differently, this discrepancy does not alter the time frame from Adam to the Exodus.

The calculations are based on the assumption that the year of birth of the child is considered a partial year and is therefore not included in the age. In this way, the year of birth is regarded as a zero year, as the child would not have celebrated their first birthday. Moreover, it is evident that the indicated age of the father corresponds to the year of his life. This approach is consistently applied to both the child and the parent, as referenced in the scriptures.

The correlation between the birth of Arphaxad, the flood, and the age of Shem serves to underscore the functionality of the chronological records. According to Genesis 5:32, Noah is five hundred years old when he has his first of three sons, Shem, Ham, and Japheth. The great flood, as delineated in Genesis 7:6, commenced in Noah's six hundredth year, and the waters of the flood covered the earth when he was six hundred years old. Two years after the flood, Arphaxad was born, when Shem was one hundred years old, as recorded in Genesis 11:10. Therefore, Shem was born when Noah was five hundred and two years old, and thus he would not be considered the oldest.

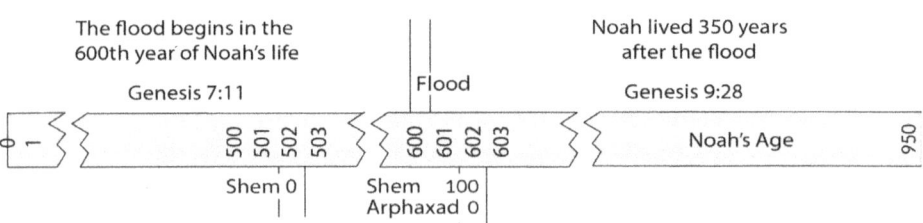

Additionally, according to Genesis 9:28, Noah passed away at the age of nine hundred and fifty, three hundred and fifty years following the conclusion of the flood. The conclusion of the flood, as outlined in Genesis 8:13, is understood to mark the first day of the first month when the waters had receded. The reference point for the calculation of three hundred and fifty years is also employed for the birth of Arphaxad. Therefore, it can be deduced that the birth of Arphaxad would have occurred during Noah's six hundred and second year.

Strangers in a Strange Land

There are several different timetables for when the children of Israel left the land of Egypt that may seem impossible to reconcile. According to Exodus 12:40-41, the children of Israel were in the land of Egypt for four hundred and thirty years. Genesis 15:12-16 states that Abram was told his descendants would be strangers in a land they do not know for four hundred years, but in the fourth generation, they would return to the place where he is. The reference to the four hundred years is also mentioned in Acts 7:6. The timelines presented in these verses are reliable, but they must be arranged cohesively to create a comprehensive chronology.

In Genesis 15:18, God establishes a covenant with Abraham concerning his descendants, who will receive the land. However, as stated in Genesis 15:13, they will first endure four hundred years of oppression. The chronology in the following illustration shows that this period begins with the year of Isaac's birth and ends with the Exodus. Starting with Isaac's birth is appropriate because God makes His covenant with Isaac, not with Ishmael, according to Genesis 17:21. Therefore, the use of the phrase "four hundred years" distinguishes between the descendants of Abraham.

The second fundamental aspect of the covenant is the return of the descendants of Abram to the land in the fourth generation. Moses, the son of Amram, was chosen by God to guide the Israelites in their exodus from Egypt, and because of this connection, Moses is associated with the fourth generation. The first generation is represented by Levi, who, at approximately forty-eight years of age, arrived in Egypt with his father, Jacob. According to Genesis 46:11, Kohath, the son of Levi, was approximately nine years old, when he moved to Egypt. Amram, the son of Kohath, represents the third generation and resided in Egypt throughout his life.

The reference to four generations pertains to the period of four hundred and thirty years. The calculation of this time is based on the yearly accumulation in the genealogy of Moses from the time Levi

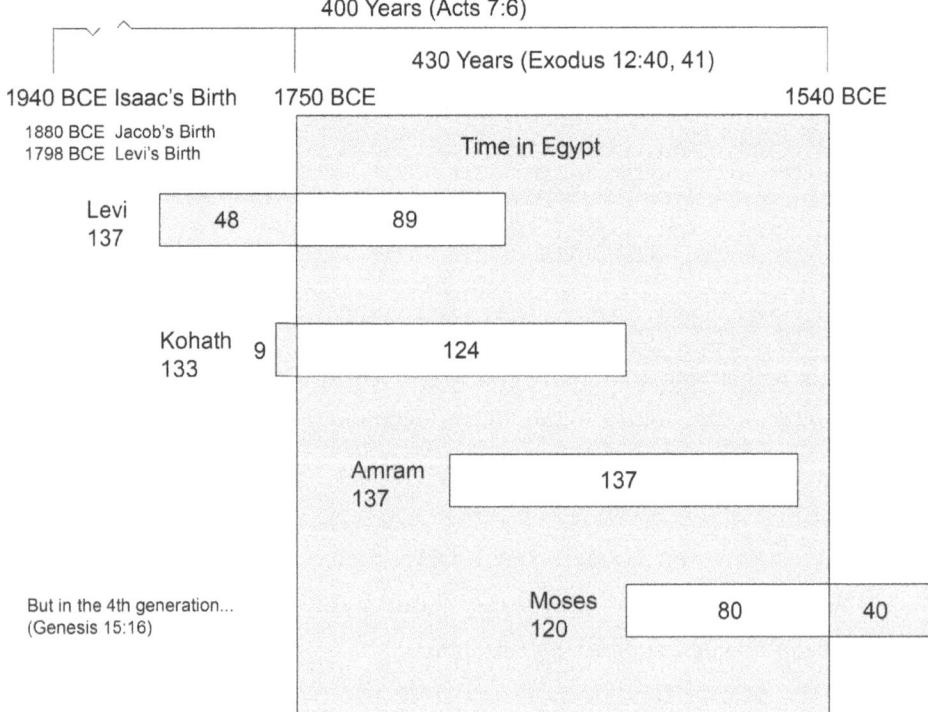

arrived in Egypt to the time of the Exodus. The total number of years in this time frame with regard to the four generations is eighty-nine years for Levi, one hundred and twenty-four years for Kohath, one hundred and thirty-seven years for Amram, and eighty years for Moses. The chronology, when viewed in its entirety, spans approximately two hundred and ten years. Therefore, the reference to four generations suggests that, according to the lineage of Moses, each generation spent more time living in Egypt than outside of it.

Time Keeping of the Judges and Kings

Following the Exodus, genealogical records were no longer utilized for the purpose of establishing a general chronology. Instead, the focus shifted to the children of Israel as a nation. The reference for keeping time became the number of years that a judge presided, a king reigned, or an event lasted. These records were also aligned with scriptural passages, including Acts 13:20, Judges 11:26, 1 Kings 6:1, and Ezekiel 4:5, which make reference to specific durations of time: four hundred and fifty years, three hundred years, four hundred and eighty years, and three hundred and ninety years, respectively. During these periods, the Israelites carefully kept track of their chronological record.

In the context of the post-Exodus chronology, the non-accession year method is employed to maintain the chronology. According to this method, the first and last years of a king or judge are each considered

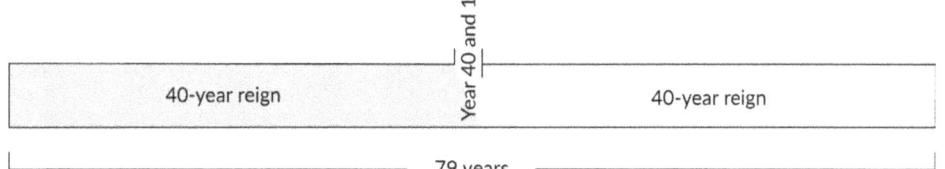

a full year, with no co-regency. This non-accession year method is applicable to all judges and kings of Israel, even during periods when other nations ruled over them. In the event that two rulers each held power for forty years in succession, the total duration of their combined rule would amount to seventy-nine years, rather than eighty. Therefore, the specific point in the year at which the ruler's reign commences or concludes, whether it signifies the inaugural or final year, is not a factor under consideration.

Samuel, Saul, and David

In the book of Acts, chapter thirteen, the author identifies three consecutive periods in the history of the Hebrews, which equals a total of five hundred and thirty years. The three periods of interest are the forty years in the wilderness, the four hundred and fifty years that include the judges down to Samuel, and forty years to David's reign as king over Israel. The period of four hundred and fifty years begins with the entry of the Israelites into the land of promise and ends with the judge before Samuel. During the period in which Samuel served

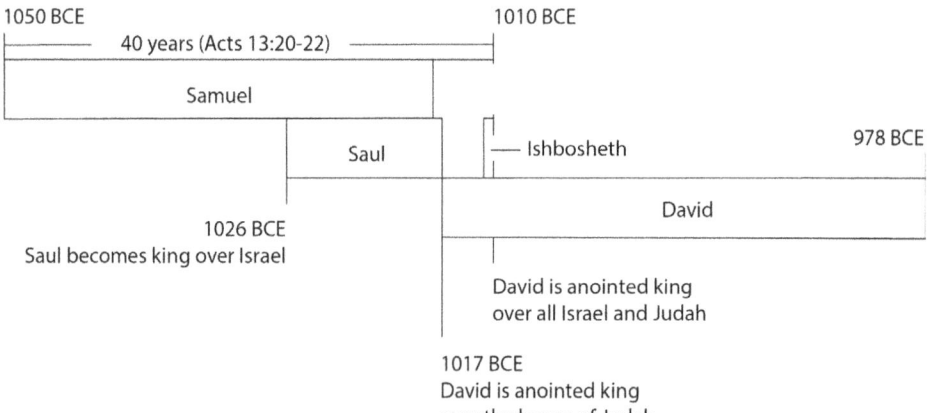

as judge, Saul was anointed king of Israel, and by the conclusion of the forty-year period, David ascended to the throne as king of Israel. Therefore, the author of Acts intends to cover the entire chronology by differentiating three distinct periods of time from the Exodus to the reign of David.

According to Acts 13:20-21, the second forty-year period begins in 1050 BCE with the appointment of Samuel as judge, encompasses the rule of Saul, and ends in 1010 BCE. While the Old Testament does not provide information on the length and beginning of Saul's reign, it can be inferred that he may have reigned for up to ten years. This inference is based on the fact that the Ark of the Covenant was kept in the house of Abinadab in the city of Kiriath Jearim for twenty years, according to 1 Samuel 7:1-2. The ark was there prior to Saul becoming king, and Samuel was said to be old at that time.

Following the death of Saul, David became the king of the house of Judah, reigning for a period of seven years and six months, as recorded in 2 Samuel 2:11. The house of Israel anointed Ishbosheth, the son of Saul, as their king, and he reigned over Israel for a period of two years, as stated in 2 Samuel 2:10. Following the death of Ishbosheth, David became the king over all of Israel and Judah, ruling over both houses for thirty-three years. Therefore, the conclusion of the forty-year period signifies a pivotal moment in which David assumed kingship over both Israel and Judah.

Correlation of the 480-, 450- and 300-Year Periods

This period of four hundred and fifty years also overlaps with the periods of four hundred and eighty years and the three hundred years mentioned in 1 Kings 6:1 and Judges 11:26, respectively. The two periods under consideration begin with the appointment of the first judge of Israel, Othniel, while the period referenced in Acts begins with the Israelites' entry into the land. The conclusion of the four hundred and eightieth year references the start of the construction of the temple in Jerusalem. The period of three hundred years is referenced in a message from Jephthah to the king of Ammon regarding how long the Israelites had been in the land. When considered collectively, these timelines present an integrated chronological sequence, spanning from when the Israelites entered the land of promise to the commencement of the construction of the temple.

The illustration delineates the relationship between the periods of four hundred and eighty years, three hundred years, and four hundred and fifty years. As documented in 1 Kings 6:1, the construction of the temple was initiated in the fourth year of Solomon's reign. This verse also references the beginning of its construction in the four hundred and eightieth year since the departure of the Israelites from Egypt; nevertheless, the appointment of Othniel as judge appears to align instead with the beginning of this period.

This appointment also marks the beginning of the three-hundred-year period referenced in Jephthah's message to the king of Ammon. Jephthah, the judge of Israel, provides an overview of the number of years that Israel was governed by the judges, citing specifically Heshbon and Aroer, along with their respective villages situated along the Arnon

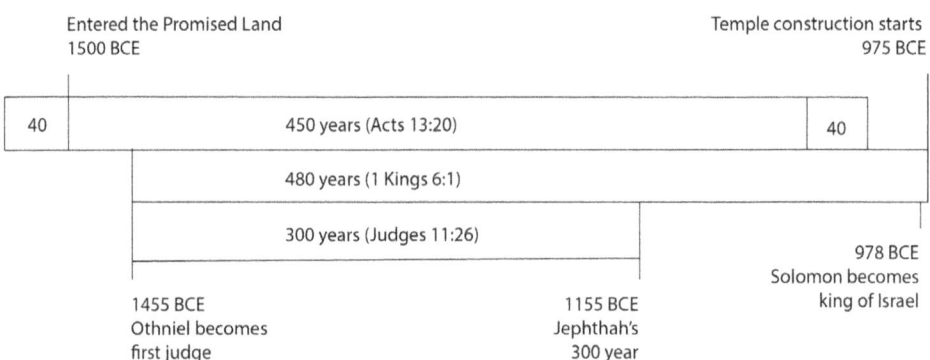

River. The non-accession year method establishes that the first year of Othniel corresponds to the periods mentioned in the Book of Judges and 1 Kings. This correspondence aligns with and therefore references their starting reference point.

Time Keeping during the Divided Kingdom

	Israel		Judah
Year	Name (length of rule)	Year	Name (length of rule)
939	Jeroboam I (22)	939	Rehoboam (17)
918	Nadab (2)	923	Abijah (3)
917	Baasha (24)	921	Asa (41)
894	Elah (2)	881	Jehoshaphat (25)
893	Zimri (7 days)	857	Joram (8)
893	Omri (12)	850	Ahaziah (1)
882	Ahab (22)	849	Queen Athaliah (6)
861	Ahaziah (2)	844	Joash (40)
860	Joram (12)	805	Amaziah (29)
849	Jehu (28)	777	Uzziah or Azariah (~~52~~ 38)
822	Jehoahaz (17)	740	Jotham (16)
806	Jehoash (16)	725	Ahaz (~~16~~ 7)
791	Jeroboam II (41)	719	Hezekiah (29)
751	Zechariah (6 months)	714	6th year of Hezekiah
751	Shallum (1 full month)		
751	Menahem (10)		
742	Pekahiah (2)		
741	Pekah (20)		
722	Hoshea (9)		
714	Fall of Samaria		

Following the death of Solomon, his son, Rehoboam, ascended to the throne. At that juncture, Jeroboam and all of Israel petitioned Rehoboam to ease the yoke that Solomon had imposed upon them. However, he rejected their request and instead elected to increase their burden, a decision that would ultimately lead to a revolt and the division of the kingdom. The ten northern tribes of Israel seceded from the house of David, and Jeroboam became their king. Consequently, the kingdom was divided in the same year as Solomon's death.

The table presents a chronology of the kings of both Israel and Judah until the fall of Samaria. In the majority of cases, the year in which a person became king is correctly linked to the year of a king from another kingdom. In instances where the information does not align, other verses are referenced to determine an applicable outcome. The scriptural references, including the length of the reign and its commencement year, along with the non-accession year method, are used to resolve the few questions concerning the timeframe during the period of the divided kingdom.

Divided Kingdom Corrections in Time

The kingdom of the ten northern tribes of Israel concludes when its capital city, Samaria, was captured by the Assyrians in 714 BCE. This year is determined by working the timeline backwards with the kings of Judah from the fall of Jerusalem in 586 BCE. The table at the end of this chapter delineates this information. The chronology given for the kings of Israel is considered accurate and without any necessary adjustments. Therefore, the house of Israel would have existed for two hundred and twenty-five years from the time of Jeroboam.

The following chart illustrates a chronological adjustment in the reigns of Jehoshaphat and Jehoram, the kings of Judah, with regard to Ahaziah and Joram, the kings of Israel. According to 1 Kings 22:51, Ahaziah reigned for a period of two years, beginning in the seventeenth year of Jehoshaphat's reign. Joram, his successor, began his reign in the eighteenth year of Jehoshaphat's reign, as stated in 2 Kings 3:1. The discrepancy in the chronology can be attributed to the ascension of Jehoram to the throne during the fifth year of Joram's reign, whereas 1 Kings 22:42 stipulates that Jehoshaphat reigned for a period of twenty-five years. Therefore, it is evident that the sum of the eighteenth year of Jehoshaphat and the fifth year of Joram cannot equal the twenty-five years of Jehoshaphat's reign.

The chronology of the house of Israel and the twenty-five years of the reign of Jehoshaphat are determined to be accurate. However, the reference to which king of Israel or in what year corresponds to the start of the reign of Jehoram, king of Judah, is incorrect. The non-accession year method is employed in the reign of Ahaziah, which is depicted as beginning in the seventeenth year and ending in the eighteenth year of Jehoshaphat. The illustration demonstrates an applicable correction, indicating that the fifth year since the commencement of the reign of Ahaziah, or perhaps the fourth year of Joram, corresponds to the reign of Jehoram, the king of Judah.

Chronological adjustments are also necessary for references to the king of Judah, Uzziah, in 2 Kings chapter fifteen: the reference to the

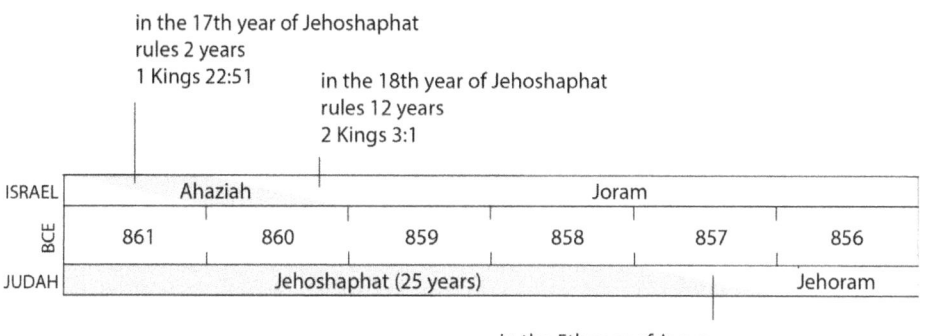

twenty-seventh year of Jeroboam II, king of Israel, and the reference to the king of Israel, Zechariah, in the thirty-eighth year of Uzziah, as well as to his reigning for fifty-two years. The reference to Uzziah in the reign of Zechariah is inaccurate because it suggests that Uzziah's reign began in the third year of Jeroboam II's reign. The most likely solution is that Uzziah reigned over Judah for a period of thirty-eight years, and in his twenty-seventh year, Zechariah ascended to the throne of Israel. Thus, the reference to Uzziah reigning over Judah for fifty-two years is corrected to show thirty-eight years.

BCE	N. Kingdom Israel	BCE	S. Kingdom Judah
791	Jeroboam II - 41 years 2 Kings 14:23		in the 15th year of Amaziah (r. 805-777)
	in the 27th year of Jeroboam II	777	Uzziah - ~~52~~ 38 years 2 Chronicles 26:3
751	Zechariah - 6 months 2 Kings 15:8		in the 38th year* of Uzziah (r. 777-740)
751	Shallum - 1 month 2 Kings 15:13		in the 39th year* of Uzziah (r. 777-740)
751	Menahem - 10 years 2 Kings 15:17		in the 39th year* of Uzziah (r. 777-740)
742	Pekahiah - 2 years 2 Kings 15:23		in the 50th year* of Uzziah (r. 777-740)
741	Pekah - 20 years 2 Kings 15:27		in the 52nd year* of Uzziah (r. 777-740)

BCE	N. Kingdom Israel	BCE	S. Kingdom Judah
	in the 2nd year	740	Jotham - 16 years
	of Pekah (r. 740-721)		2 Kings 15:32, 33

*of Jeroboam II

There are multiple instances of kings who reference Uzziah; however, these references are actually to Jeroboam II. The reference to Uzziah's reign, spanning fifty-two years, is presumably an indication of the year in which Jotham, the king of Judah, assumed the throne in relation to Jeroboam II, the king of Israel. The reference to Uzziah should be understood to refer to Jeroboam II in 2 Kings 15:23, which states that Pekahiah reigned over Israel for a period of two years, beginning his reign in the fiftieth year of Uzziah's rule. According to 2 Kings 15:27, Pekah began his reign over Israel in the fifty-second year of Uzziah, and 2 Kings 15:32 indicates that Jotham began his reign over Judah in the second year of Pekah. Thus, it can be deduced that the reign of Pekah began in the fifty-first year of Jeroboam II, taking into account Pekahiah's two-year reign and Jotham's ascension to the throne in Pekah's second year.

The chart delineates the chronological adjustments for the reigns of Hoshea, Ahaz, and Jotham. According to 2 Kings 15:30, the reign

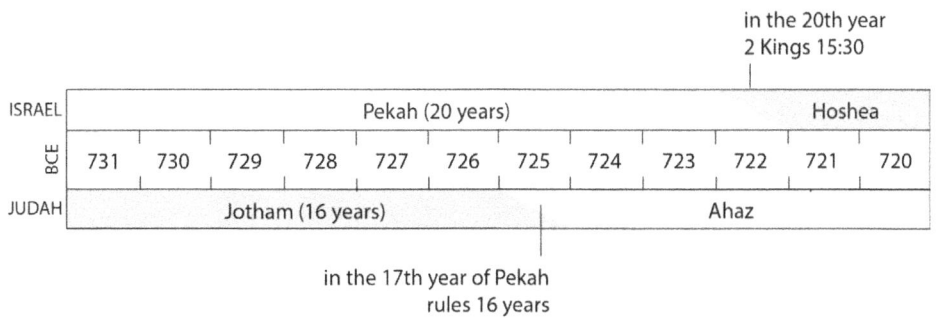

of Hoshea commenced in the twentieth year of Jotham's reign. The reign of Jotham commenced in the second year of Pekah and lasted for sixteen years, which is when Ahaz began his rule in the seventeenth year of Pekah, as stated in 2 Kings 16:1. Therefore, the reference is to Pekah, who ruled for a period of twenty years until he was assassinated by Hoshea.

According to 2 Kings 17:1, the reign of Hoshea also began in the twelfth year of Ahaz. It is noteworthy that this reference may instead refer to the twelve years between the beginning of the reign of Ahaz and the fall of Samaria.

Judah	
Year	Name (length of rule)
719	Hezekiah (29)
691	Manasseh (55)
636	Josiah (31)
606	Jehoahaz (3 months)
606	Jehoiakim (11)
596	Jehoiachin (3 months)
596	Zedekiah (11)
586	Fall of Jerusalem

16
Adam to the Fall of Jerusalem

T he period from 3520 BCE to 3330 BCE is characterized by the development of numerous civilizations. Evidence from archaeological excavations and findings indicates that the Egyptian civilization was a highly developed culture during the Pre-dynastic period, which lasted until approximately 3100 BCE. This advancement in civilization can be traced back to Genesis, specifically chapter six, and the Book of Enoch, which makes references to the Nephilim and their influence on humanity. According to Genesis 6:4, the offspring of the sons of God and the daughters of men were regarded as mighty men of renown, called Nephilim. Therefore, the sons of God, along with their descendants, played a pivotal role in shaping various cultures across the world.

This interaction between humanity and the fallen angels appears to have lasted for approximately one millennium, until the great flood. During the period of the Nephilim, the construction of pyramids, including the Pyramid of Khufu, was widespread throughout Egypt until the conclusion of the fourth dynasty. At that juncture, there was a significant decline in the quality of pyramid construction, as if all the skilled masons just disappeared. Despite the absence of any Egyptian literature describing a flood, the chronology of this study places the great flood at approximately 2332 BCE, which is roughly two hundred years after the construction date of the Pyramid of Khufu.

Born	Patriarchs	Scripture	Died	Age
3988	Adam	Genesis 1:27; 5:5	3058	930
3858	Seth	Genesis 5:3-8	2946	912
3753	Enosh	Genesis 5:6-11	2848	905
3663	Cainan	Genesis 5:9-14	2753	910
3596	Mahalaleel	Genesis 5:12-17	2698	895
3528	Jared	Genesis 5:15-20	2566	962
3366	Enoch	Genesis 5:18-24	3001	365
3301	Methuselah	Genesis 5:21-27	2332	969
3114	Lamech	Genesis 5:25-31	2337	777
2932	Noah	Genesis 5:28-32; 9:28-29	1982	950
2430	Shem	Genesis 11:10-11	1830	600
2330	Arphaxad	Genesis 11:10-13	1892	438
2295	Salah	Genesis 11:12-15	1862	433
2265	Eber	Genesis 11:14-17	1801	464
2231	Peleg	Genesis 11:16-19	1992	239
2201	Reu	Genesis 11:18-21	1962	239
2169	Serug	Genesis 11:20-23	1939	230
2139	Nahor	Genesis 11:22-25	1991	148
2110	Terah	Genesis 11:24-26, 32	1905	205
2040	Abraham	Genesis 11:26, 25:7	1865	175
1940	Isaac	Genesis 21:5, 35:28	1760	180
1880	Jacob	Genesis 25:26, 47:28	1733	147
~1798	Levi	Genesis 29:34; Exodus 6:16	1661	137
~1759	Kobath	Exodus 6:16; 6:18	1626	133
~1685	Amram	Exodus 6:18, 6:20	1548	137
1620	Moses	Deuteronomy 34:7	1500	120

The table lists the patriarchs from Adam to Moses, with Moses representing the twenty-sixth generation. The first column indicates the BCE year of their birth, while the fourth column denotes the BCE year of their death.

◊

According to Jewish tradition, Nimrod, the great-grandson of Noah, led his men in the construction of a tower at Babel that was intended to reach the heavens. Although the scriptures do not explicitly attribute Nimrod to the Tower of Babel, it is noteworthy that the city of Babel was a part of his kingdom during that period. During the course of its construction, God declared that there were no obstacles that could restrain man from accomplishing whatever his aspirations might be. In response, Genesis 10:24 indicates that the earth was divided during the days of Peleg, suggesting that before the birth of Reu, God had dispersed the people across the face of the earth.

◊

Jacob, with the assistance of his mother Rebekah, secures the rights associated with the firstborn from his father Isaac, as well as the promises of the land and of descendants originally given to Abraham. After Esau discovers that his blessing has been given to his younger twin brother, Rebekah petitions Isaac to send Jacob to her brother Laban in Padan Aram in order to find a wife, as described in Genesis 28:2. She does this out of concern for Jacob's safety. Upon learning of his father's displeasure regarding the daughters of Canaan, Esau went to Ishmael and married his daughter, Mahalath, according to Genesis 28:6-9. The timing of these events suggests that Ishmael is still alive, and that Isaac would live for almost sixty more years.

In the illustration, the Book of Jasher is referenced, although it is not considered authentic. The rationale behind the reference is the hypothesis regarding the period of fourteen years, which is noteworthy, as it introduces a degree of coherence to the timeline, as approximately twelve or more years appeared to be unaccounted for. The reference is to Jacob's journey to Eber and the duration of his stay, which is not included in the Bible. The fundamental premise underlying this reference is to ensure that Ishmael is still alive at the time Esau goes to marry his daughter. While the reference in the Book of Jasher is not generally regarded as authentic, in this instance, this hypothesis would explain how the chronology could have been.

Upon arriving in Padan Aram, Jacob encounters Rachel, a daughter of Laban, and expresses his intention to marry her. However, he is unable to pay the customary bride price, leading to an agreement between him and Laban whereby he could marry her after seven years

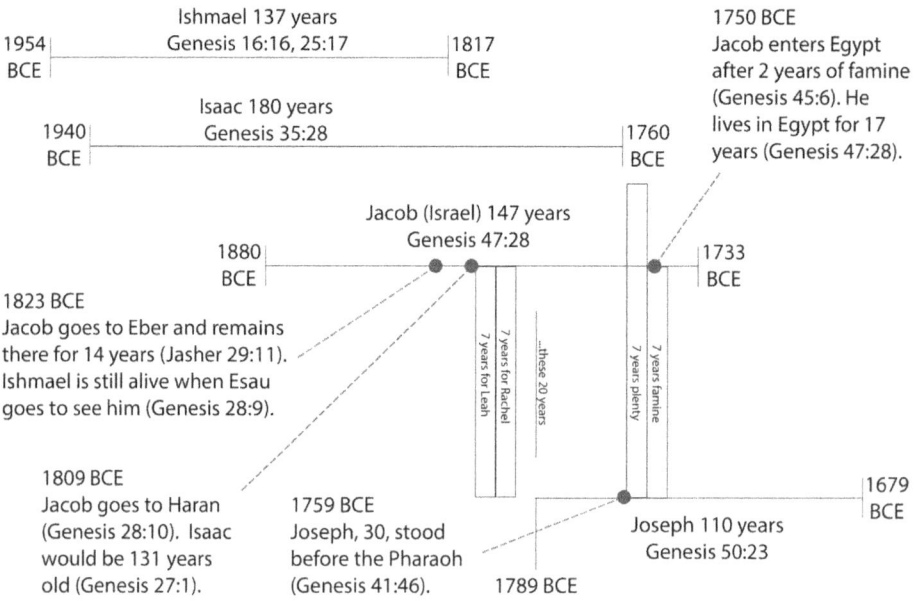

of service. After the stipulated period, Jacob married Leah, unaware that Laban had desired his older daughter to be married first. Following a week-long wedding celebration for Leah, Jacob was given Rachel as a wife with the condition that he perform an additional seven years of service, as indicated in Genesis 29:30 and 31:38. Following the fulfillment of his obligation for Rachel, Jacob was persuaded by Laban to prolong his stay. Jacob resided in Padan Aram for another six years, for a total of twenty years.

The following table provides an overview of the twelve children of Jacob, who were born while he was in Padan Aram. As Jacob's arrangement with Laban did not permit him to marry his daughter for a period of seven years, it can be deduced that his firstborn, Reuben, was likely born at the end of the eighth year. Joseph was born prior to Jacob and his family's flight from Laban. In alignment with the twenty years Jacob spent in Padan Aram, the table lists the birth years of his children, with each child born one year after the other.

BCE	Leah	Bilhah	Zilpah	Rachel	Verses
1800	Reuben				Genesis 29:32
1799	Simeon				Genesis 29:33
1798	Levi				Genesis 29:34
1797	Judah				Genesis 29:35
1796		Dan			Genesis 30:5-6
1795		Naphtali			Genesis 30:7-8
1794			Gad		Genesis 30:10-11
1793			Asher		Genesis 30:12-13
1792	Issachar				Genesis 30:17-18
1791	Zebulun				Genesis 30:20
1790	Dinah				Genesis 30:21
1789				Joseph	Genesis 30:23-24

In Genesis chapter forty-one, Joseph is thirty years old when he interprets Pharaoh's dream of seven fine-looking, fat cows being eaten by seven ugly, gaunt cows. Joseph predicts seven years of abundance followed by seven years of scarcity and famine. It should be noted that Scripture does not explicitly delineate the time between Pharaoh's dream and the beginning of the seven years of abundance. However, since Pharaoh had a second dream about the grain, this study suggests that the seven years of plenty had just begun. The two dreams imply that the Egyptians were compelled to act quickly and store up during the years of abundance for the years of scarcity.

The onset of the famine appears to coincide with the start of the Second Intermediate Period of Egypt, which dates from 1750 BCE to 1550 BCE, and encompasses the fourteenth through the seventeenth dynasties. It is noteworthy that the conclusion of this period in Egyptian history coincides with the timing of the Exodus, as evidenced by the chart in the previous chapter on the four generations. Furthermore, this same period of time also saw the establishment of Avaris as the capital of the Hyksos, which lasted until the last king, Apophis. Therefore, the period between the seven-year famine and the Exodus appears to parallel the time of the Hyksos until their expulsion after the Israelites had already entered the wilderness.

◊

Following the forty years of wandering by the children of Israel in the wilderness, Joshua led them across the Jordan River opposite the city of Jericho. During the Middle Bronze Age, Jericho was constructed with a very large wall surrounding the city. As presented in Joshua chapter six, the Israelites besieged the city, and on the seventh day the wall of the city was destroyed. The proposed date of its destruction is argued to have taken place at some point during either the Middle Bronze III or Late Bronze Age I periods, which would place its occurrence on either side of 1550 BCE. Therefore, according to the chronology presented in this study, the destruction of Jericho would have occurred approximately fifty years after the start of the Late Bronze Age I period.

BCE	Event	Verses
~1463	Joshua dies at the age of 110	Judges 2:7–10
1462	Mesopotamian rule for 8 years	Judges 3:8
1455	Othniel judges for 40 years	Judges 3:9-11
1416	Moabite rule for 18 years	Judges 3:14
1399	Ehud judges, 80 years of peace	Judges 3:15-30
1320	Canaanite 20-year rule	Judges 4:1-3
1301	Deborah judges, 40 years of peace	Judges 5:31
1262	Midian rule for 7 years	Judges 6:1
1256	Gideon judges, 40 years of quiet	Judges 6-8
1217	Abimelech's conspiracy, judges 3 years	Judges 9:22
1215	Tola judges 23 years	Judges 10:1, 2
1193	Jair judges 22 years	Judges 10:3
1172	Philistine/Ammonite rule 18 years	Judges 10:6-8
1155	Jephthah judges for 6 years	Judges 11:26, 12:7
1150	Ibzan judges for 7 years	Judges 12:8-10
1144	Elon judges for 10 years	Judges 12:10-12
1135	Abdon judges for 8 years	Judges 12:13-15
1128	Philistine rule for 40 years	Judges 13:1
1108	Samson judges	Judges 16:31
1089	Eli judges for 40 years	1 Samuel 4:18
1050	Samuel judges	
~1026	Saul anointed king, reigns 10 years	1 Samuel 10
1017	David anointed king, reigns 40 years	1 Kings 2:11
1011	Ishbosheth reigns for 2 years	2 Samuel 2:10
978	Solomon reigns for 40 years	1 Kings 11:42

In the time of King Solomon, Jeroboam consulted a prophet named Ahijah, who prophesied that Jeroboam would eventually become the ruler of the ten northern tribes of Israel. Solomon became aware of the prophecy and attempted to kill Jeroboam, as recorded in 1 Kings 11:40. Nevertheless, Jeroboam was able to evade capture and flee to Egypt, where he took refuge with Shishak, the pharaoh of Egypt.

Following the death of Solomon, his son Rehoboam was anointed king in Jerusalem. The expectation was that he would alleviate the burdens imposed on the ten tribes. However, this commitment was not realized. Consequently, following his return from exile, Jeroboam ascended to the throne as king of the ten northern tribes of Israel.

The Israelites were divided into two houses: the house of Judah, comprising the tribes of Judah and Benjamin, and the house of Israel, comprising the remaining ten tribes, as recorded in 1 Chronicles 10:18-19. Jeroboam led the people of Israel to forsake the worship of the Lord in favor of false idols. This strategic decision by Jeroboam was designed to distance the house of Israel from the house of David, as well as their participation in the pilgrimages to Jerusalem. In response, the tribe of Levi departed from the cities belonging to the ten tribes and relocated to Jerusalem and the Kingdom of Judah.

BCE	N. Kingdom Israel	BCE	S. Kingdom Judah
939	Jeroboam I - 22 years 1 Kings 14:20	939	Rehoboam - 17 years 1 Kings 14:21
	in the 18th year of Jeroboam (r. 939-918)	923	Abijah - 3 years 1 Kings 15:1, 2
	in the 20th year of Jeroboam (r. 939-918)	921	Asa - 41 years 1 Kings 15:9, 10

BCE	N. Kingdom Israel	BCE	S. Kingdom Judah
918	Nadab - 2 years 1 Kings 15:25		in the 2nd year of Asa (r. 919-879)
917	Baasha - 24 years 1 Kings 15:33		in the 3rd year of Asa (r.919-879)
894	Elah- 2 years 1 Kings 16:8		in the 26th year of Asa (r. 919-879)
893	Zimri - 7 days 1 Kings 16:10		in the 27th year of Asa (r. 919-879)
893	Omri - 12 years 1 Kings 16:23		in the 27th year of Asa (r. 919-879) 1 Kings 16:15-16
882	Ahab - 22 years 1 Kings 16:29		in the 38th year of Asa (r. 919-879)
	in the 4th year of Ahab (r. 882-861)	881	Jehoshaphat - 25 years 1 Kings 22:41, 42

◊

The Kurkh Monolith of Shalmaneser III and the Black Obelisk provide a chronological correlation between the reign of King Shalmaneser III of Assyria and that of the kings Ahab and Jehu of Israel. The Kurkh Monolith of Shalmaneser III provides one of the earliest accounts of the Israelites and offers detailed information about his conflict with Ahab, who was the king of Israel. This stele provides an account of the first six years of the Assyrian ruler's reign, concluding with an inscription enumerating the number of men in Ahab's army who engaged in combat against him. The Black Obelisk commemorates the achievements of Shalmaneser III and provides an account of tribute presented by Jehu, the King of Israel, during the eighteenth year of his reign. The reconciliation of the two stelae is possible through the application of the non-accession year method, which would indicate that the conflict with Ahab occurred in 861 BCE, marking his final year as king, and the tribute by King Jehu of Israel in 849 BCE, the first year of his reign.

Year	N. Kingdom Israel	Year	S. Kingdom Judah
861	Ahaziah - 2 years 1 Kings 22:51		in the 17th year of Jeh. (r. 880-856)
860	Joram (Jehoram) - 12 years 2 Kings 3:1		in the 18th year of Jeh. (r. 880-856)
	2 Kings 1:17 'in the 2nd year' of Ahaziah (Israel king)		
	in the 5th year of Joram (r. 860-849)	857	Joram - 8 years 2 Kings 8:16-17
	in the 12th year of Joram (r. 860-849)	850	Ahaziah - 1 year 2 Kings 8:25-26
849	Jehu - 28 years 2 Kings 9:27, 10:36	849	Queen Athaliah - 6 years 2 Kings 11:3-4
	in the 7th year of Jehu (r. 849-822)	844	Joash - 40 years 2 Kings 11:21, 12:1

Year	N. Kingdom Israel	Year	S. Kingdom Judah
822	Jehoahaz - 17 years 2 Kings 13:1		in the 23rd year of Joash (r. 844-805)
806	Jehoash - 16 years 2 Kings 13:10		in the 37th year of Joash (r. 844-805)
	in the 2nd year of Jehoash (r. 806-791)	805	Amaziah - 29 years 2 Kings 14:1-2, 17
791	Jeroboam II - 41 years 2 Kings 14:23		in the 15th year of Amaziah (r. 805-777)
	in the 27th year of Jeroboam II	777	Uzziah - 5̶2̶ 38 years 2 Chronicles 26:3
751	Zechariah - 6 months 2 Kings 15:8		in the 38th year* of Uzziah (r. 777-740)
751	Shallum - 1 month 2 Kings 15:13		in the 39th year* of Uzziah (r. 777-740)
751	Menahem - 10 years 2 Kings 15:17		in the 39th year* of Uzziah (r. 777-740)
742	Pekahiah - 2 years 2 Kings 15:23		in the 50th year* of Uzziah (r. 777-740)

*of Jeroboam II

The findings of this study indicate that the Syro-Ephraimite War may have commenced as early as 725 BCE and that Jotham, the king of Judah, was no longer alive at the time. In the twenty-seventh chapter of 2 Chronicles, Jotham is described as having attained great power and having been successful in numerous battles. However, there is no mention of his involvement in a war against King Rezin of Syria and Pekah, king of Israel, nor is there any mention of gold and silver being taken from the house of the Lord and the treasuries of the king's house to be given to the king of Assyria. According to 2 Kings 16:5-6, the war took place during the reigns of Pekah and Ahaz, kings of Judah. Therefore, it can be deduced that the invasion of Judah by Pekah and Rezin must have occurred following the death of Jotham.

Ahaz offers gold and silver to Tiglath-Pileser, the king of Assyria, with the objective of forming an alliance and subsequently waging war against Rezin and Pekah. As a result, Damascus was captured, Rezin was killed, and many of the inhabitants of the city were deported by the Assyrians. Pekah was assassinated by Hoshea in 722 BCE, and Tiglath-Pileser then appointed Hoshea as ruler of a considerably weakened house of Israel. The military conflict between the kingdom of Judah and the kingdoms of Israel and Syria came to an end, and Judah became a tributary state to Assyria.

At some point following the death of Tiglath-Pileser, Hoshea ceased to pay tribute to Assyria. Consequently, the Assyrian king Shalmaneser V launched a military campaign against Israel, resulting in the imprisonment of Hoshea. Sargon II, the successor of Shalmaneser V, captured Samaria in 714 BCE, which corresponds to the ninth year of Hoshea's reign, according to 2 Kings 17:5-6.

The scriptures clearly mention the cities of the Medes. However, it is important to note that the Assyrian did not take control of those cities until around 715 BCE. This reference means that the ten northern tribes of Israel were deported after that time. According to this study and this reference to the cities of the Medes, Samaria could have fallen and its people could have been deported in 714 BCE.

Year	N. Kingdom Israel	Year	S. Kingdom Judah
741	Pekah - 20 years 2 Kings 15:27		in the 52nd year* of Uzziah (r. 777-740)
	in the 2nd year of Pekah (r. 740-721)	740	Jotham - 16 years 2 Kings 15:32, 33
	in the 17th year of Pekah (r. 740-721)	725	Ahaz - ~~16~~ 6 years 2 Kings 16:1-2
722	Hoshea - 9 years 2 Kings 15:30		in the 20th year of Jotham (r. 739-724)
	in the 3rd year of Hoshea (r. 721-714)	719	Hezekiah- 29 years 2 Kings 18:1, 2
			*of Jeroboam II

◊

According to the non-accession year method, Nebuchadnezzar became king of Babylon in the year 603 BCE. He continued his military campaign against Syria and Palestine and successfully secured these territories. He then initiated an invasion of Egypt.

The defeat of Egypt may have appeared inevitable to the prophets Jeremiah and Ezekiel, who both prophesied that it would be conquered by the Babylonian king Nebuchadnezzar: Jeremiah in Jeremiah 46:14-26 and Ezekiel in Ezekiel 29:10-12. However, this military campaign was unsuccessful. Nebuchadnezzar would return to Babylon to regroup and replenish his forces.

This outcome likely emboldened King Jehoiakim of Judah to rebel against the Babylonians. As a result, Jerusalem was besieged. In 596 BCE, in the eighth year of King Nebuchadnezzar, King Jehoiakim died before the siege ended, and was succeeded by his son, Jehoiachin, as documented in 2 Kings 24:5-12. Following a period of three months, Jehoiachin surrendered and was then taken into captivity. According to Jeremiah 52:1, Nebuchadnezzar appointed Zedekiah as the new king of Judah when he was twenty-one years of age.

In the ninth year of his reign, the kingdom of Judah would openly revolt against the Babylonians, which resulted in a swift siege of Jerusalem by Nebuchadnezzar in 588 BCE. Zedekiah had sought military assistance from Egypt, having formed an alliance with them, but they were unable to provide substantial support. The Babylonian army constructed a mound against the city, and in the eleventh year in the reign of Zedekiah, the city was captured, as documented in 2 Kings 25:1-2. In 586 BCE, during the eighteenth year of Nebuchadnezzar's rule, Zedekiah was killed, and eight hundred and thirty-two were deported to Babylon, according to 2 Chronicles 36:17-21 and Jeremiah 52:29.

Year	King	Ruled	Scripture
691	Manasseh	55 years	2 Kings 21:1
637	Amon	2 years	2 Kings 21:19
636	Josiah	31 years	2 Kings 22:1
606	Jehoahaz	3 months	2 Kings 23:31
606	Jehoiakim	11 years	2 Kings 23:36
596	Jehoiachin	3 months	2 Kings 24:8; 2 Chronicles 36:9
596	Zedekiah	11 years	2 Kings 24:18; 2 Chronicles 36:11